ANTRIM

ALSO AVAILABLE IN THIS SERIES:

Sligo, Michael Farry (2012)
Tyrone, Fergal McCluskey (2014)
Waterford, Pat McCarthy (2015)
Monaghan, Terence Dooley (2017)
Derry, Adrian Grant (2018)
Limerick, John O'Callaghan (2018)
Louth, Donal Hall (2019)
Kildare, Seamus Cullen (2020)
Leitrim, Patrick McGarty (2020)

Antrim

The Irish Revolution, 1912–23

Brian Feeney

FOUR COURTS PRESS

Set in 10.5 on 12.5 point Ehrhardt for
FOUR COURTS PRESS LTD
7 Malpas Street, Dublin 8, Ireland
www.fourcourtspress.ie
and in North America for
FOUR COURTS PRESS
c/o IPG, 814 N. Franklin St, Chicago, IL 60610.

A catalogue record for this title
is available from the British Library.

ISBN 978-1-84682-860-7

Printed in England
by CPI Antony Rowe, Chippenham, Wilts.

Contents

LIST OF ILLUSTRATIONS   vii

LIST OF ABBREVIATIONS   ix

ACKNOWLEDGMENTS   x

The Irish Revolution, 1912–23 series   xi

1   Belfast and County Antrim in 1912   1

2   Unionism in Belfast and County Antrim, 1910–14   11

3   Nationalist politics in Belfast and County Antrim before 1914   27

4   The Easter Rising and the split in northern nationalism   39

5   Belfast and Antrim, 1917–20: unionist redoubt   47

6   The 'Belfast Pogrom', 1920–2   60

7   Belfast: operations and elections in spring 1921   88

8   The IRA campaign in County Antrim, 1919–21   97

9   Election, truce and partition in Belfast and Antrim, 1921–2   107

10   Endgame: Belfast and Antrim in 1922   125

NOTES   150

SELECT BIBLIOGRAPHY   166

INDEX   173

Illustrations

PLATES

1 Postcard of Sir Edward Carson reviewing three battalions of the UVF Central Antrim Regiment at Drumalis, County Antrim, 11 July 1914.
2 UVF parade at Balmoral Showgrounds, Belfast, 27 September 1913.
3 Joe Devlin, MP for West Belfast.
4 Parochial house, Lisburn, August 1920, with loyalists standing in the burnt-out shell.
5 Donaghy's Boot Factory, Lisburn, gutted in the anti-Catholic riots of August 1920.
6 Seán O'Neill, O/C Belfast Brigade IRA, 1920, later ADC to Michael Brennan, chief of staff, National army.
7 Funeral of riot victims, Leeson Street, Falls Road, Belfast, 1920.
8 Roger McCorley, O/C Belfast Brigade IRA, 1921, and Tom Fitzpatrick (alias Bob O'Donnell), O/C Antrim Brigade IRA, 1921.
9 Staff members, 3rd Northern Division, 1921. *Left to right*: Séamus Woods, Tom McNally, Joe McKelvey, Frank Crummey.
10 'B' & 'C' companies, 1st Battalion, Belfast Brigade IRA, 1921, on Hannahstown Hill.
11 'D' company, 1st Battalion, Belfast Brigade IRA, 1921, on Black Mountain.

Credits
Illustrations 1, 2, 7: Linen Hall Library (Belfast) Postcard Collection; 4, 5: Pearse Lawlor and Linen Centre & Lisburn Museum; 3, 6, 8, 9, 10, 11: Jim McDermott.

MAPS

1 Places mentioned in the text   xii
2 Distribution of the Crown forces   6
3 Parliamentary constituencies   13
4 Belfast   61

Abbreviations

AOH	Ancient Order of Hibernians
ASU	Active Service Unit
BMH	Bureau of Military History
CI	County Inspector (RIC)
CO	Colonial Office
DI	District Inspector (RIC)
DORA	Defence of the Realm Act
DT	Department of An Taoiseach
FJ	*Freeman's Journal*
GAA	Gaelic Athletic Association
GNR	Great Northern Railway
Hansard	House of Commons debates
IHS	*Irish Historical Studies*
IG	Inspector General (RIC)
IMA	Irish Military Archives
INF	Irish National Foresters
INV	Irish National Volunteers
IPP	Irish Parliamentary Party
IRA	Irish Republican Army
IRB	Irish Republican Brotherhood
ITGWU	Irish Transport and General Workers' Union
ITUC	Irish Trade Union Congress
MSPC	Military Service Pensions Collection
NAI	National Archives of Ireland
NLI	National Library of Ireland
PRONI	Public Records Office of Northern Ireland
RIC	Royal Irish Constabulary
RUC	Royal Ulster Constabulary
SF	Sinn Féin
TNA	National Archives, London
UCDA	University College Dublin Archives
UIL	United Irish League
USC	Ulster Special Constabulary
UUC	Ulster Unionist Council
UVF	Ulster Volunteer Force
UWUC	Ulster Women's Unionist Council
WS	Witness Statement to Bureau of Military History

Acknowledgments

This book has been several years in the making since Daithí Ó Corráin asked me to take it on. The material on County Antrim 1912–23, particularly Belfast, is vast. There have been several interruptions, not least the completion of a biography of Seán Mac Diarmada in time for the 2016 centenary and journalistic work as a result of Brexit. However, the delay turned out to be a blessing in disguise for it meant that the tremendous work of the Bureau of Military History in digitizing witness statements from the War of Independence and the Military Service Pensions applications and brigade reports was completed: a boon for all researchers. The documents could all be accessed online and, in the case of the witness statements, are searchable. Anyone interested in the history of that period owes a debt of gratitude for those labours. In my case online access avoided multiple trips to Dublin and the time and expense involved.

I owe a personal debt of gratitude first and foremost to my wife Patricia for her unswerving support throughout the period of research and writing. She gave me the time and space and understanding to enable me stick doggedly to the task.

I am grateful to the series editors, Daithí Ó Corráin and Mary Ann Lyons, for the meticulous reading of drafts and countless suggestions of areas for investigation, change and organization. I am particularly grateful to Daithí for his patient and assiduous work to correct my careless and cavalier approach to footnotes. I'm sure some errors have escaped his scrutiny, but they are mine. Martin Fanning of Four Courts Press also spotted some howlers. Thanks too to Dr Mike Brennan who produced the maps of County Antrim and Belfast by some digital magic. Dr Éibhlín Mhic Aoidh of St Mary's University College, Belfast deciphered Irish orthography used by some participants a century ago before simplified spelling came into vogue. I should also like to thank my colleague and friend Dr Peter Collins for his advice and help at various stages of the work. I am indebted to Jim McDermott, Danny Morrison and Pearse Lawlor for their help locating photographs.

It is also important to acknowledge the work of the ever-helpful staff in the various libraries and institutions where I consulted documents, especially Monica Cash, Deputy Librarian at the Linenhall Library in Belfast, the National Library of Ireland in Dublin, Military Archives in Cathal Brugha Barracks, Dublin, the Public Records Office of Northern Ireland and the other archives listed in the bibliography.

The Irish Revolution, 1912–23 series

Since the turn of the century, a growing number of scholars have been actively researching this seminal period in modern Irish history. More recently, propelled by the increasing availability of new archival material, this endeavour has intensified. This series brings together for the first time the various strands of this exciting and fresh scholarship within a nuanced interpretative framework, making available concise, accessible, scholarly studies of the Irish Revolution experience at a local level to a wide audience.

The approach adopted is both thematic and chronological, addressing the key developments and major issues that occurred at a county level during the tumultuous 1912–23 period. Beginning with an overview of the social, economic and political milieu in the county in 1912, each volume assesses the strength of the home rule movement and unionism, as well as levels of labour and feminist activism. The genesis and organization of paramilitarism from 1913 are traced; responses to the outbreak of the First World War and its impact on politics at a county level are explored; and the significance of the 1916 Rising is assessed. The varying fortunes of constitutional and separatist nationalism are examined. The local experience of the War of Independence, reaction to the truce and Anglo-Irish Treaty and the course and consequences of the Civil War are subject to detailed examination and analysis. The result is a compelling account of life in Ireland in this formative era.

Mary Ann Lyons
Department of History
Maynooth University

Daithí Ó Corráin
School of History & Geography
Dublin City University

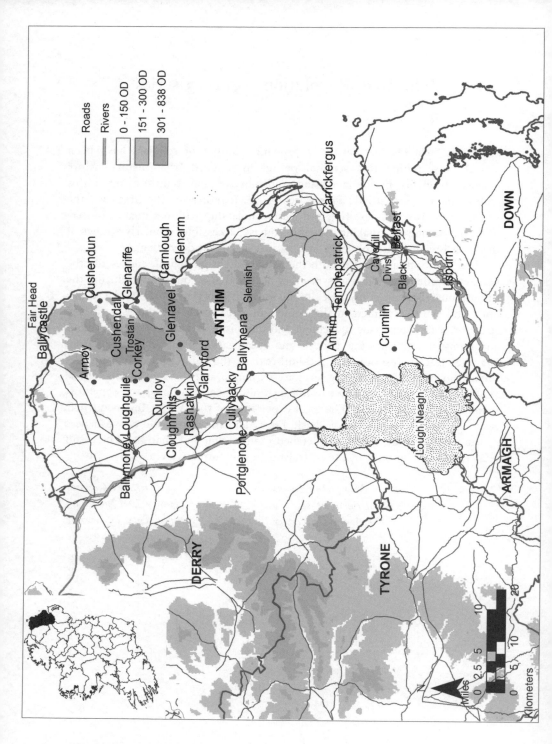

1 Places mentioned in the text

1 Belfast and County Antrim in 1912

'See Belfast, devout and profane and hard
Built on reclaimed mud, hammers playing in the shipyard
Time punched with holes like a steel sheet, time
Hardened the faces ...'

Louis MacNeice, *Valediction.*

County Antrim forms a rectangle in the north-east corner of Ireland. Its borders on the north and east are sharply defined by the Atlantic, the North Channel and the Irish Sea (see map 1). Lough Neagh takes a bite out of the western border of the rectangle, which then follows the line of the Lower River Bann north to the Atlantic. The south-western corner of the rectangle is elongated where it follows the River Lagan, which flows through Lisburn and Belfast. Most of Belfast city, straddling the River Lagan, is in Antrim. The county is about ninety kilometres north to south and has an area just over 3,000 square kilometres. It is unique in Ireland geographically, geologically, politically, economically, religiously and socially. Its proximity to Scotland, only nineteen kilometres away at its closest point, the Mull of Kintyre, has meant a constant interchange between Scotland and Antrim throughout history.

Antrim was not included in the Plantation of Ulster after 1609 when the lands of O'Neill of Tyrone and O'Donnell of Tyrconnell were confiscated. However, the county was deeply affected by the adoption of the Reformation in Scotland, which became fiercely Presbyterian. In common with Ulster counties west of the River Bann, where English Protestants were planted, large tracts of Antrim were also peopled by Protestants but of the militantly Presbyterian variety, deeply hostile to Catholicism. Successive waves of Scots Presbyterians moved to Antrim, a migration peaking in the years 1696–8 when tens of thousands were driven from the Scottish Borders by famine.[1] By the second decade of the eighteenth century, Presbyterians were the absolute majority in Antrim, making the county unique in Ireland in its religious affiliation. This huge Scottish migration also resulted in the local dialect that even today in places is indistinguishable from the accent of western Scotland and has been formally recognized as 'Ulster-Scots'. Nevertheless, a substantial native population of Irish-speaking Catholics remained. They were mainly concentrated in the inaccessible Glens, on Rathlin Island and in the north-east coastal strip of the county from Ballycastle south to Carnlough. A Gaeltacht survived on Rathlin Island and in some Glens until the end of the nineteenth century, finally petering out in Glenariffe in the 1920s.[2]

I

In 1911 Antrim's population was 193,000, half of whom were Presbyterian, 21.7 per cent Church of Ireland and 20.5 per cent Catholic: other Protestant sects, principally Methodist, made up the rest.[3] Antrim was by far the most Presbyterian and the most homogeneous Protestant county in Ireland and remains so to this day. At the other extreme, County Waterford had a combined Presbyterian and Methodist population of just 0.5 per cent.[4]

Agriculture in the form of livestock farming, with cattle on the better grasslands, sheep on the higher parts of the plateau and in the steep-sided Glens, was the county's main occupation. That remained the case into the twentieth century, but only just, for urbanization was attracting people from the land into the factories of Belfast and Lisburn. Of a total male population of 93,651 in 1911, 27,619 were employed in agriculture compared to 23,065 in industry. Over 13,000 women worked in textile mills. The county town, Antrim, situated where the Six Mile Water flows into Lough Neagh, had decayed throughout the nineteenth century as workers headed for the industries of Belfast thirty kilometres south.

The county's transport infrastructure was an important determinant of economic prosperity. In the north, the towns of Ballymena with a population of over 11,000 in 1911 and Ballymoney with 10,000, on the main road from Belfast to the north coast, flourished in contrast to the decay of towns in the south and stagnation in the less accessible Glens and on the coast. Railway links supplied Belfast with milk, meat and vegetables, and boosted the prosperity of Ballymena and Ballymoney. Both were also on the railway line opened in 1855 to Portrush, a rapidly growing seaside resort on Antrim's north coast. In addition, Ballymoney had a railway line to Ballycastle on the north coast. There was also a railway line from Belfast to the busy port of Larne, where ferries crossed to Stranraer in Scotland several times daily carrying passengers and goods. Between 1901 and 1911 Larne's population grew by 9 per cent to 12,080.

Lisburn, in the south-western corner of the county, was the second-most populous town with 12,388 people in 1911, three-quarters of whom were Protestant. It was a busy commercial centre on the River Lagan that benefitted from an important railway junction linking it to Belfast, Portadown, Dungannon and Dublin. It owed its prosperity to the textile industry and was the birthplace of the Irish linen industry at the end of the seventeenth century. Not much smaller was Crumlin, twenty kilometres west of Belfast, also a textile manufacturing town with a population of 11,878 in 1911.[5]

What really set Antrim apart was the city of Belfast, the largest in Ireland in the early twentieth century with a population in 1911 of 386,937 compared to Dublin's 304,802.[6] More importantly, it was the only industrial city on the island. With its huge shipyards, iron foundries, chemical plants and textile mills, streets of red-brick terrace houses and smoking chimney stacks, it looked more like the industrial powerhouses of Manchester or Glasgow than a city in Ireland.

Like other industrial cities in Europe, Belfast's growth in the nineteenth century had been exponential. Its population grew from 19,000 in 1800 to 350,000 in 1901. By 1911 it had expanded a further ten per cent. From 1840 to the turn of the century Belfast had been the fastest growing city in the United Kingdom. In 1888 it received a royal charter from Queen Victoria establishing it as a city. In fact, it was more than just a city. It became what geographers call a 'city region' like Trieste or Helsinki with a gravitational pull on the surrounding countryside. In Belfast's case, this extended as far as the Atlantic coast of Donegal 140 kilometres away.[7] By 1905 thirty per cent of the population of the region that would later constitute the six counties of Northern Ireland were concentrated in the city. By 1920 eighty per cent of Ireland's industrial output was generated in Belfast and the three counties nearest the city: Antrim, Down and, to a lesser extent, north Armagh. The size of that population and the wealth that Belfast generated dominated the whole region, not only economically but politically too. Many Protestants in Ulster saw Belfast as their capital – created, built, and developed by them, and in its prosperity and modernity, a statement of their difference from and superiority to the rest of an overwhelmingly rural, Catholic Ireland.

In Belfast's docks and along the Victoria Channel, the dredged channel of Belfast Lough, there were 105 craft on the night of the 1911 census, all moored well clear of the slipways of the shipyards that gave onto the Victoria Channel which could float liners requiring a ten-metre draft. Belfast had the largest shipyard in the world, Harland & Wolff, though that was not the only one. Workman Clark, known as 'the wee yard', was the fourth-largest shipyard in the UK. In 1909 it employed 9,000 men and produced the largest tonnage of ships in the UK.[8] Unlike any other place in Ireland, just under half of Belfast's male population worked in engineering, shipbuilding and textiles.[9] Forty-three per cent of Belfast females over the age of ten worked, 60 per cent of them (27,935) in textiles, mainly in linen mills. The city had the largest rope works in the world and the world's largest tobacco factory, producing millions of cigarettes and tons of pipe tobacco annually. Belfast also boasted whiskey distilleries, mineral water bottling plants, chemical works and hundreds of small to medium-sized engineering plants and workshops supplying the shipyards with components.[10]

The demand for labour, raw materials (including tens of thousands of tons of coal weekly) and industrial equipment meant that Belfast was at the centre of a complex transport system. Three railway companies operated from separate stations: the Belfast and County Down Railway, the Great Northern Railway (GNR) and the Midland Railway Company. The Midland line ran north to Ballymena with an offshoot to Carrickfergus harbour. The GNR ran to Dublin through Lisburn and Portadown. Regular ferries of the Belfast Steamship Company crossed from Belfast to Heysham, Liverpool, Stranraer, Glasgow and Ardrossan, some more than once a day with passengers and industrial cargo.

The city's large industries and commercial businesses produced an immense rateable income for Belfast Corporation, which enabled it to fund high-quality public services like gas street lighting, electric trams, public swimming baths and parks. Most of the city was piped for gas which was used for cooking and domestic lighting, as well as for industrial purposes. The income from the municipal gasworks was colossal and funded the most extravagant public statement of the city's wealth, its ostentatious city hall that opened in August 1906.[11]

The political composition of Belfast Corporation reflected the city's 75 per cent Protestant and unionist population.[12] Since the 1850s Belfast was divided geographically after sporadic intense bouts of lethal rioting. These disturbances erupted in reaction to the continual influx of Catholics from Ulster's countryside and further afield in search of work in its mills and shipyards. They found themselves in hostile territory as Belfast's Protestants guarded their skilled industrial jobs vigilantly against incoming competition.[13] These Catholics tended to congregate in an enclave beyond Townsend Street in the west of the city, which was often attacked. Riots frequently followed contentious Orange marches close to, or threatening to enter, this Catholic district that spread west along the Falls Road. On other occasions, political developments prompted disturbances, such as the conflicts instigated by unionists in 1886 and 1893 against the first and second home rule bills.[14]

Other small numbers of incoming Catholics also settled in Carrick Hill close to Townsend Street, in the nearby Docks district known as Sailortown, and around the giant tobacco and rope works in York Road to the north of the city centre. There were also some Catholic outliers around textile mills on the north-west outskirts of the city at the Marrowbone – or Bone – district and in nearby rapidly growing Ardoyne. On low land near the River Lagan bridge were the Markets, a Catholic district where livestock to supply the city's industrial population were slaughtered and other comestibles traded. On the east of the River Lagan, facing the Markets across the Albert Bridge, was the Short Strand, an isolated tiny green blob in a vast sea of orange. During the deadly sectarian onslaughts of 1920–2 these small Catholic enclaves, almost completely surrounded by loyalist districts, bore the brunt of attacks by loyalists and the Ulster Special Constabulary (USC) established in 1920.

Before the formation of the USC, Belfast was policed by the RIC under a city commissioner whose salary was partly paid by the corporation. Given the particular difficulties of policing Belfast, due to frequent sectarian clashes and the danger of deadly rioting, the number of police per head of population was the highest in Ireland at one policeman to 400, twice as many as most counties.[15] In Belfast in 1914 there were 1,041 constables, 51 acting sergeants, 141 sergeants, 28 head constables and 7 district inspectors in five districts, A – E, as well as a headquarters district overseen by the office of Thomas Smith, the city commissioner.[16] They were housed in twenty-six barracks, many very large and purpose built; for example, Mountpottinger covering the Short Strand had 82 police, Springfield Road barracks in west Belfast had 65, Musgrave Street in the city centre had 59; Glenravel Street, one of the largest barracks with 80 men, headquarters of D district, covered Dock ward, the scene of some of the most ferocious violence in the 1920–2 period.[17] On the other hand, some, like Andersonstown on the western outskirts of the city, had half a dozen policemen. In total, the Belfast RIC amounted to one ninth of the entire force.

By comparison, County Antrim outside Belfast, notably quiet and undisturbed, had one of the smallest complements of police in 1911: 239 housed in 40 barracks, about one policeman per 500 population.[18] There were five RIC districts in the county (see map 2): Antrim, Lisburn, Ballymena, Ballymoney and Larne. Each DI commanded seven or eight barracks. The county inspector (CI) was based in Lisburn. The county had forty barracks including three 'police huts' manned on an occasional basis. All the barracks were small – the largest, the district headquarters in Lisburn and Ballymena, each having eight men. Four or five police was the usual number elsewhere.[19]

It should also be noted that during serious rioting in July 1912 the British army was deployed. The biggest garrison in Belfast was Victoria Barracks, North Queen Street. The 1911 census recorded 1,007 troops there.[20] However, there were other troops available in nearby barracks such as Holywood in County Down and Carrickfergus in County Antrim. Apart from the ferocity of the rioting, the deployment of troops was due to the antipathy of the majority unionist population towards the RIC, whom they regarded as biased because they were predominantly Catholic.

Although a quarter of the city's population was Catholic by the end of the nineteenth century, 93 per cent of the 20,000 shipyard workers were Protestant. As Tony Hepburn observed, Belfast's Protestants regarded the industrial city as their creation and viewed Catholics arriving from the countryside as immigrants, 'the Irish in Belfast', incomers, much as the Irish in Glasgow or Liverpool were regarded.[21] Excluded from skilled engineering work and apprenticeships, the only jobs available to Catholics were unskilled: labouring, dock work, bar work, work on the trams or domestic service. However, there was no resistance to Catholic women working in textile mills and they poured in by the thousand in the nineteenth century.

Unlike many other industrial cities in the UK, Belfast did not have extensive slums or tenements. Whereas overcrowding close to factories tended to be the norm elsewhere because people tried to live as close as possible to their place of employment, Belfast's extensive tram network enabled workers to commute across the city. Men from the Shankill travelled daily by tram

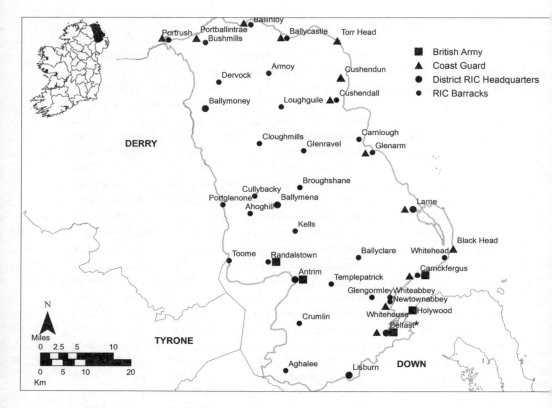

2 Distribution of the Crown forces

* The RIC barracks in Belfast were: A District – Musgrave St, College Sq North, Smithfield; B District – Springfield Rd, Andersonstown, Brickfields, Cullingtree Rd; C District – Brown Sq, Antrim Rd, Craven St, Leopold St, Ligoniel Rd, Shankill Rd; D District – Glenravel St, Chichester Rd, Greencastle St, Henry St, York Rd; E District – Mountpottinger, Ballyhackamore, Newtownards Rd, Strandtown; F District – Donegall Pass, Ballynafeigh, Lisburn Rd, Roden St.

across the River Lagan bridges to work in the shipyards and many from east Belfast travelled to work in west Belfast's engineering plants such as Mackies or the Albert Foundry.

It is true that there were slums and that a lot of housing was of poor quality – the so-called 'back-to-backs' – which were in reality one house with a gabled roof but a dividing wall in the middle. There were also 'half houses' or 'Scotch halls', where one family lived on the ground floor and another on the first storey. However, the 1911 census shows that the average number of persons per family in Belfast was 4.9 and, perhaps more surprisingly, that the average number of persons per house was five. Remarkably, there were fewer than 500 people living in one-room rented tenement accommodation and very few places with more than one person per rented room. Falls, Smithfield and Dock wards, which had the greatest concentrations of old houses in Belfast, were the most overcrowded. Smithfield had 688 families living in two-room accommodation.[22] One reason for these relatively spacious living arrangements was that Belfast's fastest period of expansion took place after the 1870s when the Artisans and Labourers Dwelling Improvement Acts (1875) applied to building regulations. At one point in the late nineteenth century, streets of houses were being built so rapidly that the builders ran out of names. The streets leading off Conway Street, between the Falls and Shankill Roads, were named simply First Street to Eighth Street. Most houses had four rooms and a scullery and were occupied by one family. The same was true in rural Antrim districts where the 1911 census report recorded the vast majority of houses as first or second class – stone or brick built with four or five rooms and four or more windows. Again, in most cases occupancy was one family per house.

As housing in Belfast was built in increasing quantity after the 1870s, adjacent schools, almost completely denominational, grew up simultaneously. The results were remarkable. In 1911 the literacy rate for the Belfast population was 94 per cent. Only 3.6 per cent were completely illiterate, far below the national average of 9.2 per cent and the Ulster average of 8.7 per cent.[23] In mainly Catholic west Belfast religious orders established several elementary schools like St Finian's on the Falls Road, run by the Christian Brothers, and St Gall's, run by the De La Salle Brothers, beside Clonard Redemptorist monastery. The Sisters of Charity and the Mercy Order founded schools for girls. Protestants were well served for secondary education by the Royal Belfast Academical Institution, Methodist College, and Belfast Royal Academy, the oldest school in the city founded in 1785. There was only one Catholic grammar school for boys, St Malachy's College on the Antrim Road in north Belfast, which also acted as the diocesan seminary. Dominican nuns ran St Dominic's on the Falls Road, the only Catholic girls' grammar school.

Like everything else in Belfast sport and recreation were divided, in the case of sport doubly so. Just as in industrial cities in Britain, soccer was the most popular recreation with local clubs competing in a league. However, the Belfast club membership and support tended to be either Catholic or Protestant, not solely because of sectarianism but because they reflected the composition of the districts where they emerged. At the apex of the sport were two semi-professional clubs which dominated the game: Belfast Celtic and Linfield. Belfast Celtic drew its players and fanatical supporters from west Belfast. The club was formed in 1891, consciously emulating Celtic football club in Glasgow with which Belfast Celtic always maintained close relations. The club's stadium, Celtic Park, in west Belfast opened in 1903. Linfield, its rival, drew its support primarily from the Protestant enclave of Sandy Row in south Belfast and Protestant west Belfast. It was founded by workers from the Ulster Spinning Company's Linfield Mill in 1886. The club moved to its present stadium, Windsor Park, located about 400 metres from

Celtic's ground, in 1905. Clashes between the two clubs were often the occasion for violent riots after (and sometimes during) games.

At the turn of the century Gaelic Athletic Association (GAA) clubs began to be established in Catholic districts in Belfast, although Gaelic games remained a minority sport among Catholics in the city. However, the clubs played an important role in raising consciousness of nationalism, both political and cultural. There was often a direct correlation between GAA membership and membership of the Gaelic League. Just as elsewhere in the country, Irish Republican Brotherhood (IRB) members worked to infiltrate both organizations, though with little success in Belfast before 1918 given the general hostility to republicanism in the city. Gaelic games, particularly hurling, were organized in north County Antrim in 1902 by Bulmer Hobson who established the Antrim County Board in that year. By 1904 there were more than a dozen clubs playing hurling in and around the Glens.[24]

Apart from sport in the shape of football, the most popular recreation in Belfast in the years before the war was attending the picture house. In 1912 there were a dozen in the city, the first being the 250-seat Electric Picture Palace, which opened in 1910. The biggest was the Coliseum, which opened in 1911 and seated 900. That was followed by the Arcadian in December 1912 with 600 seats and the Central in 1913, also a 600-seater. The Clonard Picture House on the Falls Road also opened in 1913. Another dozen opened in the next five years. Many people went to the cinema twice a week.[25] The picture houses were for entertainment but the films were silent. For news and information people devoured newspapers. For those who could not afford to buy a paper daily, Belfast's libraries and scores of public houses provided papers for their clientele, if for no other reason than it kept them in the pub while they read. Three of Belfast's four main newspapers were unionist. The nationalist *Irish News* was founded in August 1891 by Bishop Patrick McAlister of Down and Connor as an anti-Parnellite publication.[26] A long tussle for control of the newspaper between the Catholic clergy and nationalist politicians ended in 1905 when Joe Devlin prevailed.[27] He became a member of the board of directors. After the 1906 general election when Devlin became MP for West Belfast the *Irish News* became his reliable mouthpiece. It sustained its support for the Irish Parliamentary Party (IPP), but Devlin, in particular, until 1921. For most of the period of the Irish Revolution the editor was Tim McCarthy, a close friend of Devlin. However, the paper had a wider readership than Belfast nationalists because it provided a northern perspective on national politics. Perhaps just as importantly, it supplied notice of births, deaths and marriages in the Catholic community across Ulster. People joked that they checked the *Irish News* in the morning to check if they were still alive!

Of the unionist papers the *Belfast Newsletter*, founded in 1737, had the distinction – which it still retains – of being the oldest continuously published daily newspaper in English. It was staunchly establishment (Conservative and Unionist) and provided the same service as the *Irish News* for the unionist community, though with a greater consciousness of its role as the organ of Ulster politics. Like the *Irish News*, it was read across the north. The *Newsletter* was purchased by the influential Henderson family in 1846 and remained in that family until the 1990s. Throughout the period covered by this book, brothers Trevor and Charles ran the paper.[28] The liberal unionist tradition was catered for by the *Northern Whig* which generally presented a more Presbyterian ethos than the *Newsletter*. Again, the paper sold more widely than merely in Belfast, but by the opening years of the century it no longer had the clout it previously enjoyed as it took a less strident line against home rule than the *Newsletter*. Nevertheless, when its editor, Joseph Fisher, was appointed unionist commissioner of the Irish Boundary Commission in 1924, unionists did not object.

The *Belfast Telegraph* (known as the *Belfast Evening Telegraph* until 1918), also a strong unionist newspaper, took a more modern and populist approach than the other two. Owned by the Baird family who poured huge sums of money into its production, the *Telegraph* had the most up-to-date production facilities.[29] As well as news, the paper majored on advertising. It published four updated editions daily except on Saturdays when it published a fifth, initially entitled *Ulster's Saturday Night*. It was printed on pink paper and endeavoured to give all the results of the day's sport in Britain and Ireland. In 1896, it was restyled *Ireland's Saturday Night* so that a special edition could be rushed by rail to Dublin covering the following day's Gaelic fixtures across the country. Although the *Saturday Night* was really the fifth edition, last minute changes could be incorporated and it came to be known as 'the eighth', giving rise to the newsboys' cry, incomprehensible to strangers, 'Tally ate'. Robert Baird, who died in 1934, ran the paper during the tumultuous second decade of the twentieth century.

Elsewhere in County Antrim every large town had at least one newspaper of its own. There was the *Ballymena Observer* and *Ballymena Weekly Telegraph*, the *Ballymoney Free Press and Northern Counties Advertiser*, the *Carrickfergus Advertiser*, the *Larne Times* (also run by the Baird family), the *Lisburn Herald*, *Lisburn Standard*, *Lisburn Weekly Mail*. Given the predilections of their readership, all of these had a unionist editorial line and were strictly local in their coverage. Anyone who wanted a wider perspective on national or world events turned to one of the big four from Belfast, but in Antrim outside the north-east of the county, that perspective would seldom include the *Irish News*.

Among the unionist middle and upper classes in the county and in Belfast the reliably unionist *Irish Times* was read for the official government position on national affairs, for analysis, commentary and information about high society in Ireland. Perhaps surprisingly, English newspapers like the *Times,* the *Daily News* and *Daily Mail* also circulated extensively in greater Belfast among the unionist middle class because many looked to London rather than Dublin as the centre of their interest. More generally, the English newspapers, especially the popular ones like the *Daily Mail,* were regarded as slightly *risqué* in the strict Presbyterian ethos of the city and county. Presbyterian sabbatarianism governed society in Belfast and Antrim so that people did not read Sunday newspapers, and in any case there would have been nowhere to buy them because on Sundays Belfast, and other Antrim towns, were like ghost towns except when the various Christian denominations made their way in their Sunday best to their respective places of worship, in many cases up to three times each Sunday.

The unique circumstances of the city and county, its concentration of the largest self-consciously Presbyterian population in the world outside Scotland, the enormous wealth greater Belfast's industry generated, its dense population, the clout in London its political leaders wielded, all combined to enable this city region to thwart the Irish Revolution. However, those same circumstances also combined to produce another, unforeseen unionist revolution: the partition of Ireland and the creation of a self-governing region in the north-east in 1922, which had been adumbrated a decade before but which no one in London or Dublin took seriously, even when Belfast unionists set up a provisional government of Ulster in September 1913.

This book aims to demonstrate that the process of defying the will of parliament at Westminster and creating a new state in the north-east of Ireland was driven largely by Belfast unionists who formed their own military wing, the Ulster Volunteer Force (UVF), in 1913, which they armed with modern weapons in 1914. Confronted with the 1918 Sinn Féin electoral triumph and the IRA campaign in 1919, the same Belfast unionist leaders were able to take complete control of the city and county. The emergence of Northern Ireland from 1920 to 1922 occasioned ferocious urban violence with over 450 dead in Belfast, the worst in twentieth-century peacetime Europe, until the recurrence of violence in the same streets in the 1970s. The conflict in Belfast in 1920–2 to all intents and purposes took on the character of a separate civil war between Catholics and Protestants, despite the attempts of the IRA in Belfast to maintain they were part of a national struggle.

The Irish Revolution that took its course in most of the rest of the country between 1912 and 1923 had limited success in the north-east in counties west of the River Bann, but never got off the ground in Belfast and County Antrim. There, its protagonists were faced with overwhelming odds – political, military and paramilitary – but also, in contrast to elsewhere in Ireland, an overwhelmingly hostile population, both nationalist and unionist.

2 Unionism in Belfast and County Antrim, 1910–14

This chapter assesses the development of unionist opposition, both political and military, to the sudden, unforeseen and real threat of home rule after 1910. With almost universal support for home rule in the rest of the island outside the north-east since the mid-1880s, Ulster Unionists began to develop a siege mentality. Nowhere was this stronger than in Antrim and in Belfast, where serious civil disturbances erupted in both 1886 and 1893 following the first and second home rule bills. Strength in numbers – what Alvin Jackson called 'the peculiar concentration of opposition' in the north – gave unionists in Antrim and Belfast the confidence and security to take the lead in opposing home rule.[1] Also significant was the nexus between the aristocracy in Antrim, the English aristocracy, links to the vice-regal lodge in Dublin, senior British military figures, wealthy industrial magnates in Belfast and leading British politicians. While there were other examples elsewhere in the north, most notably the Tyrone-based duke of Abercorn, and the marquess of Londonderry in County Down, in some respects the role of big house unionism in Antrim, using its powerful links to business and commerce, is the last stand of the ascendancy in Ireland, ultimately successful in that they thwarted the Irish Revolution, attained control of their own destiny and retained their estates, though not their political influence.

In Belfast, the sharp geographical and economic sectarian divisions, already described, also dictated the politics of the city, which were unique. In other Irish cities there tended to be a Church of Ireland élite who controlled business, banking and commerce with a majority Catholic proletariat. In Belfast, by contrast, many of the wealthy businessmen were Presbyterian and the proletariat were self-consciously militant Protestant, outnumbering the Catholic working class by three to one. While elsewhere in the country the IPP dominated parliamentary and council elections, and in Dublin a number of Sinn Féin (SF) councillors had been elected after 1906, in Belfast (and Antrim) the 1884 Reform Act and the 1898 Local Government Act made no difference. There was no SF political presence anywhere and in Belfast there were just three nationalist councillors and one IPP MP, the charismatic Joe Devlin.

The city had four Westminster constituencies, North, South, East and West, created by the Redistribution Act of 1885. Until 1906 North, East and West were held by wealthy unionists. From 1889 to 1895, Belfast North was represented by Sir Edward Harland, one of the owners of Harland & Wolff, and for 1907–10 by George Clark, a prominent Orangeman and part owner of Workman Clark. From 1892 to 1910, Belfast East was held by Gustav Wilhelm

Wolff, the other joint owner of Harland & Wolff. Belfast West was represented by Hugh Oakley Arnold-Foster, an English lawyer, who was secretary of state for war. Often these wealthy Unionist MPs were elected unopposed.

From 1902 to 1910, Belfast South was an exception. Thomas Sloan, a shipyard worker, won a by-election in 1902 and retained the seat in the 1906 general election. Despite all the Belfast constituencies having densely populated working-class districts with a large industrial proletariat, Labour politicians got short shrift. While the rest of Ireland outside Ulster had swung to home rule since Gladstone's conversion in 1885 and had ousted the landed gentry from parliamentary seats, in Belfast, politics was characterized by an ever-more-virulent defence of the Union. Liberals and even Liberal Unionists never fared very well in Belfast. Labour politicians, especially Protestants, were regarded as a dangerous threat to unionist solidarity.

Sloan was the exception that proved the rule. A lay Methodist preacher, he was a powerful orator and strong advocate of workers' rights. However, although he was a trenchant critic of employers and wealthy unionists, and spoke a left-wing political vocabulary, he was a staunch unionist. He founded the Independent Orange Order in 1903 and later led the virulent anti-Catholic Belfast Protestant Association.[2] Sloan was ambivalent about the 1907 Belfast dockers' strike and concerned at the overt socialism of its leader, James Larkin.

By contrast, the best-known Labour man in Belfast was William Walker, a joiner in Harland & Wolff, a Protestant, and a socialist, who was president of the Irish Trade Union Congress. Elected to Belfast Corporation for Duncairn in north Belfast in 1905, he contested the North Belfast parliamentary seat in a by-election in 1905 and in the 1906 general election, losing by fewer than 500 votes on each occasion.[3] However, like other Labour candidates, Walker fell foul of the opposition of Sloan's Belfast Protestant Association and the Orange Order, both organizations determined to assert that each election was a plebiscite on the Union. To them, willing tools of the industrialists, Labour politics were a dangerous distraction from the main objective – defence of the Union. Anyone who threatened to 'split the vote' and thereby minimize total Protestant opposition to home rule was regarded as a traitor or, as Protestant Labour men and trade unionists were known in Belfast, 'rotten prods'. Walker was required to emphasize his Labourite unionism and his opposition to home rule, and in 1911 was bitterly attacked by James Connolly, then living in Belfast, for succumbing to sectarianism.[4]

To enhance unionist solidarity, the Ulster Unionist Council (UUC) was established in March 1905 as an all-encompassing ethno-political bloc to oppose home rule. With offices in Belfast, the UUC brought together in an all-class alliance, politicians, businessmen, farmers, industrial workers, the Orange Order – all shades of unionist opinion which, until faced with home

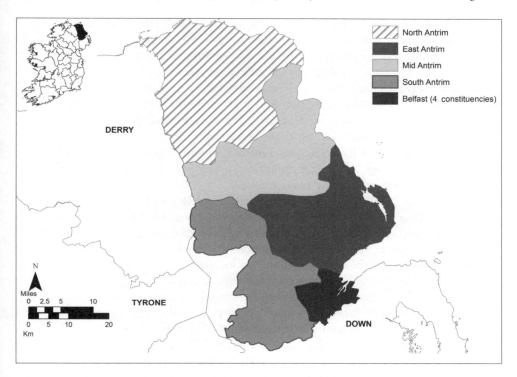

North Antrim
East Antrim
Mid Antrim
South Antrim
Belfast (4 constituencies)

DERRY

N

Miles
0 2.5 5   10

0   5   10   20
Km

TYRONE

DOWN

3 Parliamentary constituencies

rule, was notoriously fissiparous. Home rule was feared to be increasingly likely as a general election was due in 1906 and the odds were that the Conservative and Unionist Party would lose after a decade in power. Unionists feared that would leave the door open to the Westminster alliance between the Liberals and the IPP, which had led to home rule bills in 1886 and 1893.[5]

The 200-strong UUC comprised all Unionist MPs and peers, 100 representatives from Unionist constituency associations in the nine Ulster counties, as well as fifty from the Orange Order. The real power lay in the standing committee, thirty men drawn from across the north but based in Belfast, established to run the UUC on a day-to-day basis; a permanent staff was appointed to service the standing committee. Most people take this to be the origin of the Ulster Unionist Party. Its standing committee, dominated by Belfast Unionists, was also the embryo of the political organization that resisted home rule after 1912, formed the UVF in 1913 and organized gun running in 1914. The establishment of the UUC in 1905 marked a formal separation from unionists in the rest of the island who developed their own leadership through the Irish Unionist Alliance, although that organization too became dominated by Ulster Unionists.[6]

Catholics and nationalists in Belfast had nothing to compare with unionist wealth and power or, after 1905, their organization. The same was true for County Antrim outside the city. The county had been given four constituencies under the 1885 Redistribution Act: North, South, East and Mid-Antrim (see map 3). All were held by Unionist MPs of various stripes, often elected unopposed. Such contests as there were came from other varieties of Unionism, including the occasional Liberal Unionist. No nationalist stood in County Antrim until SF put up candidates in 1918, all of whom were soundly defeated by margins as great as six to one.[7]

From 1903 South Antrim was represented by Charles Craig MP, brother of James Craig, MP for East Down, who would lead Ulster Unionism and become Northern Ireland's first prime minister. Charles scraped in with a majority of 849 against a Liberal Unionist in a by-election but subsequently held it easily until the seat was abolished in 1922. North Antrim was more unpredictable. Some Presbyterian home rulers and the nationalists in the Glens made the seat a Unionist/Liberal marginal. In 1906 a Liberal Unionist won, but in 1910 an Ulster Unionist squeaked in with a majority of 384 and held the seat in the increasingly fraught political climate of 1910.

The other two County Antrim MPs epitomized the old ascendancy class swept aside in the rest of the country after 1885 and they usefully demonstrate how radically different Antrim was from anywhere else in Ireland. They had minimal connection with Ulster Unionism, being firmly based in English society. East Antrim was held by Colonel James McCalmont, a product of Eton and the Hussars. As aide-de-camp to the viceroy, the duke of Marlborough, he was an important link to Dublin Castle. McCalmont held the seat from 1885 until his death in 1913 when he was succeeded by his son, Robert, who during the First World War served with the Irish Guards and rose to the rank of brigadier-general. After 1906 the McCalmonts were unopposed in elections.[8]

Mid-Antrim was, in effect, the family seat of the O'Neills. It was held from 1910 by Arthur Edward Bruce O'Neill who was elected unopposed. The O'Neills were substantial landed aristocracy, based at Shane's Castle near Antrim town. Arthur O'Neill was an officer in the Life Guards, having received his commission in 1897. He died in November 1914, the first MP killed in the First World War. His youngest son, Terence, then just two months old, became prime minister of Northern Ireland in 1963.[9]

After the 1906 general election it looked as if unionism was safe for the foreseeable future since the new British Liberal government's large majority meant that it did not need IPP support. Furthermore, the leaders of the Liberal government appeared to see no political advantage in promoting home rule.[10] Yet suddenly, out of left field, in 1909 a hitherto-unimagined connection between home rule and social reform emerged. The House of Lords rejected the government's budget and caused the biggest constitutional crisis of twentieth-century Britain. From being surplus to requirements after the 1906 general election, the IPP unexpectedly found itself holding the balance of power in the House of Commons after two general elections in 1910. As had been the case since 1886, the price of Irish support was home rule.

While the majority of people in the rest of the country were delighted with this prospect, in Belfast and County Antrim the unionist majority was horrified. As a result of the crisis the so-called 'People's Budget' had provoked in 1909, the Liberal government proposed to remove the Lords' veto on legislation, substituting instead a maximum two-year delay for contentious items passed by the Commons. After two general elections, the outcome of the December 1910 contest was a dead heat – 272 Conservatives and 272 Liberals. H.H. Asquith, the Liberal prime minister, needed the support of John Redmond's party to govern, but also to push through his plan to reform the House of Lords.

The result of the second election in December 1910 had obvious consequences. In return for helping to overturn the Lords' veto in the Parliament Act of 1911, the IPP was promised a home rule bill, which in theory would pass after the mandatory two-year delay. This turn of events produced consternation among Ulster unionists. In Belfast with its huge population, its concentration of vast wealth, its business and commerce tied tightly into the British industrial and financial system, there was particular outrage. There was genuine horror among industrialists and property owners at the prospect of being governed by a Catholic-dominated, backward, agriculturally oriented parliament in Dublin. They were determined to use all means available, all their connections with senior Conservative Party figures at Westminster, their enormous disposable wealth, and, if necessary, armed resistance, to prevent it.

Unionists had seen the way the wind was blowing after the Liberal victory in the January 1910 election formally removed the power of the Lords to amend a money bill. Even before the December election, called to give Liberals a mandate to remove the Lords' veto on any legislation, members of the UUC standing committee had begun to resurrect the structures that had been developed to oppose the 1893 home rule bill. Immediately the result of the December 1910 election was known, unionists publicly expressed their opposition in no uncertain terms, although their determination to resist home rule, by force if necessary, was never taken seriously by the IPP and completely ignored by republicans who were not interested in home rule. As far as the British government was concerned, any concessionary move towards unionists at this early stage even before the Parliament bill was tabled would, in the words of Nicholas Mansergh, have 'affronted [Redmond] beyond measure'.[11] In the circumstances, Ulster Unionist party opposition seemed unnecessarily hyperbolic.

On 10 January 1911 James Craig MP told the British *Morning Post* 'of the silent preparations that are being made to meet by armed resistance the encroachment on their [Ulster unionist] civil and religious liberties that would naturally follow the establishment of a parliament in Dublin'. His warning went unheeded. Nevertheless, he was speaking the truth about preparations already under way. There had been some armed groups and drilling in both 1886 and 1893. One of the instigators of the 1893 opposition, Fred Crawford, who formed the Young Ulster Society in that year and later became infamous to nationalists as the main gun runner for the UVF, began to revive armed opposition in 1910.[12] A lot of the initial planning in 1910 seems to have been based on what happened in 1893. That included the revival of Unionist Clubs, originally established in 1893 but suspended in 1896.

The purpose of resurrecting the clubs in 1910 was to unite and focus opposition against any proposed third home rule bill. Many officers of clubs and their members were also in the Orange Order but the point of the clubs was to mobilize maximum participation among unionist men because while all Orangemen were unionists, not all unionists were Orangemen. Membership of the clubs grew rapidly. In April 1911 the Council of Unionist Clubs of Ireland met to coordinate opposition. Many council members would become leading figures in the UVF, organizing drilling on the estates of 'big houses' across Ulster. By December 1911 there were 164 clubs, rising to 316 in August 1912, all but ten in Ulster.[13] In Antrim the RIC noted in March 1911 that Unionist Clubs had been formed in most of the major towns of the county and were being set up in rural districts.[14]

The female counterpart of the Unionist Clubs was the Ulster Women's Unionist Council (UWUC) established on 23 January 1911.[15] By the end of that year there were 40,000 members and by 1913 the number had risen to over 115,000. It was the largest women's political association in Ireland but was concentrated in the north-east. By comparison, there were 4,425 women in Cumann na mBan in 1914 but only about thirty in Belfast at the time of the 1916 Rising.[16] The first UWUC president was the duchess of Abercorn. She was succeeded in 1913 by Theresa, marchioness of Londonderry, wife of the enormously wealthy coal magnate Lord Londonderry, president of the UUC. The importance of these aristocratic women in the opposition to home rule cannot be underestimated. The marchioness of Londonderry was the eldest daughter of the premier earl of England, the nineteenth earl of Shrewsbury. She had unrivalled connections with the British royal family and with the Conservative Party – hence her sobriquet 'Queen of Toryism'. Her husband had been viceroy of Ireland from 1886 to 1889 and it was during those years in Dublin that the marchioness's appetite for politics was whetted. She had thrown herself into opposition to Gladstone's 1893 home rule bill and organized a petition with 20,000 women's signatures against the measure.

By the time of the third home rule bill, the marchioness was perhaps the leading political hostess in England. She was a patron of Sir Edward Carson and a personal friend of Andrew Bonar Law, from 1911 leader of the Conservative Party.[17] As MPs, Craig, Carson and other important Unionist figures were personally friendly with senior Conservative MPs like Bonar Law and Balfour, met them regularly in Westminster and engaged socially with them at the Carlton club. The role of Walter Long from Wiltshire, MP for South County Dublin, chief secretary from 1905 until 1910, leader of Irish Unionist MPs until 1910 and president of the UUC, was invaluable in advocating the unionist cause in the Conservative Party. Long would later chair the cabinet Irish committee 1918–20 as the Government of Ireland bill went through parliament. Carson, who took over from Long as Unionist leader, was especially close to Bonar Law. In Belfast Craig entertained British senior military officers in his home 'Craigavon'. For example, Brigadier-General Lord Edward Gleichen, officer commanding British troops in Belfast from 1911, and a grand-nephew of Queen Victoria, played bridge at Craigavon with Craig's wife as partner.

In parallel with this political organization and agitation, the leaders of the UUC began planning armed resistance should home rule be enforced. Craig had been surprisingly open in his January 1911 interview with the *Morning Post* when he mentioned 'armed resistance'. On 22 November 1910 Fred Crawford, believing the direction of travel at Westminster to be inevitable, had already begun his quest for guns. Using the *noms de plume* 'H. Matthews' and 'W.H. Jones', he wrote from the offices of his Belfast starch manufacturing company to four arms manufacturers in England, Germany and Austria to ask if they could supply, 'for immediate delivery 20,000 Military Rifles with and without bayonets, and one million rounds of ammunition'. In case his requests were unsuccessful, Crawford placed adverts in six European newspapers in Paris, Brussels, Berlin and Vienna: 'Wanted, 20,000 good second-hand small-bore military rifles with one million rounds of ammunition for same.'[18] It is quite clear that Crawford's activities were authorized and paid for by the UUC. His diary indicates there was an 'Inner Committee of the UUC formed to look into the question of physical force' – the arms committee.[19] As he put it in a letter to a friend in the Royal Irish Rifles, the committee consisted 'of the leading men in this part of Ulster, and men who have practically unlimited means to carry this thro.'[20]

By the end of 1912 as the UVF was being established, the secret arms committee of the UUC, composed of men based in Belfast, included some leading figures in Ulster Unionism such as James Craig MP. The other members were Crawford, retired General Richardson, later commanding officer of the UVF, Colonel Hackett Pain, chief of staff of the UVF, Captain Wilfrid Spender, UVF quartermaster, George Clark of the 'wee yard' Workman Clark, who was chairman, James Cunningham, a wealthy stockbroker whose family owned an extensive estate, Fernhill, at Glencairn in north-west Belfast, Richard Cowzer, an employee of Cunningham who acted as messenger and general factotum for the committee, Captain Frank Hall, secretary of the Unionist Clubs, Dawson Bates, honorary secretary of the UUC, Alexander McDowell, a solicitor, and Samuel Kelly, coal importer and ship owner.[21] All leading men in Ulster Unionist politics were therefore fully aware of what was going on: Crawford recounts how, in 1911, he had displayed specimens of his purchases – 'cold steel' as he said – for their approval.

Craig, Cunningham and Cowzer looked after the finances. Both Craig and Cunningham were personally vastly wealthy and had important connections with other financiers and bankers. Craig had inherited £100,000 in cash in 1900 (about £12 million today) from his father, a millionaire whiskey distiller. As well as continuing the distillery business, Craig became a stockbroker. He had five mansions around the greater Belfast area, the most substantial called Craigavon on the County Down shore of Belfast Lough.[22] Craig organized businessmen to subscribe substantial sums to the movement and Cunningham wrote out the cheques to pay for Crawford's arms purchases, which arrived at Larne on 24 April 1914.

The results of these preparations soon became evident in Belfast. The years 1912–14 were fraught with danger for Catholics in the city, whether home rule supporters or republicans. Ulster unionists were organizing frenetically throughout 1911 to resist home rule proposals. By early 1912, as it became clear a bill would be introduced at Westminster, unionist opposition became more belligerent and militarist, encouraged by ferocious rhetoric from Carson and Craig, and aided and abetted by the leader of the Conservative opposition in Westminster, Andrew Bonar Law. The unionist majority in Belfast looked on the city's Catholic population as the enemy within, scapegoats, hostages for the actions of the home rule leaders in Dublin and Westminster. If the precedents of the lethal civil disturbances in 1886 and 1893 in response to earlier home rule bills were anything to go by, there would be death and destruction in Belfast as a third home rule bill made its way through parliament.[23]

As the introduction of the bill in Westminster approached in April 1912, unionists mounted an enormous show of strength on the southern outskirts of Belfast at Balmoral in fields belonging to the Royal Ulster Agricultural

Society. Seventy special trains brought men from various parts of Ulster. An estimated 300,000 people attended. What was said to be the biggest union jack ever woven was flown from a thirty-metre flagpole as 100,000 men marched past, exhibiting the results of drilling over the previous months. On the reviewing stand, beside Unionist leaders stood Bonar Law, and around the platform, seventy Conservative MPs from England, Scotland and Wales. A strident resolution was passed opposing home rule. The lines were drawn that day for a lengthy and bitter battle between two alliances, on the one hand the Liberal government and the IPP, on the other the Conservative opposition and Ulster Unionists.

Two days after the Balmoral demonstration, the home rule bill was tabled in Westminster on 11 April. Four days later, unionists were dealt a terrible, psychologically demoralizing blow. The *Titanic*, the pride of Belfast's Harland & Wolff shipyard, sank on its maiden voyage to New York after striking an iceberg. It went down with the loss of 1,500 lives. Building passenger liners at the forefront of modern technology for the White Star shipping line was what set Belfast apart from the rest of Ireland. Some of these ships competed for the 'blue riband', the unofficial title of the fastest ship across the Atlantic. The *Titanic*, the largest ship in the world, was the very symbol of Belfast's and Ulster unionism's superiority over backward, rural, Catholic Ireland, a demonstration of Belfast's world-class engineering that provided some legitimacy for opposition to home rule. Had the *Titanic* completed the Atlantic crossing in record time, unionists would have used the ensuing publicity to ask how Dublin-based politicians, who knew nothing about modern technological society, could propose to govern modern industrialized Belfast. For the *Titanic*, the very emblem of northern Protestant superiority, to sink in the same week as the home rule bill was introduced seemed an ominous omen.

Nevertheless, symbolic as it may have been for many unionists, the tragedy in the North Atlantic did nothing to deter the militaristic preparations evident at Balmoral. Unionist Clubs had proliferated in Antrim and Belfast and drilling proceeded on the estates of prominent unionist landowners. In May the future British Labour leader, George Lansbury MP, asked Augustine Birrell, the Irish chief secretary, whether he intended to do anything about drilling.[24] By May 1912 in Belfast and Antrim there was drilling at Balmoral, Carrickfergus, Whitehead and Mossley.[25] Rumours also spread about large imports of guns. As the Orange marching season began in the summer, tensions heightened, reaching a climax in July when serious violence erupted in the Belfast shipyards.

On 29 June there was a minor clash in Castledawson, County Derry, between a Hibernian band returning from a home rule rally in Maghera, County Derry, and a Protestant Sunday school outing from Whitehouse in north Belfast, mainly children and teenagers. Local unionists came to the aid of the Belfast excursion and fighting broke out. There were no serious injuries but eventually seven local unionists and twenty-three Hibernians stood trial for the day's events.[26] Apprentices from Workman Clark, which had a small shipyard near Whitehouse, attacked Catholic workers and chased them out of the yard on 2 July after emotional accounts of the Castledawson incident appeared in the press the day before. Another version is that an argument between a riveter, whose son had been injured in Castledawson, and a Catholic worker sparked the trouble. Disturbances quickly spread to the main Workman Clark shipyard in east Belfast and then to other engineering works and linen mills. About 2,000 men, mainly Catholic, were expelled from the shipyards with great violence but also along with them about 500 Protestants. The latter were mainly trade unionists and Protestant workers who had refused to join Unionist Clubs.[27] Attempts by the men expelled to return to work after the July holidays were violently repulsed: they faced destitution.

Castledawson is often taken to be the sole cause of the expulsions from the Belfast shipyards in July 1912 but it was not the only incident that took place in the highly charged atmosphere of June 1912. Before the minor riot in Castledawson there were attacks on Catholics in Lisburn, Carrickfergus and Ballyclare, County Antrim, which Joe Devlin raised in the House of Commons when condemning the shipyard expulsions. In Lisburn, on 25 June, children had pelted priests and nuns taking Catholic children on an outing to Ardglass with mud and stones.[28] There had also been violence in other parts of the north, for example in Kilrea, County Derry, and the city of Derry.[29] All these incidents took place in the context of scurrilous, irresponsible rumours in the unionist press, allegedly predicting the dire fate of Protestants in a home rule Ireland. It was said Catholics were organizing ballots for the property of Protestants that would be taken over on the day home rule came into force; that a massacre of Protestants by Hibernians was planned.[30] In his response to Devlin, Birrell claimed that tensions had been rising in the shipyards for some time before the Castledawson incident, which he roundly condemned.

Devlin raised the expulsions in the Commons on 31 July and went into some detail about the events which he called 'shocking and unparalleled atrocities'.[31] He read a graphic report in the London newspaper *The Star* into the record:

> The reign of terror continues in Belfast, and matters have arrived at such a stage that either a Catholic or a man possessed of progressive ideas is not safe walking in the streets. Night after night the streets are paraded by Orange mobs looking for victims, and it matters little whether they are male or female, the same brutality is meted out.

There was much more in the same vein. Devlin pointed out that on 23 July when Harland & Wolff reopened after the holidays it had been arranged that those expelled at the beginning of the month could return safely. However, when they tried to do so they were prevented from entering and fights had broken out on the road to the shipyard. After an hour, 400 troops of the Cheshire Regiment, with fixed bayonets, and 200 RIC were deployed, to no avail.[32] The chief secretary reported that while there had been eighty assaults since 2 July inside or near the shipyards, only two men had been arrested.[33] Devlin gave examples of the violence meted out to those attacked in the yards – one man was held naked over an open furnace, another thrown into a barrel of tar, and several had to dive into the River Lagan to escape being pelted with rivets. Individuals caught by gangs were badly kicked and beaten. According to Devlin, the trouble began in Workman Clark's yard when the heads of departments asked workers to join Unionist Clubs and 'to take part in the pantomimic performances which those who live in Belfast know to their cost'. He maintained that the Catholics and 500 Protestants who refused were 'marked men'. Devlin went on to apportion blame. He named Carson who had announced that he was 'going over to Ireland to break every law' but who stayed in England and allowed 'his wretched dupes in Belfast' to break every law and Bonar Law, who told a rally at Blenheim Palace in July that he 'could imagine no length of resistance to which Ulster will go that I will not be ready to support'. Next came the duke of Norfolk, 'the mighty Catholic Duke of England', who also attended what Devlin described as 'the saturnalia at Blenheim' and who declared there were no lengths that opponents of home rule would go to that he was not prepared to defend. Devlin was supported in a lengthy contribution by Ramsay MacDonald, the future Labour prime minister, who had met a deputation of workers, Catholic and Protestant and neither, from Belfast. In a powerful speech MacDonald explicitly blamed Carson and Charles Craig MP for inciting violence against home rulers.

Conditions for Catholics in Belfast continued to deteriorate during the remainder of 1912 as the home rule bill progressed through Westminster. The climax of polarization in Belfast was the signing of the Ulster Covenant on 28 September, so-called 'Ulster Day', a gigantic display of politico-ethnic solidarity by northern Protestants. In a demonstration of their complete dominance in Belfast, Ulster Unionists took over Belfast City Hall for the occasion. All factories, shipyards and mills closed for the day as did all shops in the city centre to enable workers to attend the ceremony. The immense crowd was marshalled by 2,500 members of the Unionist Clubs and the Orange Order, wearing white armbands and carrying white staves. Using a silver, square-sided pen specially made and engraved by Sharman D. Neill of Donegall Place, Carson was first to sign, followed by Lord Londonderry, viceroy of Ireland at the time of the first home rule bill in 1886 and in 1912 president of the UUC, then James Craig, followed by representatives of the Protestant Churches in Ireland. Across Ulster, 237,368 men signed the Covenant and 234,046 women signed a declaration couched in similar terms. While Belfast was the most spectacular venue, arrangements were made in 500 Protestant parish halls and presbyteries across Ulster for signing ceremonies.[34]

This immense show of strength did nothing to impede the progress of the home rule bill. By January 1913 it had passed the Commons and would inevitably be defeated in the Lords, but under the terms of the Parliament Act of 1911 would automatically become law in September 1914. To frustrate that progress, buoyed up by the ethnic solidarity of Ulster Day, the Ulster Unionist response was to intensify extra-parliamentary opposition which was not taken seriously either by the police or Dublin Castle. Since such activity had begun in earnest in 1911 both the RIC and the government remained very relaxed. The Antrim CI reported in 1911 that unionists were confident home rule would not be enacted, 'for many years, if ever', and therefore that there was no need to prepare for armed resistance. The first stage of opposition would be 'passive resistance to taxation', only then followed by 'active resistance if necessary'.[35] A year later the RIC deputy inspector general, W.H. O'Connell, reported to Dublin Castle that the only evidence he had of illegal importation of weapons was 200 rifles from Germany, which had been seized.[36]

On the other hand, there was suspicion at the top levels in the RIC that no effort was being made to monitor drilling or uncover weapons caches. In September 1912 Colonel Sir Neville Chamberlain, RIC inspector general, instructed CI Holmes of the Special Branch to draw to the attention of county and district inspectors in Ulster suspicions that large quantities of rifles were being stored in the north of Ireland. Each was to be asked to reflect on his position if 'it transpired that arms and ammunition had been collected and hidden away, in his county or district, unknown to him'.[37] Birrell felt no urgency. As late as August 1913 he wrote to Asquith about reports from the RIC that 'they are all obviously onesided. Sir Neville Chamberlain himself is a true blue + the majority of the Reporting Officers (probably) would be themselves Covenanters, were they not policemen'.[38]

Meanwhile unionist preparations proceeded apace. By 13 December 1912 members of Ulster Clubs aged between seventeen and sixty-five had been transformed into units of paramilitary volunteers. On 13 January 1913 they were formally constituted by the UUC as the Ulster Volunteer Force. A prerequisite for enrolling was to have signed the Covenant (which could be signed retrospectively) and numbers were restricted to 100,000. There was no difficulty recruiting. In Belfast units were either based on the workplace or on streets. Command was at grassroot level, with the men who ran the local Orange lodge often playing a dual role. The smallest unit, a squad, was based on a street and consisted of a dozen men, including the squad leader. Two squads made up a section. The warrens of tiny streets in Belfast quickly produced hundreds of squads.

As in the rest of Ulster, the senior UVF officers in Belfast and County Antrim tended to be from the aristocracy or prominent businessmen. For example, Lord Castlereagh commanded the North Belfast UVF Regiment, which had six battalions, a total of more than 8,000 men, and Captain the Hon. Arthur O'Neill MP the North Antrim Regiment. In Lisburn A.P. Jenkins, owner of a major linen mill, established the UVF and commanded the 1st South Antrim Battalion.[39] The overall commander of the Antrim UVF was retired Major-General Sir William Adair, from a prominent Antrim landed family, formerly deputy adjutant-general of the Royal Marines. In 1914 he was in charge of landing and dispersal of the guns brought into Larne.[40]

Unsurprisingly, during this period of increasingly frenzied unionist opposition to home rule, the nationalist minority in Belfast and Antrim kept very quiet indeed. Their sentiments were expressed through the main nationalist newspaper, the *Irish News*, which kept up a tirade of mockery and derision about the unionist tactics. The paper's response to the vast demonstrations at the time of the Covenant gives a flavour of the attitude of nationalists, an attitude which, of course, remained mute in factories and mills. The newspaper dismissed Ulster Day as 'a silly masquerade'.

> At last the curtain has been rung down on the Ulster Day farce … The Carson circus having toured North East Ulster … gave its final and greatest performance entitled, 'Signing the Covenant', in Belfast on Saturday, and wound up its fantastic career in a paroxysm of flag waving and noise, emblematic of the meaningless nonsense of the whole grotesque scheme from start to finish.[41]

Nationalists north and south confidently presumed that the parliamentary process would take its course, that home rule would inevitably be enacted in 1914, and that unionist opposition and threats, verbal or militaristic, should not and would not be taken seriously. Given the highly charged atmosphere in Belfast and the violence of summer 1912, it was prudent for nationalists to keep quiet and allow Redmond and the leadership of the IPP to challenge unionists. However, as 1913 wore on, unionists began to turn their fire away from their cowed victims in Belfast towards the British government and threaten insurrection.

From its formal inauguration in January 1913 the UVF became more open in its preparations and organization across north-east Ulster. Its greatest numbers were in Belfast and the leadership, both civil and military, was based in the city's old town hall, where the UUC had its central office. Fred Crawford, Carson's gunrunner, had rented the premises from Belfast Corporation for the UUC at the end of 1911 for £500 a year.[42] Parades in and through Belfast's main thoroughfares were impressive for their numbers and propaganda. However, they masked patchy organization and questionable efficiency. By summer 1913 the retired Lieutenant-General Sir George Richardson was appointed general officer commanding the UVF. He had a distinguished military record but was largely a useful figurehead. Most of the administrative work was carried out by Colonel George William Hackett Pain, the UVF's chief of staff, and Colonel McCammon, who also illegally retained his command of the 5th Special Reserve Battalion of the Royal Irish Rifles until the UVF was transformed into the 36th Ulster Division in 1914.[43] The men who really directed the activities of the UVF were the political wing, those running the UUC inner committee, principally Carson and Craig.

Hackett Pain and McCammon naturally modelled the UVF on the British army and created companies, battalions and regiments. Each county was to provide a regiment made up of several battalions, while Belfast was to have a regiment for each of its four parliamentary constituencies. That was the theory. In reality, whereas on paper Belfast had four regiments, the totals in the different parts of the city were lopsided, but taken together could have supplied double that number of regiments. East Belfast with more than 8,000 men, perhaps as many as 10,000 by the end of 1913, was the largest in the city. North Belfast grew to have eight battalions in its regiment, while west Belfast, essentially the Shankill, never produced more than two battalions totalling 3,500 men.[44] South Belfast had four battalions comprising 2,800 men and was commanded by Fred Crawford, appropriately the UVF's director of ordnance.[45] Also, while a British army battalion had four companies, the number of companies in UVF battalions varied extensively as did the number of men in each company.

Although each county was supposed to produce one regiment, in County Antrim there were initially four: South, East, Mid and North Antrim, closely based on local districts. Together they were taken to constitute a division. In 1914 the County Antrim division was reduced to three regiments: North, Central and South.[46] Each regiment varied widely in size. South Antrim was by far the largest. In August 1913 its 3rd Battalion alone had nine companies comprising 1,567 men. Its commander was the egregiously named Algernon William John Clotworthy Skeffington, twelfth Viscount Massereene and Ferrard. The battalion's district ran from Antrim town through Randalstown, south to Crumlin and Glenavy. The 1st South Antrim Battalion was based in Lisburn and the 2nd ran through rural areas from Dunmurry to Aghalee on the south-western boundary of the county. North Antrim was the next biggest regiment, but as an example of the variation in organizational structure it had only two battalions: 1st ('Ballymena'), and 2nd ('Ballymoney'). However, they both had regiment-like numbers with almost 2,500 in 'Ballymena' in ten companies and 1,200 in 'Ballymoney' in nine companies. 'Ballymoney' covered the area from Ballycastle to Portrush on the north coast and south to Ballymoney. 'Ballymena' was based on the town and surrounding district, including Galgorm, Braid, Cullybackey and Ahoghill.[47] In August 1913 the total in County Antrim's four UVF regiments was 6,285 men, but by 1914 the figure was likely to have been in excess of 10,000.[48]

On paper Belfast and County Antrim had over 40,000 men in the UVF by 1914, almost half the organization's total. The reality on the ground was rather different. At the time of a large UVF parade at Balmoral on 28 September 1913, the anniversary of the Covenant, the RIC believed the number of UVF in Belfast was 10,390, organized in fourteen battalions, mainly in East and North Belfast, nothing like the almost 30,000 on the muster rolls. There were similar discrepancies in Antrim, where many members were only nominal. Large numbers failed to turn up for any parades or drill and were threatened with dismissal. In the case of the North Antrim Regiment, as many as 1,100 (out of 3,700 on the roll) had defaulted by May 1914. In 'A' company of the regiment, 'the CO reported in February 1914 73 "effectives" and 58 "non-effectives". A large proportion of the above have never attended any drills and it is questionable whether these men intend to turn out in any capacity.'[49]

Nonetheless, regardless of their preparedness or expertise, there were still thousands of men in Belfast and Antrim willing to turn out for parades and drill sessions, to pay for their uniforms and buy rifles. They presented a formidable force, albeit as yet, largely unarmed. Their parades and demonstrations along the highways and byways had an intimidating effect, especially in Belfast where the nationalist population deeply resented the UVF's apparent impunity from arrest or investigation by the RIC.

The sequence of events in the north of Ireland from 1911 to 1914 is well known and well documented. As tension rose to fever pitch with the introduction of the home rule bill in April 1912, the signing of the Ulster Covenant in September that year by 470,000 Ulster Protestants, the formation of the UVF at the end of the year, and the announcement of plans for a provisional government of Ulster, put Belfast at the epicentre of Ulster Unionist seditious activity. With nationalists in Belfast unanimously in support of home rule, which seemed certain to become law, and unionists in total opposition, there was no space for republicans. As the next chapter will show, in Belfast those supporting the republican cause numbered only a few dozen. Given the tightly strung emotions and intense hostility of the city's dominant unionist majority, these republicans only very cautiously followed the example of Dublin in forming an Irish Volunteer unit in response to the mobilization of the UVF.

3 Nationalist politics in Belfast and County Antrim before 1914

In many respects the cradle of Irish republicanism was Belfast and County Antrim, where the political philosophy emerged and flourished in the 1790s. Its leaders were Presbyterians and it was a predominantly Presbyterian force of about 4,000, led by Henry Joy McCracken, which faced British troops and Irish militia at the battle of Antrim in June 1798. United Irishmen, almost exclusively Presbyterian, had already taken the County Antrim towns of Larne, Ballymena and Randalstown before McCracken's main force was defeated at Antrim.[1] A century later circumstances could not have been more different. In Antrim republicanism was regarded as a threat to Protestants' way of life, their prosperity and political domination. Presbyterians themselves had split in the 1830s into liberal and conservative wings and other offshoots, but ultimately by the end of the nineteenth century, all Presbyterian factions, as well as Anglicans, were united in their opposition to home rule and, it goes without saying, to the more advanced version of separatism exemplified by Irish republicanism.[2] Given the political and religious complexion of Antrim as a whole and Belfast, in particular, republicanism was a tender plant at the beginning of the twentieth century. As a political presence, it was invisible. What public manifestation there was of an Irish Ireland tended to be strictly cultural and, outside the authentically Gaelic areas of north Antrim, even that was viewed with hostility. In the prevailing anti-Irish climate of the county, one of the advantages the late nineteenth-century Gaelic cultural revival had in north Antrim was the tradition of Gaelic-speaking descendants of Presbyterians from Scotland and *Innse Gall* who lived there. Appreciation of Gaelic culture in the Glens of Antrim was, therefore, not necessarily subversive as it was elsewhere in the county.

The Gaelic revival was late arriving in Antrim, even though Eoin MacNeill, one of the movement's originators and chief proponents, hailed from the Glens of Antrim where there was still a Gaeltacht at the beginning of the twentieth century, chiefly in Glendun, Glenariffe and on Rathlin Island. To preserve and celebrate the Irish language, traditions, music, songs and games of the Glens, Feis na nGleann was established. The driving force behind the project was Francis Joseph Bigger, a lawyer and historian from north Belfast who holidayed in Cushendun. He assembled an interested group of friends, comprising Protestant and Catholic professionals, ascendancy types from 'big house' society in north Antrim, along with others, including poet Joseph Campbell, who was Presbyterian, and Denis McCullough, a piano tuner and music shop owner from Belfast, and a leading light in the IRB. On 28 February 1904 they met with a group of people from the Glens and planned the cultural festival that became the inaugural Feis na nGleann on 30 June 1904; it subsequently became an annual event.[3]

There was no equivalent display of political nationalism to match that annual idyll of cultural nationalism in the Glens. The outward sign of political nationalism was support for home rule and that was tightly restricted to west Belfast and pockets in north Belfast. Catholics in north Antrim around Ballycastle and Cushendall did support home rule but generally kept their allegiance to themselves. The only overt support for home rule in the north of the county came from individual Presbyterians, mainly around Ballymoney, the traditional centre for Liberal or Gladstonian Protestants. The most notable was the Presbyterian minister, Revd John B. Armour, who was prominent in the Ulster Liberal Association, which was resurrected in 1906 before the general election of that year. However, despite a Liberal Unionist winning the North Antrim seat in 1906, by 1910 Liberals and Liberal Unionists had been swept aside in all constituencies by the Conservative and Unionist tide.[4] In May 1912 Liberal Unionists and Conservatives bowed to the inevitable and formally merged after meeting in the Carlton club becoming the Conservative and Unionist Party.[5]

The mainly Presbyterian Liberal followers of Armour were appalled at the belligerent campaign led by Carson after 1912 and organized an alternative campaign that reached its climax in October 1913 when Armour and Liberal supporters joined with nationalists like Roger Casement and Alice Stopford Green to hold a home rule rally in Ballymoney to protest against the 'lawlessness of Carson' and Ulster Unionists' talk of a provisional government of Ulster. Between 400 and 500 attended the meeting, where speakers urged people to sign an alternative covenant extolling the virtues of home rule and, in reference to the machinations of Carson and the UUC, urged people to stand together and 'help one another when our liberties are threatened by any non-statutory body that may be set up in Ulster or elsewhere'. They managed to gather about 12,000 signatories over some weeks, mainly in north Antrim.[6] However, the signatories were not nationalists but liberals, supporters of the British Liberal government, very much a minority compared to the tens of thousands in Antrim who had signed the Ulster Covenant.

Even in west and north Belfast overt support for home rule was carefully managed, first by the Catholic Church and then after his election in 1906, by Joe Devlin, the only IPP MP in Belfast or County Antrim. The certainty of instant violent retribution for overstepping the accepted position of nationalists in Belfast was only too well embedded in recent local experience. Elsewhere in the county, nationalists were such a minority that they offered no political threat. Migration by workers seeking jobs in the city's industries had produced a dense Catholic population in the west of the city which, if properly organized and harnessed, had the numbers to elect an MP. Born in 1871 in Hamill Street in the Falls district of west Belfast, Devlin was first elected as MP for Kilkenny North in 1902. For many years he worked to win the only available nationalist seat in his native city, prevailing by a whisker in 1906. It took Devlin years of manoeuvring to wrest control from the Catholic clergy, both of nationalist politics in Belfast and of the *Irish News*. As a consequence, while endorsing home rule politics, his main emphasis was the social and economic welfare of his Catholic constituents. Second, he also had to promote openly Catholic policies and avoid antagonizing the city's unionist establishment which, after all, controlled the employment of his constituents in the mills of the Falls Road. The Ancient Order of Hibernians (AOH) was Devlin's main instrument for advancing the dual aims of his constituents' welfare and home rule for Ireland. In many respects, it mirrored the Orange Order. Whereas Orangemen had to be born Protestant, AOH men had to be Catholic. The AOH marched on Catholic holy days carrying banners honouring Irish saints and the Virgin Mary. By the turn of the century the AOH had been integrated into the IPP in many parts of the country. Its delegates played a major role in party selection conventions.

Devlin harnessed the AOH as an electoral machine having witnessed the activities of its American counterpart while on a fundraising trip to the US in 1902. He transformed the AOH into a mass movement and became its grandmaster for life in 1904. Under his tutelage, the governing body of the AOH, the 'Board of Erin', publicly adopted the IPP's policy on home rule in 1905 by which time the order had 10,000 members. That number climbed to 64,000 in 1909.[7] The Hibernians also received an enormous boost in 1911 when the AOH was recognized as an 'approved society' (as was the Orange Order) for the purposes of the National Insurance Act of that year. This recognition entitled the AOH to an annual fee from the government of 3s. 8d. per member for administering the insurance system. In 1911 the AOH had 433 divisions in Ulster totalling 130,000 with the largest membership in County Tyrone.[8] By 1915 the AOH employed 1,400 people and had 122,000 in its insurance section.[9]

Thanks to Devlin the AOH was especially strong in west Belfast. There, Devlin used it as the IPP organization doling out patronage, registering voters, and in the 1906 election, getting out the vote and organizing personation on an industrial scale. He won Belfast West by a mere sixteen votes with a suspiciously high turnout of ninety-five per cent. However, Devlin's appeal was consciously populist rather than nationalist. His public priorities were always directed towards improving the conditions of the thousands of (mainly female) millworkers in west Belfast. That was acceptable to the unionist city fathers. Stridently advocating home rule in Belfast could lead to dangerous retribution for his constituents. The same was true for the rest of Antrim and what was the point in taking the risk in the county outside Belfast when there was no hope of any success? Banging the home rule drum was best left to the leaders of the party safe in faraway Dublin or London: John Redmond and John Dillon.

However, Devlin's activities were not confined merely to west Belfast. He was also the general secretary of the United Irish League (UIL), which ran the IPP's constituency organization in Ireland. As AOH grandmaster and UIL secretary Devlin had a critical hand in the selection of Westminster candidates for the IPP. In this dual capacity he denied access to supporters of rival nationalist politicians like William O'Brien and Tim Healy. He was accused of packing selection conventions and was not averse to using strong arm tactics by deploying his 'baton men' – usually sent from west Belfast – to places where there was a prospect of trouble.

By the time of the crucial elections in 1910 Devlin was the dominant nationalist figure in Ulster. A charismatic, inspiring orator, full of wit and invective, he was much in demand as a speaker. T.M. Healy dubbed him 'the pocket Demosthenes' because of his small stature – praise indeed from Healy, himself an acclaimed speaker – but in west Belfast Devlin was simply 'Wee Joe'.[10] One of the top three figures in the IPP with Redmond and Dillon by the time of the home rule crisis, it was to Devlin that Winston Churchill turned in February 1912 when he made his ill-advised visit to Belfast to speak at a home rule rally organized by the Ulster Liberal Association in the Ulster Hall, regarded in Belfast as the temple of unionism. With the prospect of serious rioting, the organizers turned to Devlin, who provided Celtic Park on the edge of west Belfast as an alternative venue.

Devlin had been able to demonstrate his influence in west Belfast, but in doing so exposed the extreme limitations of nationalists' influence in the city. He could offer the first lord of the Admiralty a tent to speak in but nothing else, and no safety elsewhere. Unionists showed beyond doubt who controlled Belfast and demonstrated the subservient political status of nationalists.

Circumscribed as home rulers were in Belfast by the power of unionism, republicans, or 'advanced nationalists' as they were known, were literally an endangered species in the city and Antrim. The only public manifestation was an annual commemoration of Roddy McCorley and other local heroes of the 1798 Rising. This event, at the elaborate 'Temple of Liberty' in Toome, was organized by the Ulster IRB leader, Neal John O'Boyle, a farmer and publican from nearby Staffordstown.[11] This commemoration was countenanced partly because of Presbyterian involvement in the 1798 Rising and also because of its location, Toome, or Toomebridge, a Catholic town on the north shore of Lough Neagh where the Lower Bann flows out to form the western border of Antrim and Derry. Although being the leader of the IRB in Ulster may seem an important position, in fact at the turn of the century O'Boyle was the nominal head of a dormant organization that had only a handful of members in Antrim, mainly based in west Belfast and around Toome. O'Boyle's commemorations epitomized the role of the IRB in Ireland at the beginning of the twentieth century: middle-aged to elderly men meeting to remember past events. The police correctly did not regard them as any threat to the peace.[12]

However, in Belfast during the first decade of the new century a younger generation of men in their twenties began to reorganize the IRB, at first working through cultural groups like the Gaelic League and the GAA. The two leading lights in this reorganization were Denis McCullough and Bulmer Hobson, both of whom were to play important roles in the Irish Revolution. They were joined in 1906 by Seán Mac Diarmada, later one of the signatories of the 1916 Proclamation.[13] The three were all born in January 1883, though in very different circumstances. Hobson came from a comfortable, middle-class Quaker family that supported home rule. McCullough, a Catholic from west Belfast, grew up in a staunchly republican family, his father, grandfather and brother, all members of the IRB. McCullough was sworn into the organization at the age of eighteen in 1901. Belfast IRB meetings took place in the McCullough family home in Divis Street at the city end of the Falls Road.[14] Mac Diarmada, from a farming family in County Leitrim, came to Belfast to look for work in 1904.[15] There, he fell in with Hobson and McCullough who had met in 1901 in the Tír na nÓg branch of the Gaelic League in Albert Street off the Falls Road.

By 1901, aged eighteen, Hobson was a dedicated republican, learning Irish and engaging enthusiastically in the GAA and other Irish cultural activities. By 1902, in an illustration of the fate of anyone in Belfast engaged in nationalist activities, he had been sacked from his job at a printer's when the owner discovered he was organizing the Feis Uladh. Undeterred, Hobson set up hurling clubs in Belfast and helped establish the GAA's Antrim County Board in 1902. He also formed Na Fianna Éireann, the republican scouts, in June 1902.[16] McCullough introduced Hobson to the IRB and in 1904 Patrick Dempsey, the Belfast IRB centre, swore Hobson in. Together with McCullough they set about purging the organization of its middle-aged and elderly drinkers who seemed to constitute the IRB membership in Belfast. The purge included McCullough's own father, an alcoholic.[17] McCullough succeeded Neal John O'Boyle as Ulster IRB centre in 1908.[18]

In March 1905 Hobson and McCullough set up their own republican ginger group in Belfast, the Dungannon Clubs, named after the convention that met in Dungannon in 1782 to push for Irish legislative independence. However, it was clear that the Dungannon Clubs supported a far more radical view of Irish politics than either the Dungannon Convention or the type of home rule the leaders of the IPP sought. One club member in Belfast, Liam Gaynor, also an IRB member and later in the IRA, recalled that the objectives of the Dungannon Clubs were 'the complete independence of the country by physical force and the study and spread of Irish and the fostering of support of Irish industries.'[19] Rapidly, the original Belfast club spawned other Dungannon clubs in Derry and Tyrone, then London and Glasgow. Mac Diarmada joined the Belfast club in early 1906 and was soon sworn into the IRB. By that time Hobson was publishing a newspaper, titled *Republic*, to expound the ideology of the clubs.

Mac Diarmada was sacked from his job as a tram conductor in July 1906 for smoking on the tram's platform and was unemployed. Ernest Blythe, a member of the Belfast club, later a minister in the Irish Free State government, explained many years later how they appointed Mac Diarmada full-time organizer for the clubs in 1907. 'They simply got thirty members of the [Belfast] Dungannon club to agree to pay a shilling a week each ... and without more ado Seán went on the road.'[20] The Belfast club supplied him with a bicycle. This account of the club's appointment of Mac Diarmada is revealing in a number of ways. Almost all members later joined the Irish Volunteers in Belfast or elsewhere, mainly Dublin, and some later served in the IRA during the War of Independence. Second, the total membership of the Belfast club – about thirty – constituted pretty much the number of active republicans in the city in 1907. Political opinion among nationalists overwhelmingly favoured home rule and political activists strongly supported Devlin and were most likely to join his aggressively anti-republican AOH rather than support the IRB. Blythe recalled that when he went to Belfast in 1907 the number of IRB was 'very small, about fifteen members or so, and [they] met in the workshop at the back of Denis McCullough's premises'. They met weekly, 'sitting on benches and dismantled pianos'.[21] Their fortunes were not about to improve.

The 1906 British general election had dealt a severe blow to the hopes of Redmond and the IPP; the Liberal Party had won with a massive majority and did not need Redmond's support. Nevertheless, there was no consequent swing of support in Belfast or Antrim away from the IPP, much less towards Sinn Féin (SF), the new movement Arthur Griffith had formed. By 1908 there were eleven SF councillors on Dublin Corporation out of a total of eighty members. In Belfast, there were no SF candidates, let alone councillors. As a political party in the city and Antrim county, SF was non-existent. There was intense hostility towards republicans and they risked physical violence, both from unionists and Devlin's Hibernians. Devlin's West Belfast parliamentary seat was so precarious that any prospect of a split vote that might jeopardize it could not be contemplated.

By 1908 the young men who had been reorganizing the IRB and revitalizing republicanism in Belfast had decided it was barren ground. Hobson needed employment and had little chance of finding any in Belfast where unionists regarded him as worse than a Catholic nationalist; he was an apostate. He moved to Dublin where he remained at the centre of republican activity until the Rising. By 1908 Mac Diarmada had become national organizer for SF and later the IRB and was also living in Dublin. McCullough remained in Belfast and would become the Ulster representative on the IRB's supreme council and in 1915 its president, but to all intents and purposes overt republican activity in Belfast and Antrim ceased until the founding of the Volunteers in 1913.[22]

While nationalist home rulers were spectators at the ever-growing aggressive public displays of unionist resistance after 1912, republicanism was at its lowest ebb, regarded as an irrelevance. It appeared home rule had triumphed politically and would shortly be a reality. In Dublin in 1912, SF had difficulty filling a room at its annual ard fheis. There was no ard fheis at all in 1913.[23] Away from the limelight Mac Diarmada, secretary of the IRB supreme council, was secretly working full tilt in Dublin to reorganize the IRB and managing a new IRB newspaper *Irish Freedom* funded by American money, but it looked a futile exercise that even the RIC did not take seriously.[24] In Belfast the numbers of IRB men remained tiny. They now met in a room in Berry Street in the city centre to discuss copies of the new newspaper; they called themselves the Freedom Club. The members were the usual suspects: McCullough, Rory Haskins, Seán Cusack, the eccentric Herbert Moore Pim, Archie Heron, Sam Heron, Seán Dempsey, Seamus Cullen, Harry and Paddy Osborne, Seán O'Sullivan, Seamus Dobbyn and Liam Gaynor.[25] Some of these men were prominent in the IRA in Belfast after 1919 and Cusack was later a senior officer in the National army. Blythe also remembered Seán Lester, later secretary-general of the League of Nations, Alf Cotton, Cathal O'Shannon, Dan Turley, shot by the IRA as a spy in 1922, and Harry Shiels, who was one of the guard over Bulmer Hobson when Volunteers held him prisoner prior to the Rising.[26] Not all were present at every meeting and some such as Cotton and Turley and Blythe himself had left Belfast by 1913 but the core group was a dozen strong.

According to Blythe there were two sluaithe or companies of Fianna Éireann in Belfast; there were between sixty and seventy boys in one while the other was the only girls' slua in Ireland.[27] From about 1910 they met in one of what was known as the 'Willowbank Huts' – disused, dilapidated premises off the Falls Road, formerly used by a British cavalry squadron. The huts were on a four-hectare site that ran from the Falls Road down to the Bog Meadows where the M1 motorway now runs into Belfast. West Belfast GAA clubs also used the site.[28] These activities constituted the sum total of republicanism in Belfast during the home rule crisis. The contrast with the numbers, money, influence and status enjoyed by Ulster unionist opposition to home rule could not have been greater.

   The enormous and increasingly belligerent UVF displays throughout 1913 in opposition to the home rule bill had produced unease among nationalists in the rest of the country. Detailed plans for a provisional government of Ulster announced by the UUC in Belfast were ominous. A proposal to take control of the administration of Ulster had been adumbrated as early as September 1911 when Carson told a vast crowd of fifty thousand men from the Orange Order and Unionist Clubs assembled in the grounds of James Craig's mansion 'Craigavon': 'We must be prepared … the morning Home Rule passes, ourselves to become responsible for the government of the Protestant Province of Ulster'.[29] Two years elapsed before these proposals were fleshed out. Addressing 500 members of the UUC in Belfast's Ulster Hall on 24 September 1913, Carson received support for a provisional government of seventy-five run by a five-strong committee, chaired by himself, to take over (six-county) Ulster the day home rule became law. A shadow administration would be established in the meantime covering all the departments of state such as education, commerce, law and taxation.[30] A military council was also set up alongside the civilian arrangements. Meanwhile, UVF parades across the north-east culminated in a massive demonstration at Balmoral on 27 September when the Belfast regiments of the UVF paraded.[31]

   These treasonable actions unnerved nationalists who were also aware of discussions behind the scenes to find some way to accommodate Ulster Unionists but did not know what those discussions entailed. Rumours abounded. A motion in the Commons in 1912 about exclusion of some northern counties from home rule, talk of arrangements, whereby individual counties could vote to opt out (the county option) on a temporary basis, and the apparent freedom of the Unionists' paramilitary force to march at will, all produced anxiety and unease throughout Ireland. An important article by Eoin MacNeill, 'The North Began', on 1 November in *An Claidheamh Soluis*, the newspaper of the Gaelic League, provided the catalyst for the creation of a body of nationalist volunteers as a counterpart to the UVF to advocate home rule lest the case went by default. MacNeill's article struck a chord and on 25 November thousands turned up at the Rotunda Rink in Dublin to enrol in the Irish Volunteers; over 3,000 did so on the first night.[32]

   Support for the Irish Volunteers was slower in Belfast and Antrim than in other parts of Ireland for the obvious reasons. The first public stirrings of any republican sentiment in Belfast and Antrim did not emerge until four months after the establishment of the Irish Volunteers in Dublin. From his position on the IRB supreme council, McCullough was aware of developments in Dublin and the role IRB men like Mac Diarmada played in organizing the Volunteers, placing IRB men in key positions.[33] McCullough was quickly active in Tyrone and Derry along with other IRB men like Pat McCartan and Cathal O'Shannon who encouraged IRB cells to establish Volunteer companies. By the spring of 1914 there were twelve companies in east Tyrone totalling about 600 men.[34] In west Tyrone there were about 750 Volunteers by January 1914.[35] By March there were eleven companies with about 1,250 Volunteers in County Derry with drilling in Magherafelt and Newbridge near Castledawson.[36] In Donegal Volunteer recruiting grew rapidly from the new year 1914 and by March there were eleven companies comprising 2,600 men.[37]

Replicating such activities in Belfast was a very different matter. Apart from the danger of attack by unionists and harassment by the police, most nationalists in Belfast were suspicious of the men organizing the Irish Volunteers, if not even hostile to them because the initiative was taken by McCullough and members of the Freedom Club, known republicans. Nationalists in west Belfast, and it was only there that Volunteers could really operate, would not support anything associated with republicanism. Devlin strongly discouraged support for the Volunteers and strenuously opposed drilling. It was only after the Curragh incident in March 1914 and the Larne gun running on 24–5 April 1914 that numbers grew in Belfast and Antrim, although again nothing like elsewhere in the country.

From April 1914 home rulers belatedly woke up to the seriousness of unionist resistance. They had already been deeply unsettled by various proposals from British government figures to placate unionists which by spring 1914 had taken on concrete form, including temporary partition of the whole of Ulster (though Ulster Unionists had already by 1913 settled on six counties) or a 'county option', whereby each county would be given a vote on home rule. Belfast (like Derry city) would be regarded as a unit equivalent to a county and the result would be pretty clear.

After the Curragh incident nationalists in the north-east of Ireland also decided they needed an army of their own since it was now apparent that the British army would not secure or defend home rule. Many had also lost confidence in the government's determination to see the policy through. The landing of a significant consignment of guns and ammunition at Larne, County Antrim, and County Down ports, Bangor and Donaghadee – over 25,000 rifles and 3 million rounds of ammunition – was the decisive moment. Units of the Irish Volunteers were established in almost all nationalist towns in Ulster, and even in Belfast 150 men enrolled in April. By June the number had risen to 600, a paltry figure when compared to that of west of the Bann and Derry.[38]

According to Seán Cusack, commandant of the Antrim and East Down IRA Brigade in 1919, the Irish Volunteers in Belfast were formed in St Mary's Hall in March 1914, significantly four months after the first enrolment in the Rotunda in November 1913. Cusack remembered that men joined because they felt the need to resist Carson and the UVF.[39] The senior officer in charge of the Volunteers was McCullough, who had no military experience. Cusack, who was a reserve NCO in the British army and had joined the IRB in 1912, was appointed chief instructor. In Antrim some men set up a Volunteer unit in Ballycastle but they were home rulers. There was no SF or republican activity in the county, according to Liam McMullan, who later became a captain in the Volunteers and engineer to the Antrim Brigade in 1921.[40] He maintained there was no republican activity until the conscription crisis in 1918 when some people in north Antrim began to support SF.

In Belfast, numbers remained very low until the IPP instructed the UIL to join the Volunteers in May 1914, after the third reading of the home rule bill. Devlin encouraged his supporters to join the Volunteers and moved to take control of the Irish Volunteers in Belfast in June 1914. It had become clear to Redmond that the leaders of the Volunteers were IRB men. As a result of Devlin throwing his weight behind the Volunteers, numbers in Belfast grew to between three and four thousand.[41] By June 1914 Devlin's supporters had taken over the Belfast executive of the Volunteers. Devlin made himself honorary colonel and took the salute at a march past in Shane's (now MacRory) Park in west Belfast on 7 June.[42]

Within a month, larger events on a European scale had overtaken the home rule crisis and the fear of a conflict between the UVF and the Irish Volunteers. After the assassination of Archduke Franz Ferdinand on 28 June and Russia's mobilization to defend Serbia against an Austrian attack, Britain's obligations under the Triple Entente came into play. After war was declared on 4 August there was a period of indecision surrounding the fate of the Government of Ireland Act 1914 (home rule) due to come into force in September. Both Carson and Redmond expressed their support for the British war effort but the role of the rival Volunteer forces remained unclear. Redmond initially offered the Irish Volunteers as a home defence force. However, Carson quickly outbid him by unequivocally committing the UVF to join the British army en masse. Asquith, the prime minister, had to consider the fact that there were almost 180,000 Irish Volunteers, the vast majority determined to have home rule, and that if their loyalty could be assured, they would provide a valuable reservoir of manpower for the British army. The support of the Volunteers would also mean the British government could reduce the size of the garrison in Ireland necessary to prevent a *coup de main* by the Volunteers. Asquith finally gave in to Redmond and placed home rule on the statute book on 18 September, although it was suspended until the end of the war. Redmond responded with his infamous Woodenbridge speech on 20 September when he urged the Irish Volunteers to join the war effort and go 'wherever the firing line extended'.[43]

Redmond's advice caused an immediate split in the Volunteers across the country. The vast majority supported the IPP leader and many joined the

British army. Meetings took place across the north in October 1914 to decide whether to support Redmond. In Belfast the Volunteers met in St Mary's Hall, where both Devlin and McCullough spoke. Seán Cusack believed, correctly as it turned out, that Devlin, true to form, would pack the meeting. Cusack asked for membership cards to be required as Volunteers entered the hall.[44] In the event, huge numbers of Devlin supporters arrived, all carrying cards, which Cusack was convinced were bogus. The only item on the agenda was whether to support Redmond's Woodenbridge speech. Devlin's short address in favour was met with 'long and loud applause'. After being shouted down and heckled for fifteen minutes, McCullough realized the result was a foregone conclusion and gave up. After the meeting the Volunteers split with only about 150 out of over 3,000 staying loyal to McCullough. At the first muster of Irish Volunteers at the Willowbank huts, about three weeks after the split, only forty-six men turned up.[45]

Many of the others, about 1,200, joined what became the 16th Irish Division of the British army in 1914, but far more nationalists enlisted than were members of the Volunteers. Redmond came to Belfast on 25 October 1914 and, with Devlin, drove up a Falls Road festooned with union jacks and other allied flags, a sign of the gratitude to Britain for having apparently granted home rule. Redmond spoke at a rally of Volunteers in the Clonard cinema, urging the men to enlist, 'to strike a blow for Ireland where the real fighting is going on'. Devlin told the rally that 'the war is Ireland's war quite as much as Great Britain's or any other part of the Empire's. However it may have been in the past, England today is fighting the battle of Ireland's liberty.'[46] The RIC inspector general commented in his report for August–September that there was no anti-recruitment activity in Belfast, 'except by a small IRB group' which handed out seditious leaflets discouraging recruitment and attacking Redmond.[47]

Indeed, Catholics in Belfast were four times more likely than elsewhere in Ulster to enlist. In 1914 Catholics, just under a quarter of Belfast's population, made up 23.1 per cent of the city's 16,800 recruits. In 1915 that percentage increased to 27.3 of the 14,500 going to France, a total of 7,800 Catholics in the two years. As many Catholics enlisted per head of population as Belfast's Protestant population, perhaps because of poverty, perhaps because many had been expelled from their jobs over the previous two years, perhaps out of loyalty to Devlin's appeal. There is also the suggestion that some signed up believing the war would be over by Christmas.[48] Many enlisted in August after continental markets for linen products were cut off, resulting in heavily reduced working hours and in some cases unemployment. Steel production was also hit initially. For example, Combe Barbour's foundry on the Falls Road closed on 11 August, laying off 1,800 workers and Mackies Albert Foundry shut many of its sections.[49]

Most Catholics were unskilled and enlistment offered financial attractions. Average earnings for an unskilled man were 15–20s. a week. Basic army pay was 7s. a week but food and accommodation were free. For married men half – 3s. 6d. – went to their wives. However, more importantly, their wives also received a 'separation allowance' of 12s. 6d., increasing per child. So, the wife of a man with three children received £1 a week plus 3s. 6d., substantially more than if he worked in Belfast. The number of Belfast nationalists who rushed to enlist in 1914 and 1915 contrasts sharply with other counties in the north-east. By mid-1916 only 2,123 men from Tyrone had signed up, 1.5 per cent of the population, on a par with Fermanagh at 1.75 per cent, but behind Derry city and county (2.68 per cent), although the Derry figure included the large unionist population of the city that had a tradition among unemployed males (both Protestant and Catholic) of joining the British army.[50]

As for the few dozen Belfast Volunteers who rejected Redmond's and Devlin's injunctions to support the war effort, they continued to drill rather forlornly at the Willowbank huts, went on weekly route marches on the plateau behind Divis mountain and carried out rifle practice in a disused quarry there. As McCullough later put it, they waited for something to happen.[51]

Despite the horrors of the workplace expulsions of summer 1912, nationalists in Belfast remained confident in 1914 that there were better days ahead. They had returned 'Wee Joe' Devlin twice in 1910 and they trusted him that home rule would be delivered after the war, which none of them imagined would last four years and would produce unprecedented casualties in working-class districts. After an initial dip in the autumn of 1914 when there was a shortage of raw materials for the textile mills, many of which relied on flax from Belgium, and reduced demand for manufactured steel goods, business confidence returned and there was full employment with the shipyards also taking back men who had been laid off in the weeks after war was declared.[52] There was no internal debate within nationalism in Belfast or Antrim. Devlin's supporters remained solidly behind the IPP and continued to do so after the 1916 Rising and into 1918 when other parts of the north-east began to repudiate Redmond's party. Republicanism in Belfast remained the choice of a tiny minority within the minority.

4 The Easter Rising and the split in northern nationalism

For more than eighteen months after war was declared in August 1914 there were no political developments in Belfast or County Antrim. The balance of forces remained exactly the same, overwhelmingly in favour of unionism. Among nationalists, republicans made no further inroads into the massive support for home rule. Recruiting among Belfast and Antrim nationalists for the war effort actually increased in 1915, despite growing casualties that spring. An uneasy, unspoken political truce between unionists and home rulers seemed to be in operation and remained intact through the 1916 Easter Rising mainly because the contribution of Belfast republicans took place sixty-five kilometres west of the city in Tyrone. However, in the aftermath of the Rising the British government tried hastily to cobble together a compromise version of the suspended 1914 Government of Ireland Act that involved the partition of the six north-eastern counties. The outworking of the failed negotiations around that compromise split northern nationalism forever and signalled the beginning of the end of the IPP.

By May 1915 it was clear that Churchill's brainchild, the Dardanelles operation, was becoming a fiasco. Also, in May, the second battle of Ypres ran into the ground with enormous casualties; the Royal Dublin Fusiliers were almost wiped out. There were many Belfast and Antrim men in regular army regiments like the 1st and 2nd Royal Inniskilling Fusiliers, the 1st Royal Irish Fusiliers and the 1st and 2nd Royal Irish Rifles.[1] All of these regiments, part of the 10th Irish Division, were to suffer badly at Suvla Bay in the disastrous landings at Gallipoli in July 1915. The serious losses in Flanders, shortage of munitions for artillery barrages, and the failure of the Dardanelles campaign led to the creation of an all-party coalition on 25 May 1915. This new government included the Conservative leader Bonar Law, Balfour, former Irish Unionist leader Walter Long, the Unionist leader in the Lords, Lord Lansdowne, and, the biggest shock to Irish nationalists, Ulster Unionist leader Sir Edward Carson as attorney-general. All Redmond's greatest political enemies and the enemies of home rule were now in the British government.[2] The arrival of this powerful group of staunch Unionist figures in the government changed British policy towards Ireland fundamentally. No longer did Asquith depend on the IPP for a majority, but more importantly, in the new bipartisan climate, no longer was there a division between Conservatives and Liberals on Irish policy. Redmond stood outside the government, having refused the place he was offered. As Tim Healy MP predicted: 'Redmond's hold on the balance of power has now disappeared and he will be, I fear, treated accordingly.'³ In the event of a disagreement on Irish policy, in the words of Ronan Fanning, 'there was a powerful incentive towards compromise ... The impetus in short was towards agreement on Ireland where previously it had been towards disagreement, and agreement, in the context of coalition, meant partition.'⁴

As bad news about the progress of the war in France and Turkey became frequent, Dublin Castle had begun to take a stern view of attempts to undermine the war effort and spread pro-German attitudes. The hard line against those in Ireland opposed to the war was also not unconnected with the creation of the coalition government containing staunch Unionist members such as Carson. Using the Defence of the Realm Act (DORA), passed on 8 August 1914, and wartime censorship, newspapers and periodicals criticizing the war were banned and people making speeches attacking recruitment were prosecuted. DORA included the power to deport people from Ireland to Britain if it was thought they were encouraging anti-war sentiment. Not surprisingly, a number of leading IRB men fell foul of DORA.

In summer 1915 Denis McCullough was handed his deportation order requiring him to move to England. After consulting with the leaders of the Volunteers in Dublin, including Eoin MacNeill – who wanted him to travel to America to do propaganda work for the Volunteers – and Tom Clarke for the IRB, McCullough decided to defy the order. As a result, he was arrested and sentenced to four months imprisonment in July 1915.⁵ Shortly after his release in November, the pace of events began to quicken. He attended a meeting of the IRB supreme council in Clontarf town hall. The main item of business was to elect a new IRB president. The election was overdue because the supreme council secretary, Mac Diarmada, like McCullough, had been in jail after making a seditious speech in Tuam in May. Much to McCullough's surprise and despite his protestations, the two dominant figures on the council, Tom Clarke and Mac Diarmada, engineered McCullough's election as president. He recalled protesting in vain.⁶

With hindsight it is easy to see Clarke and Mac Diarmada's motive. According to the IRB constitution, decisions between council meetings could be taken by any two of the three officers, president, secretary and treasurer. McCullough ran his own music shop business in Belfast, which he could not leave very often. His absence in Belfast meant in effect that Clarke as treasurer and Mac Diarmada as secretary ran the IRB; at the end of 1915 they had urgent business in hand.

According to his statements to the Bureau of Military History, McCullough did not know until early 1916 that an IRB military council had been established.⁷ Despite being president of the supreme council, he was kept out of the loop by his long-time friend and IRB colleague, Mac Diarmada. By the end of 1915 the military council had formulated a detailed national plan for the Rising, but like other leading IRB figures, McCullough was told only the role he had to play, but not the date of the Rising.[8] McCullough was summoned to Dublin, probably in March, to meet Pearse and Connolly in the rooms of the Keating branch of the Gaelic League. Pearse gave him his orders for the Belfast Volunteers in the national plan. Once the Rising's date was revealed, McCullough and the Belfast men were to join the Tyrone companies in Coalisland and 'proceed with all possible haste to join [Liam] Mellows in Connacht and act under his command there'.[9]

The national plan was to hold the line of the Shannon as the Volunteers fell back from Dublin and Meath under the anticipated onslaught from the British army. McCullough did not think much of Belfast's part in the plan. The Belfast Volunteers had few weapons and he reckoned marching west from Coalisland through unionist towns in Tyrone and Fermanagh, even when joined by the large Tyrone Volunteer contingents, was too risky and they were likely to be attacked. He told Pearse he thought they would need to raid a couple of RIC barracks for more weapons. McCullough recalled that Connolly 'almost shouted, "You'll fire no shots in Ulster."' Connolly, who had lived in Belfast – and whose daughters Ina and Nora still did in 1916 – was well aware of the dangers of a sectarian bloodbath, and was obviously determined to avoid any attempt at insurrection in Ulster. He then repeated Pearse's orders about marching west and added, 'If we win through, we'll then deal with Ulster.'[10] It was not to be.

After that meeting, McCullough in Belfast heard nothing more but rumours of a Rising. He only managed to ferret out the date of the Rising after he travelled to Dublin on Saturday of the weekend before Easter to ask Mac Diarmada what was going on. Mac Diarmada dodged him for two days before McCullough managed to corner him in his office in D'Olier Street on Monday of Holy Week. McCullough came in and locked the door behind him and demanded to know what was going on. Mac Diarmada came clean. The Rising was to be on Easter Sunday and the plan for Ulster remained the same.

McCullough rushed back to Belfast on Tuesday and called a meeting of the Volunteer section commanders at the Volunteer premises in Divis Street. He told the officers they were going to Tyrone at Easter for manoeuvres and that the men should bring two days rations. The officers were to gather any arms and ammunition they had; that amounted to about forty sundry rifles. McCullough spent the rest of Holy Week arranging travel and accommodation. Their rifles were deposited in two dumps, one at Hannahstown, a Catholic village on the Black Mountain above west Belfast, and the other in Clonard Redemptorist monastery in west Belfast. James Tomney, the IRB leader in Tyrone, picked up the stuff from Clonard on Spy Wednesday night and Hugh Rodgers from Beragh took the rest from Hannahstown over the Black Mountain and south of Lough Neagh to Coalisland.

James Connolly's daughter, Ina, a member of Cumann na mBan, using IRB money, bought excursion train tickets in batches of six and twelve for the Volunteers to travel on Holy Saturday in three groups to Dungannon, then on to Coalisland. McCullough had arranged for one contingent to stay at Annaghmore, twelve kilometres from Coalisland, the second in a barn at Derrytresk, a townland a couple of kilometres outside the town, and the third, about 75 men, in St Patrick's Hall, Coalisland. The Connolly sisters, Nora and Ina, and four Cumann na mBan women would stay in farmhouses at Derrytresk.[11] It all worked a treat with 132 men arriving as planned, the weapons already there, though only sufficient for a third of them.

Meanwhile McCullough had travelled to Carrickmore in Tyrone on Good Friday to meet Dr Pat McCartan, also a member of the IRB supreme council, only to find two meddling priests who had heard about the planned Rising trying to persuade McCartan to stop it. The priests believed it was a communist insurrection instigated by Connolly. McCullough wasted a large part of Holy Saturday arguing with the priests that it was an IRB rebellion and trying to persuade McCartan to support the Rising. McCullough went to Coalisland on Saturday to check that the Belfast men and weapons had arrived. While there, he decided to swap his own large heavy Luger parabellum for a small Belgian FN automatic pistol. On his way back to McCartan's house he stupidly pulled the trigger of the unfamiliar gun, 'to check if it was loaded', shot himself through the hand and passed out. When he came to, he made his way to McCartan's house where McCartan bandaged him up. From then on, although he was in shock, McCullough continued to try to persuade McCartan – who was never keen on a Rising in any case – and then the Tyrone men, to join the march to Omagh and the west to no avail. By late on Saturday night news of Eoin MacNeill's countermand arrived to add to the confusion and disarray. In the end, McCullough decided it would be madness for the Belfast men to try to march west through unfamiliar territory without the large Tyrone Volunteer contingent.[12] He resolved to take his men back to Belfast on Easter Sunday.

The Belfast Volunteers mustered in Coalisland on Sunday and marched to 10.00 a.m. Mass, many of the officers disagreeing with McCullough's decision, particularly as they stood alongside hundreds of men from eleven Tyrone Volunteer companies, some from as far away as Sion Mills and Strabane, and also some companies from south Derry.[13] Nevertheless, McCullough prevailed. Joe O'Neill of Derrytresk hid the rifles in a bunker in the bog on his land. That afternoon the Belfast Volunteers marched to Cookstown for the 7.30 p.m. train to Belfast, en route fending off a unionist attack in Stewartstown, then 'a hotbed of Orangeism' as McCullough described it.[14]

So ended 'the Rising that never was' in Ulster. The only casualty was its leader, McCullough. The Belfast Volunteers arrived safely back in the city. A number of them went to work on Easter Monday as usual. Their officers, however, and some rank and file, were arrested the following weekend after the collapse of the Rising in Dublin. Most, including McCullough, were interned in Frongoch. In total, twenty-four leading Belfast republicans were arrested.[15] Until the arrests most people in Belfast had no idea what 132 Volunteers had been up to over the Easter weekend and were astonished and angry when they found out. Belfast nationalist reaction to the Rising in Dublin was shock and dismay. Initially information was scanty and confused because the national newspapers were not published and rail transport was cut off to the public. However, on 1 May the *Irish News* leader accused the insurgents of being 'German agents and intriguers' attempting to create a diversion in Ireland, 'who fought Germany's battle in the capital of this country'.[16]

The Belfast committee of Redmond's Volunteers – quiescent since 1914 – responded more quickly. On 26 April they condemned 'in the strongest possible manner the action of the Sinn Féin party in Dublin ... in playing into the hands of Ireland's enemies'.[17] Since there was no uprising in Belfast (or indeed anywhere else in the north) there was no unionist retribution visited on the Catholic population in Belfast whose universal condemnation of the Rising was accepted as genuine, which it was.

It was only after the speech by John Dillon MP, Redmond's number two in the IPP, in the Commons praising the courage of the insurgents and condemning the secret courts martial and the executions that, even in west Belfast, attitudes began to change. The RIC report on Belfast noted that 'the original feeling of disgust and annoyance changed as time went on and a feeling of sympathy with the rebels arose.'[18] The arrests and internment, not to mention the hostility from both the unionist majority in Belfast, as well as from the city's nationalist home rulers, put an end to Volunteer military operations in the city and County Antrim until 1919, though they were involved in the 1918 election campaign. Events in the months after the Rising in 1916 would once again demonstrate the exceptional political stance of Belfast and Antrim in Ireland as a whole, but particularly in the north-east.

In June 1916 Asquith, aware to some extent of the damage the Rising had done to the IPP, moved quickly to try to produce some fix to end the home rule impasse that in 1914 seemed to have been successfully set aside for the duration of the war. The prime minister believed that the best solution to save the position of Redmond's party was to implement home rule 'at the earliest practicable moment'.[19] This, of course, was easier said than done given that nationalists and unionists remained at loggerheads over the fate of Ulster. To find a way round this impasse, Asquith gave Lloyd George the task of concocting a deal – a feat that had eluded everyone for the previous five years – a deal that could satisfy the Ulster Unionists and the increasingly worried IPP who saw their support sliding away faster by the day. However, Asquith

stipulated that any deal must be based on the exclusion of Ulster. To fulfil
these terms of reference Lloyd George proposed exclusion, not of Ulster, but
of the six north-eastern counties – which had been the Ulster Unionist position since late 1912. He gave Redmond the 'most emphatic assurance' that the
exclusion would be temporary but told Carson in writing that any such settlement would have 'permanency'.[20] The prospect was held out of a final
arrangement for the excluded six counties to be reached at an Imperial
Conference after the war. For Lloyd George, the key objective was to secure
agreement on partition in principle, then work out the details later. For that,
the consent of northern nationalists, who would be most immediately affected
by partition, was needed. That consent could only be gained by the IPP per-
suading its northern supporters to agree: a tall order.[21] Redmond accepted
Lloyd George's assurances and placed his hopes in the de facto leader of
northern nationalists, Joe Devlin. Could he induce, cajole, inveigle northern
nationalists to vote themselves out of a home rule Ireland, even on a temporary basis?

As soon as Lloyd George's proposals were known, northern nationalism
split east and west of the River Bann. Tyrone, Fermanagh, most of County
Derry and Derry city with their nationalist majorities, were outraged at the
prospect of being 'excluded' from a home rule parliament. Nationalists in
Belfast and Antrim were more sanguine. Many of them had believed for some
years that, as a minority constituting about a quarter of the county's and
Belfast's population, they would end up in any compromise being dominated
by Ulster Unionists. In Belfast, many Catholic businessmen and factory workers agreed with unionists that home rule would damage the city's industry
and its integration with Britain's economy. Unlike other parts of Ulster west
of the Bann, there had been no protests in Belfast against partition or indeed
anti-recruitment rallies.[22]

The Catholic hierarchy was utterly opposed to the proposals and Bishop
Charles McHugh of Derry and Bishop Joseph MacRory of Down and Connor
made their views clear to Devlin and Jeremiah McVeagh, MP for South
Down.[23] Privately, Cardinal Michael Logue, archbishop of Armagh and primate of All Ireland, conveyed the same opinion in strong terms. While
Redmond and Devlin worked to have a conference of northern nationalists at
the end of June decide on the proposals, clergy and public representatives
participated in meetings during June across the six counties where the split
in nationalism was evident.

The conference was set for 23 June in St Mary's Hall, Belfast. Redmond,
Dillon and particularly Devlin worked assiduously all month to ensure a
majority for the Lloyd George proposals. The *Irish News* vigorously supported Redmond's line that immediate home rule for most of Ireland was
better than no home rule, and that home rule for the north would follow after

the war. The newspaper repeatedly published statements by Devlin arguing that exclusion was temporary and a final arrangement would be reached after the war. Devlin also emphasized that there would still be 103 Irish MPs in Westminster who could have a decisive effect on such arrangements.[24]

The parish clergy in Down and Connor supported Devlin's position, despite the declared opposition of Bishop MacRory. Fr McCotter, PP Antrim, a strong Devlin supporter, wrote to the *Irish News* on 17 June that he could 'not dream of a verdict [in the conference] which would prevent four-fifths of Ireland from obtaining the blessings of Home Rule.'[25] In Tyrone, Derry and Fermanagh there was strong opposition to Lloyd George's proposals. There was also opposition to Belfast as a venue for the conference given the overwhelming support for Devlin in the city and the lack of opposition there to the British proposals. In addition, there was a fear that Devlin would pack the meeting. Clergy in County Derry objected to representatives of the AOH and IPP being allowed. In the event, the Irish National Foresters (INF) and AOH were each given forty seats.[26]

Devlin held a huge meeting in Belfast on 17 June, a week before the conference, attended by almost 2,000 businessmen, clergy, lawyers and trade unionists who expressed their support for accepting the proposals. That gave him grounds for believing that he could carry the day against Tyrone and Fermanagh at the conference because, given its population, County Antrim, including Belfast, along with County Down would have over a third of the delegates and the rest in Armagh and County Derry were split. The 776 delegates would be made up of MPs, councillors, clergy, representatives from branches of the IPP, INF and the AOH.

Redmond himself chaired the conference. The only motion was on the Lloyd George proposals: that they were 'the best means of carrying on the fight for a united, self-governing Ireland'. The chairman of the *Irish News*, Councillor Patrick Dempsey, proposed the motion, which was seconded by three prominent Catholic clerics from Donaghmore in Tyrone, Camlough in Armagh and Fr John Nolan, a strong Devlin supporter, parish priest of Toome, a staunch nationalist district in south-west Antrim. At the outset, both Redmond and Devlin promised to resign if defeated. After five hours of stormy, often unruly, ill-tempered debate, the motion was carried by 475 to 265. Northern nationalists had voted for partition but were irrevocably split. Antrim and Down delegates voted overwhelmingly for the proposal, while Tyrone and Fermanagh voted against. The east of County Derry voted for, while the west and Derry city voted against; Armagh was also divided north and south. There was general agreement that a virtuoso performance by Devlin had carried the day, though others were not so sure if it was simply Devlin's oratory that secured the large majority. Recriminations erupted immediately with defeated delegates claiming the meeting had been rigged by

Devlin and the AOH. There were also claims of multiple voting, that men in favour of partition voted twice or three times in different capacities as county councillors, AOH and IPP delegates. But the voting figures were academic. *Realpolitik* swiftly took over.

The wonder is that experienced politicians like Redmond and Devlin ever imagined Lloyd George's proposals could possibly get through the coalition cabinet with its hard-line Conservative and Ulster Unionist members such as Bonar Law, Lord Lansdowne, Lord Selborne, Walter Long, Balfour and Carson. On 11 July, the day before the annual Twelfth of July parades, Lansdowne announced in the Lords that any legislation incorporating Lloyd George's proposals would have to be 'permanent and enduring'. On 22 July Lloyd George told Redmond that the cabinet had decided the plan would be permanent but worse, that the continuing representation of Ireland with 103 MPs would end.[27] Redmond and Devlin had put their leadership on the line for nothing. Without leverage in Westminster, Redmond and Devlin had been shown up as naïve, credulous and impotent. They had accepted the principle of partition. The betrayal was a shattering blow to the IPP, particularly in the north. Within a month, on 5 August, a new political organization, the Irish Nation League, was established which the following year merged into the rapidly growing SF. The IPP in the north-east never recovered. In Belfast and Antrim, the organization remained strong but it was now Devlin's party rather than a national party, and subsequent votes for Devlin in 1918 and thereafter were personal ones. The St Mary's Hall conference in June 1916, not the 1916 Rising, marked the watershed in nationalist sentiment in the north.

5 Belfast and Antrim, 1917–20: unionist redoubt

The preoccupations and priorities in Belfast and County Antrim during the four years after the 1916 Easter Rising were markedly different from those in most of the rest of the country; consequently, events there do not follow the same timeline. As internees and prisoners began to return home from Christmas 1916 onwards, SF began to organize as a national political party and in parallel the Irish Volunteers – many with dual membership of SF – also started to recruit and develop.[1] Progress in both endeavours was much slower and desultory in Belfast; in County Antrim, it was almost non-existent. Neither Antrim nor Belfast played a role commensurate with their size and population in the national campaign against conscription during spring 1918, although there was substantial opposition to conscription in nationalist districts in north Antrim and Belfast. Likewise, the national excitement in the 1918 election campaign and SF's overwhelming victory were not shared. The main feature of the campaign in Belfast was clashes in west Belfast between SF supporters and Devlin's loyal followers, but the parties elected in both city and county remained unchanged. While in January 1919 most of the country was agog with the establishment of the Dáil, the Declaration of Independence, the announcement of the Democratic Programme and the first shots fired in the War of Independence, in Belfast the biggest engineering strike of the century brought the city to a standstill. As the IRA campaign in the south and west moved into top gear in 1920, Belfast descended in July of that year into two years of bloody sectarian attacks with the IRA playing a mainly unsuccessful role as defender of Catholic districts.

In 1917, as SF began to organize and develop and the Irish Volunteers attracted growing numbers to their ranks, political, societal and economic factors inhibited growth of the movement in Belfast and Antrim. In Ulster, west of the River Bann, there was some rapid expansion, but in Belfast and Antrim the vast majority of the population, staunchly unionist, remained completely hostile to any concept of Irish independence, more so after Easter 1916.[2] It should also be remembered that among the minority nationalist population in these places, home rule and loyalty to the IPP remained the preferred political position. There was no surge to SF, as was the case west of the Bann.[3]

The numbers and composition of the Irish Volunteers (which became the IRA) in Belfast and nationalist districts of Antrim after 1919 compared to those in Dublin illustrate the different circumstances. Belfast and Dublin were by far the largest cities on the island. By the end of 1920 the IRA's Dublin Brigade composed six battalions, four in the city, plus an engineering battalion and a sixth covering south County Dublin and part of County Wicklow.

The total number amounted to around 2,100 men but those regularly active were far fewer.[4] By contrast, in 1920 the Belfast 'brigade' never had more than 200 active members. Cork city with a population of 76,673, a fifth the size of Belfast's, had eight companies in its 1st Battalion, Cork No. 1 Brigade, numbering about 800 men.[5]

Nevertheless, SF did begin to grow in Belfast, albeit slowly, especially after internees started to return from England at the end of 1916. Alongside the growth of SF there was the beginning of reorganization of the Volunteers, very often the same men. SF speakers travelled north regularly during 1917 and addressed public meetings, strongly advocating an Irish Republic and proposing that Ireland be represented at the peace conference after the war.[6]

A prime example of such meetings was one that took place on 22 November 1917. Seán MacEntee chaired a SF meeting in St Mary's Hall to commemorate the Manchester Martyrs. The main speaker, Countess Markievicz, wearing her Irish Citizen Army uniform, delivered a characteristically inflammatory speech. She addressed her audience as 'fellow rebels' and told them it was 'not the law that was respected in Ireland today but the man who broke the law'. 'No cause', she claimed, 'could be won without suffering and death and martyrdom'.[7]

By the end of 1917, following the consolidation of SF's national organization at its October ard fheis in Dublin, the RIC estimated there were eight SF cumainn in Belfast with a total membership of 780, almost certainly an exaggeration. Still, to view that number in perspective, the police put UIL numbers in the city at just under 6,000.[8] Due to constant monitoring and harassment by the RIC, those reorganizing the Volunteers used local GAA clubs as cover. An unpublished autobiography by David McGuinness, a Belfast IRA man, provides details of the links at the outset of the reorganization between the GAA and Volunteer companies in west Belfast, the only part of the city and Antrim in 1917–18 with bodies of Volunteers.[9]

According to McGuinness, four companies – A, B, C, D – were created in 1917 in west Belfast neighbourhoods, but they were only nominally companies as in reality each was the size of a platoon or smaller. They were intended to form the basis for expansion. 'A' company members tended to be in the Peter O'Neill Crowley and Michael Davitt GAA clubs, 'B' in John Mitchel, 'C' began as members of the Clan Ulaidh Pipe Band, then joined the Seán McDermott GAA club, but members of 'D' had no links to a club.[10] The aim was that when enough men had joined, the four 'companies' would form a battalion. Other Belfast districts would also form companies making another battalion, ultimately becoming the Belfast Brigade.

The numbers did not materialize until 1921. There was no one in Belfast with the clout to suggest that the IRA leadership should cut their suit to match their cloth, that it was never going to be feasible to create the structures of the British army from the small number of men available. As a result, there were always too many chiefs and too few Indians in the Belfast IRA. Although the unit names like company and battalion were inappropriate, they did at least have the merit of cohesion, being local groups based mainly on Catholic parishes. For example, 'B' company was based in the Clonard district of west Belfast, St Paul's parish; 'C' was based in St Peter's. The same parish basis was used to recruit men from Catholic enclaves in the rest of the city, not for any religious reason but because the men lived near each other and the parochial hall and school were convenient meeting places.

Thomas Fitzpatrick, alias Bob McDonnell, a former British army veteran who had served extensively in the Middle East and attained the rank of acting major, was given the task in 1919 of organizing a second battalion.[11] He set up one company in the Short Strand parish (St Matthew's), one in Carrick Hill (St Mary's) and one in the Markets (St Malachy's), as well as another based in Ardoyne and the Marrowbone (Holy Cross and Sacred Heart) nationalist enclaves in north Belfast; all were small in number and poorly armed. These 'companies' became the second battalion and by 1920 had joined with west Belfast to become the Belfast Brigade under the command of Seán O'Neill.[12] In practice, however, the Belfast Brigade was largely confined to west Belfast with its 'companies' there calling themselves the 1st Battalion. Séamus McKenna, who became O/C, recalled that at the end of 1917 the battalion had a nominal strength of around 240 but admitted that he rarely saw more than a hundred at monthly battalion meetings.[13] The small units in Ardoyne and the Bone in north Belfast, in the Markets district in central Belfast, and even smaller in east Belfast based in the Short Strand, never took any initiative. Their main purpose was defensive. The Belfast IRA saw no action until 1920. Before then the Volunteers, other than drilling at the Willowbank Huts or on Divis mountain, provided protection for SF speakers at meetings and election rallies from Devlin's supporters and Hibernians.

For a brief period during spring 1918 there was an uneasy alliance, or at least a unity of purpose, in Belfast between SF and IPP supporters in opposing conscription. Indeed, for a few short days in April it even looked as if there was a prospect of uniting Protestant and Catholic workers in Belfast to oppose conscription. When the Military Service Bill was introduced on 9 April in response to the losses caused by the massive German spring offensive, two union leaders, Thomas Johnson, president of the ITUC/ILP and leader of the Irish Labour Party, and David Campbell, a representative of the Belfast Trades and Labour Council on the ITUC/ILP executive, organized the first anti-conscription protest in Ireland at Belfast's Custom House Square near the Docks on 14 April.[14] An estimated 10,000 attended. Another rally was called for on 17 April at Belfast City Hall, but by then unionist leaders and hard-line loyalists had become alarmed because patriotism and loyalty to king and country were essential for the success of their political project. In the words of Charles Townshend, the leaders of Unionism regarded the ITUC/ILP 'as the industrial wing of the republican movement'.[15] Rumours had spread, not helped by insinuations in Johnson's speech on 14 April, that home rule was going to be applied immediately for nationalists if conscription was accepted, but that those opposed to conscription would be deployed to Mesopotamia to fight the Turks.[16] Fighting broke out at the rally when loyalists attacked the speakers and Johnson was hit on the head by a chunk of concrete; the brief solidarity had collapsed.

For unionist workers the critical confirmation of an anti-British conspiracy was the Catholic Church's formal endorsement of the anti-conscription campaign, which appeared to make the campaign a national crusade. Even worse for any prospect of solidarity was the endorsement by the Church – always the bitterest opponent of Bolshevism – of the national strike against conscription. The Church's role was roundly condemned in the British press, final confirmation for unionists of the disloyalty of opposing conscription. The national strike called for 23 April, overwhelmingly supported in the rest of the country, duly failed in Belfast and Antrim with all the factories and mills operating. The GNR was the only railway in Ireland running, albeit only north of Newry.[17]

Meanwhile, SF nationally had taken the lead in anti-conscription action and had Éamon de Valera and Arthur Griffith on the national committee. In Belfast, emboldened by this enhanced role for the party, SF and the Volunteers received an influx of recruits; 'C' company in the Falls district ballooned to 300 men. Working on a parish basis, they began to gather signatures door-to-door for a plebiscite opposing conscription. However, this 'state of affairs lasted for only a short time ... and those new members eventually dropped away'.[18]

During the rest of the year, as SF numbers grew exponentially across Ireland, there was some modest growth in Belfast.[19] The RIC estimated that in September 1918 there were 950 SF members in Belfast and 500 Volunteers – often the same people.[20] The police classified the Volunteers as 'one company' and assessed them as 'inactive'. They still constituted a very small minority among Belfast nationalists.

Alongside the Volunteers in Belfast and County Antrim was the largely unknown number of Cumann na mBan, many of whose members joined in 1916, a few like Nellie Neeson (née O'Boyle) even earlier in 1914.[21] None (except Winnie Carney) was interned after the Rising, so most remained active, visiting prisoners and carrying dispatches throughout the period 1916–22 in Belfast. The leading figures in rank were Winnie Carney and Agnes McCullough. Carney described herself as 'formerly James Connolly's aide-de-camp'. She was Cumann na mBan president in Belfast in 1917–18. Agnes

McCullough, wife of Denis, succeeded her. Annie Ward and Elizabeth Delaney commanded Cumann na mBan members in west Belfast attached to the Belfast Brigade.[22] During the 1918 election campaign they canvassed, distributed election materials and generally fetched and carried. Their crucial role supporting the IRA campaign came later.

The identity of interest that had briefly existed between nationalists and republicans during the conscription crisis in spring 1918 dissipated as the 1918 general election approached at the end of the year. There were serious clashes and street fighting between Devlin supporters and Volunteers in west Belfast during the lengthy election campaign. De Valera was the SF candidate in West Belfast but he was unavailable to campaign, being in Lincoln Jail since May 1918 after his arrest as part of Dublin Castle's so-called 'German Plot' concoction. Besides, de Valera's main interest was in East Clare, where he had won the by-election in July 1917, and in East Mayo where he was challenging John Dillon.[23]

De Valera's Belfast campaign was left to local SF speakers who were often prevented from speaking by Devlinite mobs. Apart from differences on policy, the main fear among voters was that SF would split the nationalist vote and let a Unionist in, thereby depriving Belfast of its only Nationalist MP. After decades in Belfast politics and twelve years as a Belfast MP, Devlin controlled the premises available for public meetings, especially St Mary's Hall, and of course, AOH premises. He also continued to enjoy the staunch support of the *Irish News* which published a constant stream of hostile editorials against SF.

De Valera's SF supporters had to be content with holding public rallies and meetings outside church gates, which left them open to attack by Devlin's 'baton men'. The Redemptorist monastery at Clonard in west Belfast was a particular focus for trouble. On one occasion in October 1918 several hundred SF supporters holding an election meeting were baton charged by the RIC after they refused to disperse.[24]

On 27 November SF organized a rally in Clonard Street for 9.00 p.m., the time the weekly Holy Family confraternity ended. A large crowd, mainly female mill workers, gathered, all staunch Devlin supporters; for many of them this election would be their first opportunity to vote. When the SF speakers arrived in a shooting brake (a large car used to transport shooting parties and their game) the crowd's jeering and groaning drowned out their attempts to speak. According to the *Irish News*, 'a body of Sinn Féiners, armed with bludgeons, rushed at the mill-workers and drove them some distance.' The women regrouped and broke through a cordon of SF supporters, blocking the street. Finally, the police got between both groups and the SF supporters retreated.

More fighting broke out outside the SF office at 157–9 Divis Street, where the speakers had taken refuge.[25] John Murphy was arrested and con-

victed of riotous behaviour and fined 40s.[26] This incident was just one exam-
ple of frequent street fights in the run-up to polling day between SF and
Devlin supporters in the dense network of streets off the Falls Road and
Divis Street in the Pound Loney, Albert Street and Barrack Street.[27]

In the event, Devlin was easily re-elected in December 1918, beating de
Valera by 8,488 votes to 3,245.[28] As usual, there were well-founded accusations that Devlin's election committee had organized massive personation.
They had gotten into the habit of this in 1906 and 1910. On the other hand,
since the last election in 1910 the electorate had expanded dramatically. No
one knew for certain exactly what the outcome would be; better to be sure
than sorry. The result of the election in West Belfast reinforced the constituency's different character from that of other nationalist districts in urban
Ireland. Devlin's personality, political charisma and ward organization ensured
that voters saw no merit in supporting SF which never produced a political
personality in the city, and almost no one in west Belfast had the slightest
idea who de Valera was.

While the rest of the country's attention after the 1918 general election
turned to the establishment of the Dáil in Dublin and the political declara-
tions at its first sitting in January 1919, in Belfast the priority was industrial
action for higher wages and shorter hours. The demands of the British war
effort had led to an increase in weekly hours with no corresponding rise in
pay. Now, with the war over and thousands of men being demobilized, engineering workers across the UK demanded a reduction in hours, partly to
make more jobs available to ex-servicemen. On 14 January Belfast shipyard
workers voted 22,000 to 1,100 to demand a reduction in hours from fifty-four
to forty-four. The threat to production evidenced by the huge vote immediately induced the employers to offer forty-seven hours for the same pay. The
workers held out for forty-four. Belfast workers were not alone. Shipyard and
skilled engineering workers in Belfast were members of British trade unions
who were also voting to strike in Glasgow and Liverpool and other British
industrial cities. In Glasgow the shipyard workers struck for forty hours a
week. From 25 January, 44,000 were on strike in Belfast with over 20,000
more workers laid off with no work to do as a consequence.[29]

Electricity was cut off except to hospitals, gas pressure reduced, trams
stopped, shops closed, newspapers were not printed. A strike committee, led
by a Catholic shipyard worker, Charles McKay, in effect ran the city, handing out permits to firms licensed to operate. The committee appointed 300
'special constables' to help the RIC deal with 'hooliganism'. Unlike in
Glasgow where strikers were baton-charged, troops were deployed and strikers dispersed with cavalry, in Belfast the unionist employers and political
leaders like Carson realized that coercion would be disastrous given the grip
the strikers had on the city and the overwhelming numbers involved. Troops

were confined to barracks. Dawson Bates, a senior Unionist, warned that 'Once one of the workers got injured in a melée with troops, nothing could stop Belfast becoming a scene of disorder ... the consequences of which were far-reaching.'[30] The fear of employers and Conservative and Unionist politicians was that the mass strikes in Glasgow and Belfast were really a front for Bolshevism.[31] Even more dangerous was the prospect of Belfast collapsing into turmoil as Dublin appeared to be heading out of control at the same time.

The strike lasted for four weeks into February as employers and Belfast Corporation (which ran the city's gas supply) negotiated with the strike committee and separate unions. In the end, Belfast was alone after the Glasgow and Liverpool strikes were crushed. The Belfast strike failed, but hours were reduced to forty-seven per week which also applied to council workers across the island. Dublin Corporation employees were the first to benefit. Their hours were reduced during the Belfast strike, probably to head off labour agitation there that could be exploited by SF. Demand fell in 1920 in the postwar slump, but the employers feared a repetition of January 1919 (the largest engineering strike in Ireland in the twentieth century), so although hours were reduced further, pay was maintained at the same level.[32]

In all these events, SF in Belfast were spectators. Their gaze was focused on Dublin and developments there, but the party had no presence in Belfast's engineering works apart from individual workers employed there. In any case, involvement by SF would have been counterproductive because that would have damaged the strikers' solidarity instantly. For SF, the greater goal was establishing an Irish Republic – hence they avoided becoming involved in what they saw as distracting industrial disputes led by British trade unions. The whole labour upheaval in January and February 1919 was a demonstration of how little republicans counted in Belfast.

The picture was similar elsewhere in County Antrim, where there was little or no SF activity, much less recruiting for Volunteers, after 1916. Ballycastle was the only place where there was any noticeable republican activity. That was largely instigated by Liam McMullan, who worked in a local toy factory, and by Louis Walsh, a local solicitor. A SF cumann with about twenty members emerged during the war but in his statement to the BMH, McMullan states that it was only after the conscription crisis in 1918 that developments occurred.[33] Initially, local Orangemen opposed conscription as much as nationalists. In a mainly agricultural area, everyone shared deep concern about the fate of farming if there was conscription. McMullan related the unlikely cooperation between the two sides at an anti-conscription meeting organized by Walsh in Ballycastle in April 1918. The bands of Moyarget Orange lodge and SF 'paraded through all the principal thoroughfares of the town before the meeting commenced' and the master of Moyarget lodge chaired the meeting.[34]

The *Irish News* reported the event as 'a monster meeting' of between 2,000 and 3,000, 'an immense throng of people made up of Orangemen, Hibernians, Sinn Féiners, unionists, Catholics and Protestants marching alternately to such tunes as "The Boyne Water" and "A Nation Once Again"'.[35] It was only after the 1918 general election that relations between local unionists and SF collapsed.

For republicans in north Antrim, however, the structures developed during the conscription crisis provided the basis for both political and military organization in 1919 and subsequently. As elsewhere, members of SF were usually also members of either local GAA clubs or the Gaelic League, or both. In 1919 they began to organize as IRA Volunteers. Paddy McLogan, a seasoned IRA Volunteer, came from Belfast and formed the first company of about twenty-five men in Ballycastle.[36] Liam McMullan was made O/C.[37] McLogan set about organizing in the rest of north Antrim. He established a company in Glenravel and another in Loughguile, and gave lectures on firearms and drill. There was an acute shortage of weapons: in 1919 they had just one Lee Enfield rifle and some shotguns. McLogan approached 20-year-old Feidhlim MacGuill, an ardent republican, in late 1919 to organize the IRA in Glenariffe and Cushendall.[38] MacGuill got together seven or eight friends and McLogan signed them up. That 'company' never consisted of more than fifteen who were extremely active from 1920 onwards when, as in Belfast, the IRA began operations in the north from the spring of that year.

Outside these districts in north-east Antrim, west Belfast, pockets in north Belfast, the Markets and the Short Strand in east Belfast, not only was there no IRA organization, there were no IRA members. Although there were thousands of Catholics living and working in Lisburn, there was just one Volunteer in the town. Until 1921, despite elaborate paper structures in west, north and east Belfast, there was really only one battalion in Belfast made up of four companies numbering fewer than 200 in total. The evidence for the sparse organization is that in 1921 GHQ in Dublin lumped the whole county and city together as the 3rd Northern Division covering Belfast, Antrim and also East Down, an area of desert for the IRA, but of course total numbers were not even close to a brigade size, let alone a division.[39]

Aware of their small numbers and lack of arms and training, the Belfast IRA leaders were reluctant to instigate any operations in case they provoked an overwhelming response from the police and unionist community. This policy produced tensions between the young men in the Belfast IRA and their leaders. When the Belfast Brigade did finally take action on Easter Saturday, 3 April 1920, it was only because of orders from GHQ in Dublin. In retaliation for the murder on 20 March of Tomás MacCurtain, lord mayor of Cork, and also to commemorate the Easter Rising, there was to be a concerted national operation to burn income tax and customs and excise offices, courthouses, and empty RIC barracks throughout the country. The Belfast IRA would play its part. One of those involved in the background planning for the burnings was Winifred Carney.[40]

Various members of the squads involved in Belfast provided detailed accounts of the events in their BMH statements. Séamus McKenna, later O/C 1st Belfast Battalion, was in the squad that burned the records in Belfast Custom House.[41] Those with him were Aloysius 'Wish' Fox, Séamus Woods, Joe McKelvey and Bill O'Brien. Another IRA man, O'Dowd, kept watch outside. Fox and Woods, dressed in postmen's uniforms, gained entry through the caretaker's entrance, pretending to deliver a telegram. Once inside, they proceeded to burn what documentation they could find. It did not go smoothly. It was Woods's first operation and he recalled his inexperience with petrol bombs. 'When I flung the bottle the blast from the ignition full flung me out of the room and singed my eyebrows.' He changed his damaged postman's uniform in McDevitt's the tailor's in 5 Rosemary Street, a safe haven for republicans for many years, two hundred metres from the Custom House.[42]

Other offices were attacked at the same time in Ann Street, North Street, Oxford Street and one based in the Grand Central Hotel in Royal Avenue.[43] McKelvey was particularly busy that Saturday. With others, he had tried to burn the tax office on the top floor of the imposing Scottish Provident building in Donegall Square West on the Wednesday before Easter, but the fire brigade arrived promptly and extinguished the blaze. Both McKelvey and Woods were familiar with the layout of the building since both had worked there, in Woods's case as a trainee accountant after he was expelled from Mackies engineering factory on the Springfield Road in 1918 along with other Catholic employees. They returned the following Saturday and destroyed the records.[44]

Unionist leaders were naturally furious at these events, not simply the destruction caused, but also the fact that in Belfast it had all happened in broad daylight and the perpetrators had escaped scot free. It was also the first manifestation of the IRA in Belfast and Antrim and therefore evidence that there existed in the city and county an IRA organization that obeyed instructions from Dublin and whose members were obviously participating in a nationwide operation. The other side of this coin was that the success of the attacks on tax offices in Belfast and the absence of retaliation from unionists emboldened the younger IRA men like McKenna, Woods, McKelvey and Roger McCorley, who were chomping at the bit to participate in the national campaign, which had been growing in intensity in 1920.

McCorley, one of the most prolific IRA operators in Belfast, joined the Volunteers in 1917 at the age of sixteen and rose to become O/C No. 1 Brigade, 3rd Northern Division. Dissatisfied at the lack of action, he recalled 'stormy exchanges' at company council meetings as the 'younger element felt there should be many more military activities'.[45] By contrast, the brigade staff feared that militant action would result in reprisals on the Catholic population. McCorley admitted that on a couple of occasions, 'unofficial attempts' were made to start activities, which gave 'us a bad name with the company and battalion officers.' One instance of unsanctioned activity, in March 1920, involved throwing grenades into a compound in the Markets where military vehicles were parked. McCorley had to wait until the burning of the tax records in spring 1920 for any authorized action. From then until he was wounded in May 1922, he hardly stood still.

Despite the fears of the IRA leaders in Belfast about reprisals, when violence began, the anticipated onslaught on the city's Catholic population did not come as a response to Belfast IRA activity. In truth, the burning of the tax offices in Belfast was little more than a nuisance. While it was good for IRA morale, it had no effect on the day-to-day business in the city. In fact, it exposed the lack of resources available to the city's IRA. The authorities would not have been aware that the same twenty or so men who carried out all the arson attacks were the total number of activists available to the Belfast IRA. The same was true for the attacks in Larne and Loughguile, which merely signified the presence of IRA in County Antrim but made no practical impact on daily life.

Elsewhere in the country, however, it was different. That same Easter weekend in 1920 the IRA had burned dozens of tax offices, 400 abandoned RIC barracks and fifty courthouses.[46] The IRA campaign was accelerating. The court system was collapsing. Assizes could not be held. After Easter the inland revenue ceased to function. The Dáil was beginning to tighten its grip on the country. In Belfast and Antrim, life continued as normal, but unionists were apprehensive, many convinced they were facing an existential threat.[47]

The accumulation of events, both military and political, across the country in spring 1920, rather than anything specifically to do with Belfast or its small IRA membership, culminated in a paroxysm of murder and mayhem being unleashed on Belfast's Catholic population in July. From the beginning of the year there had been growing unease among unionists after urban council elections in January. Perhaps unsurprisingly, SF carried all before them in these local elections nationally, but Ulster Unionist leaders were shocked by the results in the north-east. Nationalists won control of Derry City Council and other town councils west of the Bann. The victory of Hugh O'Doherty, to become the first Catholic mayor of Derry city since 1688, was powerfully symbolic.[48]

For unionists, worse was to follow. In June nationalists took the county councils of Tyrone, Fermanagh, South Down and Armagh. SF assumed control of thirty-six of the fifty-five rural district councils in the province of Ulster. In Belfast, Labour won twelve seats and SF five out of the sixty on the corporation. The IPP won five in Belfast. SF also had individuals elected to other councils which had previously been exclusively Unionist. Louis Walsh from Ballycastle won a seat for SF on Antrim County Council. These results were unnerving for unionists. Coupled with events elsewhere in the country, including what looked like the expansion of the IRA campaign north after a successful attack on Ballytrain RIC barracks in County Monaghan, the concept of a six-county state was in question. The ground seemed to be moving under unionists' feet.[49]

Tension had been rising in Belfast as a consequence of the election results that placed SF in control of most of the country's councils; violence in Derry; the increased frequency of IRA attacks in the rest of the country; the destruction of barracks and courthouses and the obvious disarray of the RIC in most of Ireland. In Belfast and Antrim unionists had strength in numbers and were determined to resist. Some Catholic-owned licensed premises in Belfast had been burned in spring 1920 and sporadic assaults on Catholic workers had taken place, but no major events occurred that could have sparked civil disturbance or mass attack. Unionist newspapers helped inflame emotions with reports giving the impression of a concerted SF assault on the north and non-sensical stories of men flooding in from the south. Fanciful letters, reinforcing conspiracy theories and scare stories, appeared regularly in the *Belfast Newsletter*, *Belfast Telegraph* and *Northern Whig*. Some reports raised the spectre of Protestant ex-servicemen losing their jobs in the shipyards while SF supporters took them. Undoubtedly, there was a downturn in orders in the shipyards in 1920 and some lay-offs, as part of a general UK-wide economic decline, but there is no evidence whatsoever of the unlikely scenario in Belfast of Catholics being taken on to work in preference to Protestants. That Protestant ex-servicemen were finding it difficult to get work as recession bit in 1920, while Catholics, who had not volunteered in the First World War, were in work occasioned resentment.

Timing also contributed to growing tensions and the final eruption of violence. The high point of the annual Orange marching season, 12 July, was a Monday in 1920. That meant the shipyards, engineering works, foundries and mills were closed from 10 July. Much drink had been consumed over the weekend of 10–11 July before processions to various Orange 'demonstrations' around Ulster. In Belfast, the venue was Finaghy, on the southern outskirts of the city, and the main speaker was Carson. He had participated fully in raising tensions, issuing dire warnings and spreading alarm in the run up to the summer marching season. On 30 June he had written an open letter to the government, the text of which was published in the *Newsletter*. He warned that if the government did not take harsher measures against SF and the IRA, he 'would organize our people for defence against those whose crimes are ruining Ireland'.

Speaking at Finaghy to an estimated crowd of 25,000 on 12 July, he warmed to his theme in a speech of startling incitement:

> We in Ulster will tolerate no Sinn Féin – no Sinn Féin organization, no Sinn Féin methods but we tell [the government] this – that if, having offered you our help, you are yourselves unable to protect us from the machinations of Sinn Féin and you won't take our help, well then we will take the matter into our own hands. We will reorganize in our own defence, throughout the Province, the Ulster Volunteers and those are not mere words. I hate words without action.[50]

Indeed, unknown to his audience, Carson and Sir James Craig were busily planning to reactivate the UVF. Four days after Carson's notorious speech, Craig wrote to Colonel Wilfrid Spender asking him to reorganize the UVF.[51]

However, it was events 320 kilometres away, in County Cork, which detonated the explosion of violence in Belfast the week after Carson's speech. On 19 June the RIC divisional commissioner for Munster, Colonel G.B.F. Smyth, had addressed RIC officers in Listowel barracks in north Kerry in terms that provoked what became known as the Listowel mutiny. Smyth told the police that they could shoot suspects who did not surrender and, if innocent people were killed, he would see to it that no policeman would be convicted.[52] The RIC in the barracks refused to cooperate. Many resigned and others in the district followed suit.

Smyth's speech and its repercussions were widely reported in the press. He immediately became a target for the IRA and a month later, on 17 July, he was shot dead in the County Club, Cork city, by Seán Culhane and a five-man squad from 1st Battalion, Cork No. 1 Brigade.[53] Unfortunately for Catholics in the north, Smyth was a member of a prominent business family in the largely Protestant town of Banbridge, County Down, where they owned a textile mill. The family also had important links to the UVF and had played a prominent part in the opposition to home rule in 1912–14.

To make matters worse, feelings were running very high by the day of Smyth's funeral in Banbridge since railway workers in Cork refused to transport the remains because of his infamous speech. His large impressive military funeral on 21 July in Banbridge coincided with the first full day back to work after the Twelfth holiday.[54] A special train brought mourners from Belfast along with fifty RIC men and the RIC band. One hundred men of the Bedfordshire and Hertfordshire Regiment and the regimental band were also present. That night, some Catholics were attacked and Catholic-owned houses burnt in Banbridge and nearby Dromore and Lisburn. The assaults continued for the rest of the week but that was a mere foretaste of what was to come in Belfast.

In an uncanny repeat of the events of July 1912, notices were posted on walls and fences in shipyards calling for 'Protestant and Unionist' workers to meet at 1.30 p.m. in Workman & Clark's south yard. After listening to inflammatory speeches by men from the Ulster Ex-Servicemen's Association lamenting unemployment among ex-servicemen and from the Ulster Unionist Labour Association attacking 'disloyal rotten' Protestants in the Labour movement, hundreds of apprentices (known as 'rivet boys') stormed into Harland & Wolff and chased Catholics, including Charles McKay, the leader of the strike committee in January 1919, and 'rotten Prods' out of the shipyard. Many were injured. Some had to jump into the River Lagan and swim to escape. The expulsions spread that afternoon to engineering works: Mackies, the Sirocco Works, Coome-Barbour, Gallahers tobacco factory and of course textile mills around the city. As Protestant workers made their way home that evening, they were attacked by vengeful Catholics and intense rioting broke out, followed by heavy gunfire – 'a carnival of terrorism', the *Irish News* called the events.[55] What became known as the 'Belfast Pogrom' had begun.

6 The 'Belfast Pogrom', 1920-2

Wednesday 21 July 1920 is taken as the beginning of what has been called the 'Belfast pogrom'. For the next two years until 29 June 1922, the population of certain Belfast Catholic districts was subjected to sporadic outbursts of intense violence that reached a climax in May 1922 when more than fifty people were killed in the city. Catholic districts in Belfast were not alone in having serious violence inflicted on them. There were wholesale attacks on Catholics in Lisburn and many fled from the town. However, in the case of Lisburn the onslaught was largely confined to the months of July to October 1920, whereas in Belfast it lasted on and off for two years. The course of events is well documented and the number of fatalities is generally agreed with marginal differences, depending, for example, on whether policemen and their religion are included as well as civilians. Belfast was by far the most violent place in Ireland during those two years. As the violence intensified, Ulster Unionist leaders who were members of the British government and others closely connected to senior Conservatives successfully argued for greater control of law and order through an armed special constabulary that emerged officially as the Ulster Special Constabulary (USC) in October 1920. In response to the attacks, first by loyalist mobs, then by members of the new USC, the IRA in Belfast organized itself as the defender of Catholic districts, but simultaneously tried to carry out operations against Crown forces as part of the national campaign. Reprisals duly followed. By the end of 1920 some Catholic districts had settled down to what one IRA man called 'semi-war conditions' that were to last until summer 1922.[1]

First, it is clear there was an onslaught on certain Catholic districts in Belfast from 21 July 1920 (and in Lisburn from 24 July), but there was not a generalized attack on all nationalist districts or on all Belfast Catholics. Most violence and killing in that initial week in July were concentrated in the Clonard district of west Belfast and around the Short Strand, a nationalist enclave in east Belfast, sometimes referred to as the wider district of Ballymacarrett (see map 4). There were also serious disturbances in Cromac Square near the Catholic Markets district. The violence was worst in places where blocks of segregated housing met. Nowadays in Belfast these places are known as 'interface zones' and are usually separated by interface barriers – so-called 'peace walls'. They are remarkably similar in location to the segregated frontier streets a century ago: for example, in the Short Strand/Newtownards Road and between Clonard and the Shankill, areas divided by the most elaborate interface walls today.

Nevertheless, from the onset of attacks on Catholics in July 1920, the commanders at a senior level in the army and police were less than enthusiastic

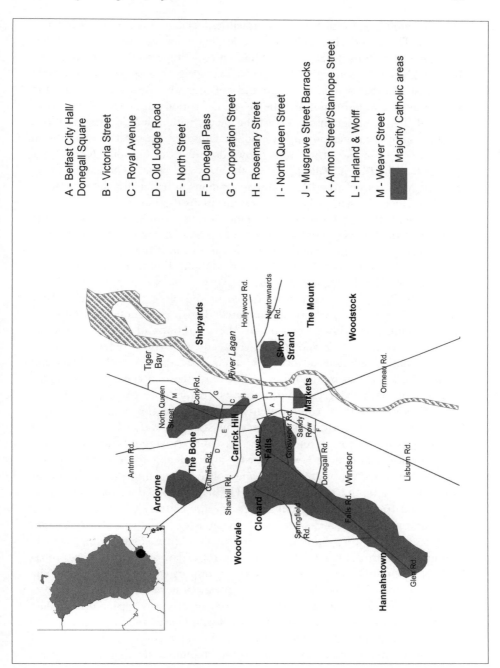

4 Belfast

about defending nationalist districts, much less taking on the mobs of unionist attackers. There were close links between leading unionists and army and police commanders, both in Belfast and Dublin, but most importantly in Westminster. They all shared the conviction that the IRA campaign was spreading inexorably north-east and that if unionists there did not urgently take control of law and order, the IRA would triumph. The belief that nationalist rioters were part of a general IRA insurrection, or at least the enemy within, led the army to direct its fire disproportionately towards Catholics. However, the most obvious reason for the hostility of the Crown forces towards crowds in Catholic districts was the fact that the IRA in Belfast fired on the army and police. The Crown forces believed, with reason, that IRA men among mobs in nationalist districts posed a mortal danger to them, whereas Protestant mobs did not.

At exactly the same time as ferocious rioting erupted in Belfast in July 1920, the British government was considering how to respond to the increasingly successful IRA campaign in the south and west of the country. The cabinet met on 23 July with Generals Macready and Tudor in attendance and significantly, Sir James Craig too. Craig was a junior minister in the Admiralty, but his presence is evidence of the close ties between Ulster Unionists and the Conservative-dominated British government. Tudor had been appointed in May to coordinate the operations of the RIC and the recently recruited Black and Tans. Macready was commander-in-chief in Ireland. Political solutions advocated by their Irish advisers, both military and civilian, were rejected by the cabinet. The only question considered was how to defeat the IRA. Macready inevitably asked for more troops, a difficulty given Britain's military commitments elsewhere in the Middle East and Russia. It was Churchill, then secretary of state for war, who asked, 'what would happen if the Protestants of the six counties were given weapons and charged with maintaining law and order and policing the country?' In his opinion that would release the troops and police stationed in the north to confront the IRA in the rest of Ireland. He also proposed raising a force of 30,000 men from Ulster to pacify the rest of the country.[2]

Some cabinet ministers were aware that Ulster Unionists, led by Carson and Craig, were busily doing exactly what Churchill was suggesting, namely planning to resurrect the UVF to take control of law and order. It is probable that Churchill was one of that select group of cabinet ministers in the know, and was deliberately raising the question at cabinet because he was aware of what was going on. That very week adverts had appeared in Belfast unionist newspapers announcing the reestablishment of the UVF and asking for recruits and former members to rejoin.[3] Unsurprisingly, Craig supported Churchill against strong opposition from the Dublin Castle civil servants present and also from Macready who would not countenance a private army being established and threatened to resign. Craig was minuted as follows:

Ulster would be glad to maintain order in the six counties and would be able to do it. Ulster would not terrorize the Roman Catholics and would not allow mob rule. Ulster would be able to prevent the Protestants running amok.[4]

Just as this cabinet meeting was taking place, precisely what Craig denied would happen – mob rule with Catholics the main victims – was occurring in Belfast. The police and army could not cope with the widespread nature of the violence or the sheer number of rioters (in the thousands) in different parts of the city.

The RIC in Belfast had been under the command of its own city commissioner. However, from November 1919 he was superseded by the appointment of a divisional commissioner of the RIC in Belfast. To the amazement and deep dismay of the city's nationalists the position was filled by Brigadier-General Sir George Hackett Pain, an ultra-unionist and former chief of staff of the UVF. In 1916 he had transferred back from the 36th Ulster Division to command of the British army's northern district in Ireland. Hackett Pain had played a critical role in organizing the 1914 Larne gunrunning and had been close to Carson and Craig ever since. Devlin complained bitterly that the chief of staff of 'Carson's army' (northern nationalists' derisive name for the UVF) was now responsible for protecting nationalists in Belfast.[5] With Hackett Pain in command there was no prospect of fair treatment for the nationalist population of the city. In retrospect, the appointment can be seen as the direction of travel that law enforcement was taking in the north-east. On paper, Hackett Pain had about 1,000 armed RIC men at his disposal in Belfast, an impressive number. However, the Belfast police were not routinely armed and were not trained or equipped to deal with serious civil disturbance. Since 1910 firearms training had been dropped from the RIC recruiting syllabus. The British army was always deployed to deal with major civil disturbances, the most recent being the shipyard expulsions in 1912. Furthermore, the Belfast police were scattered unevenly through five districts plus city headquarters. Moving men from one district to reinforce another caused administrative and command problems, apart from leaving parts of the city unprotected.

The biggest bugbear for Unionist politicians, who were increasingly determined to take control of law and order in Belfast and the north-east, was that the unionist community did not trust the RIC. As a national force by 1920 the RIC was over 70 per cent Catholic; that figure was 86 per cent for constables.[6] For example, in Glenravel Street barracks in Belfast there were only twenty-four Protestants in 1920; it was known as 'Fenian barracks' because of the large number of serving Catholics. To make matters worse, since the IRA campaign had intensified in 1920, Dublin Castle was transferring dependable loyalist RIC men to the south and west, where the RIC was disintegrating, and sending less dependable men to the north-east.[7] According to Dawson Bates, secretary of the UUC and later Northern Ireland minister of home affairs, over half of the RIC in Belfast were 'Roman Catholics, mainly from the South, and many of them are known to be related to Sinn Féin. The majority of NCOs are Roman Catholics.'[8] For all these reasons, including his military background, Hackett Pain preferred to use the military to quell disturbances, not only because of fears that the RIC in Belfast might be lukewarm, ineffective, and might provoke Protestant crowds, but because the army was more adaptable and better armed. It was easy to transport troops to places where riots were happening without having to consider district boundaries as in the case of the RIC. Furthermore, the army was under central command rather than having to take account of RIC district inspectors, each keen to maintain his own authority.

However, as with the RIC, the number of troops available on paper in a crisis was misleading. The 'Ulster brigade' covered the north of Ireland, including Donegal in 1920. The brigade was basically the 15th Infantry Brigade made up of four infantry battalions spread across the north. Each battalion usually comprised three or four companies of 200–225 men each, but although at full strength there should have been about 1,000 men in a battalion, in practice only a fraction of that number was available for operations.[9] If barrack duties, training, guard duty, sick leave and so on are taken into consideration, only about a company could be called on at short notice for active service. In the case of Belfast, although there were thousands of troops garrisoned in and around the city (not all part of the 15th Brigade or under the command of the Ulster brigadier), in reality only the 1st Battalion, The Norfolk Regiment, based at Palace barracks, Holywood, on the outskirts of east Belfast, could be deployed. The other units were a signals company, a company of Royal Engineers, two transport companies and members of the Royal Army Medical Corps. Therefore, in Belfast in July and in Lisburn in August, the Norfolk Regiment confronted the mobs.

At the outset of the communal violence on 21 July it appears that nationalist mobs were the aggressors, for many men who had been forcibly expelled from their workplaces earlier in the day stoned trams carrying unionist workers back home that evening past nationalist districts like the Markets. They also attacked workers walking home to the Shankill from Mackies factory on the Springfield Road through nationalist districts like Clonard, and walking from the shipyard past the Short Strand. The first gunfire seems to have been directed at Mackies workers from the nationalist Kashmir Road in the Clonard district, a long straight, unusually wide, street leading towards the Shankill. It was one of two main routes unionist workers used to get to the Shankill, the other being the parallel Cupar Street, one hundred metres away. British troops fired into the Kashmir Road, killing 40-year-old Francis

Finnegan from Lower Clonard Street and Bernard Devlin, an 18-year-old from the Falls district. At the Markets in the city centre the RIC fired on a nationalist crowd stoning trams and killed 27-year-old Margaret Noade.[10] Over the next three days, frenzied attacks, often fuelled by looted alcohol as well as by sectarian hatred, were directed against Clonard and the Short Strand, in particular.[11] The now exclusively loyalist workers in Mackies had come to work on 22 July with weapons to defend themselves after being attacked the previous evening. Some carried revolvers. There was an exchange of shots as they left the factory to walk home to the Shankill. Later that evening, in an eerie precursor of events in August 1969, the Shankill workers returned in numbers to attack Bombay Street on the edge of Clonard. They were determined to burn as many houses in the street as possible and were largely successful as many residents fled from the onslaught and lost every-thing when their homes went up in flames. There was considerable gunfire. Rifle rounds later gave way to machine-gun fire from the Norfolk Regiment sweeping the streets, but mainly directed towards nationalist crowds. The *Irish News* reported, 'firing from the military from 9.20 to 10.30 was intense'.[12] One of those killed was a lay brother from Clonard monastery, Brother Morgan, who was shot by the army as he helped women and children from Bombay Street move furniture. At Morgan's inquest, the jury found that 'the firing was entirely unnecessary for the purpose of suppressing a riot and was unprovoked by the action of any person in the monastery'.[13]

While Clonard was attacked that evening, unionist crowds had been ram-paging round Ballymacarrett in east Belfast all day. In the evening they descended on the Short Strand. During the day, Catholic-owned businesses, principally public houses and spirit grocers, on the Newtownards Road and nearby main thoroughfares were broken into, looted and burned. Witnesses reported men distributing bottles of beer and whiskey, breaking open barrels, and porter running along the gutters into drains. When the fire brigade arrived to extinguish the fires, their hoses were cut with axes. The mob then headed for St Matthew's church on Bryson Street and threw stones at the building until the military fired a volley to disperse the crowd. A number of attackers were killed or wounded and the inquest jury found that the military was justified in firing. Total casualties for the day in Belfast were twelve dead and forty-six wounded.

The following day, Friday 23 July, fierce rioting went on all day, again in Ballymacarrett, with concerted attempts to burn streets of Catholics houses. There were also continuing attacks on commercial premises, including some unionist-owned businesses on the main roads. Outnumbered nationalists fought desperately hand to hand to hold off the loyalist mobs from getting into the heart of the Short Strand. The *Irish News* reported a huge battle in Beechfield Street and Seaforde Street, a straight street about half a mile long, as nationalists fought with kidney pavers (cobblestones) to repel the onslaught. Troops were deployed in what must have been company strength. They set up barbed wire entanglements and posted soldiers with fixed bayonets at the corner of every street leading off Beechfield and Seaforde. Even so, the attacking mobs still found routes to their nationalist quarry. In the end, the army commandeered a house in Beechfield Street and in an upstairs room posted, incredibly, a Lewis machine-gun, a battlefield weapon capable of firing 500 rounds a minute. The Lewis gun team raked the length of Seaforde Street, shooting over the heads of the crowds. Only then did the fighting die down. However, that evening the mobs launched another foray into the grounds of St Matthew's, this time diverting to attack the nearby Cross and Passion convent where nuns who taught in the local parish schools lived. The attackers carried petrol, and after breaking into the convent, managed to set two rooms on fire before troops and police arrived. DI Sidley told an inquest in August that he, with ten police and seven soldiers in a lorry, came under attack on the Newtownards Road from a crowd of hundreds trying to prevent them reaching the convent. Constable James Carty testified that stones, bottles and other missiles were thrown at the lorry which was almost surrounded until the military fired a number of rounds to scatter the mob.[14]

With the heavy military presence, exhaustion, and a large number of funerals taking place on the Saturday, the assaults on Clonard and the Short Strand abated. On Sunday, the rival sets of Christians went to their packed churches across the city. The death toll for 21–4 July was ten nationalists and eight unionists, all but one killed by Crown forces, and a shocking three hundred wounded. Scores of houses had been burnt and families rendered homeless. Thousands of nationalists who had been thrown out of work on 21 July were now in many cases homeless as well as destitute.

It was collective violence by a majority against a largely defenceless minority, in the case of Belfast, a religious minority. However, Catholic districts were attacked not simply because of the religious beliefs of the residents, but because Belfast's unionist majority had no confidence in the police and believed that the army did not share their fear of the nationalist population, however misplaced, as 'the enemy within', namely people who harboured IRA units and who were secret supporters of the republican campaign that was creeping north as 1920 wore on. Speeches by the political leaders of Belfast's majority encouraged that view.

The posture adopted by the British army when deployed also demonstrated that the briefing officers received was not that nationalist districts were under attack and needed to be defended, but on the contrary, that while both nationalist and loyalist crowds were equally culpable, nationalist crowds were more likely to be hostile. The result was that nationalists were not defended against attacks on their homes by crowds that always outnumbered them, in the case of the Short Strand by more than ten to one. The army made strenuous and successful efforts to defend Catholic churches and convents, but no similar effort to defend Catholic-owned or rented homes, as for example in Bombay Street in Clonard, or in Seaforde Street in the Short Strand.

When the mass expulsions of Catholics from the shipyards, engineering works and textile mills took place in July 1920, followed immediately by mob attacks on nationalist districts, the IRA in Belfast was at a loss how to respond. They seem to have been left very much to their own devices with no instructions from Dublin, much less any guidance from SF. Obviously, the Belfast IRA – never more than 100 activists in early summer 1920 and fewer than thirty gunmen – was massively outnumbered, but that was not the dilemma that exercised the leaders initially. They considered themselves members of the army of the Republic, loyal to the Dáil, whose first duty was to attack and resist Crown forces, not to attack unionists or be drawn into a sectarian conflict.[15] As Roger McCorley, then a lieutenant in 'C' company 1st Battalion, recalled, many of the rank and file were of the view that 'British troops should be attacked at any and every opportunity irrespective of whether they were engaged in firing on our people or not'.[16] However, how could the IRA not defend nationalist districts coming under attack day and night by loyalist mobs? When one IRA officer was court-martialled for defending his local community his justification was that it would not be 'very dignified for an IRA officer to stand by and allow someone else to defend his home for him'.[17] IRA leaders in Belfast in 1920 were concerned that IRA attacks during and after disturbances would provoke reprisals against nationalist civilians and SF members. This internal argument continued among the Belfast IRA for several months.

McCorley regarded the brigade staff in Belfast in 1920 as too old, cautious and timorous. Others thought the staff were appointed because of their IRB membership rather than their military prowess. Joe McKelvey, later O/C 3rd Northern Division, was cited as a case in point.[18] McCorley, who never joined the IRB, was the most gung-ho, nerveless IRA man in Belfast. He had already taken action in defiance of the brigade in spring 1920. On 1 June he took part in an ambitious, official, but chaotic and unsuccessful attempt to capture the RIC barracks in Crossgar, County Down. By 1921, along with Séamus Woods, McCorley was the senior officer in the Belfast ASU and 'for coolness, courage and daring they could not have been surpassed'.[19] By the end of 1920 McCorley and other young bloods had supplanted the older men and in January 1921 McCorley was O/C 1st Battalion, but still as critical as ever of senior officers restraining him.

In July 1920 there was evidence that McCorley had ignored the prevailing policy and had engaged in gun battles with loyalists using a rifle to fire at snipers in the Shankill.[20] He had acquired his own Lee Enfield rifle in

1918.[21] After the attacks began in July, he and some others managed to acquire about sixty Lee Enfield .303 rifles from a Catholic priest who had been storing them since 1914. The priest thought he was handing them over to Hibernians to defend nationalist districts and McCorley and his squad did not disabuse him of the belief.[22] In August 1920, and later that year, they used the rifles mainly in defence of convents, schools and churches, favourite targets of loyalist arsonists.

At the outset of the violence in July, however, the IRA leaders in Belfast were too shocked and surprised to produce a coherent response. They were thrown onto the defensive, but were completely unable to protect nationalist districts from mass attacks. The policy was not to fire into loyalist crowds, for if the IRA had done so they would have been met with an overwhelming response from British troops that would have killed and wounded nationalists. Firing at unionist workers coming from Mackies on 21 July had resulted in the shooting dead of two nationalists by the army and the wounding of others.

While the nationalist population of Belfast was still reeling from the mass expulsions from factories, arson attacks on their districts, and the death and destruction of 21–4 July, once again events far away in Cork would produce devastating consequences in Belfast and Lisburn. In March 1920 Tomás MacCurtain, SF lord mayor of Cork and O/C Cork No. 1 Brigade, had been shot by an RIC murder gang. Famously, the jury at the inquest on 17 April returned a verdict of wilful murder against Lloyd George, Lord French, Divisional Commissioner Smyth and DIs Oswald Swanzy and Clayton. Swanzy was district inspector for Cork city north. Michael Collins, who had been in Frongoch with MacCurtain, was deeply affected by the killing of his friend and was determined to avenge it. On another level, Collins could not allow reprisals against senior republicans to go unanswered. He resolved to have the whole murder gang killed. By May the Cork IRA had killed two and wounded another involved in MacCurtain's assassination. As a result, the RIC divisional commissioner in Munster transferred Swanzy in mid-June to Lisburn, an overwhelmingly unionist town. Swanzy's family lived there and he moved in with his mother and sister at 31 Railway Street beside a RIC barracks and across from the Orange hall.[23]

Swanzy left Cork hurriedly by train under a false name leaving the city's IRA nonplussed. It took them some time to work out that luggage left to be forwarded to Lisburn belonged to the DI.[24] In fact, the details of Swanzy's new location came from one of Collins's sources in Belfast, RIC Sergeant Maurice (Matt) McCarthy, a Kerryman based in Chichester Street barracks.[25] McCarthy revealed that Swanzy was in Downpatrick in a temporary posting, pending his move to Lisburn. An order to kill Swanzy in Downpatrick was promptly sent to McKelvey, then O/C 1st Battalion Belfast Brigade, as there was no Down IRA brigade organization. When the IRA in Downpatrick proved incapable of recognizing their target, Collins turned to tried and trusted men in Cork No. 1 Brigade. He settled on 19-year-old Seán Culhane who led the squad that had assassinated Colonel Smyth in July. Apart from being an experienced gunman, Culhane had the advantage of knowing Swanzy by sight. He was a customer at the draper's shop, where Culhane worked, that supplied uniforms to the RIC and British army. Culhane recalled how he was interviewed by Collins, Richard Mulcahy and Cathal Brugha in Vaughan's hotel in Dublin before being given the go ahead.[26] He picked four accomplices: Dick Murphy, Dr Leo 'Stetto' Aherne, Con McSweeny and 18-year-old Jack Cody as their driver.[27]

Collins ordered Culhane to contact Matt McCarthy in Belfast and liaise with McKelvey since there was no IRA presence in Lisburn. The Corkmen travelled to Belfast and stayed in McKelvey's house at 26 Cyprus Street off the Falls Road. Culhane met McCarthy in Kearney's pub in Rosemary Street. McCarthy appears to have advised him that he needed all the help he could get from the Belfast men, not least in reconnoitring Lisburn and Swanzy's movements. It had to be Belfast men because the Corkmen had no idea of Lisburn's layout and could not ask directions because their Cork accents would have instantly aroused suspicion.

Culhane concluded that five men plus Belfast guides were too many to make successful escape possible. He reduced the team to two: Dick Murphy to accompany him with Cody as driver. Collins told Culhane to kill Swanzy with MacCurtain's gun, which had remained hidden under the mattress in his baby's cot when soldiers ransacked his house the night he was killed. The added piquancy was that Swanzy had signed the licence for the revolver for Jim Gray, transport officer in Cork No. 1 Brigade, who had posed as a loyal-ist under threat from the IRA. Gray then gave the gun to MacCurtain. Considerable work was needed over many days to establish where Swanzy lived in Lisburn and if there was any pattern to his movements. McKelvey recruited McCorley and Tom Fox, another west Belfast IRA man, to help him. Fox cycled to Lisburn with McKelvey and Culhane to show Culhane the lie of the land.[28] McCorley travelled to Lisburn daily for most of a week to monitor Swanzy's movements. McKelvey identified a weak spot in Swanzy's routine. He had a habit on Sundays of walking to church for a midday service that finished just before 1.00 p.m. and then walking home. On 15 August the Corkmen mounted an attempt to kill Swanzy. They hired a taxi, which they then hijacked from the driver. There are various accounts of what ensued. One is that the taxi broke down, another that the squad failed to spot Swanzy. It is also possible that the Cork driver got lost in the minor roads leading from the Black Mountain west of Belfast to Lisburn. Whatever happened, the hijacked taxi was abandoned at the small nationalist enclave of Hannahstown, west of Belfast.

A second attempt was made the following Sunday, 22 August with the full participation of Belfast IRA men. The same plan was followed, but the driver was 28-year-old Seán Leonard, a Belfast taxi driver and IRA member.[29] Leonard picked up Culhane, Murphy and Fox. McCorley, already in Lisburn monitoring Swanzy's movements, reported that he was in church. The IRA had to wait the best part of an hour until the service in Christ Church, Church of Ireland cathedral ended. The assassins came up behind Swanzy and Culhane shot him in the head. Dick Murphy fired too, hitting Swanzy in the body. Other shots were fired and McCorley leaned over him to give the *coup de grâce*. Swanzy died instantly. They all ran towards the waiting taxi.

Some of the churchgoers gave chase, but stopped when McCorley fired at them. Captain Woods, the Lisburn UVF commander, continued the chase swiping at McCorley with a blackthorn stick. By a fluke, McCorley shot the blackthorn out of his hand, the bullet grazing a woman's leg. Another bullet smashed through the window of the Lisburn Co-op and a third narrowly missed Thomas English, clerk of Lisburn petty sessions. This rear-guard action by McCorley left him about twenty metres behind the rest of the fleeing squad who jumped into the taxi, which began to move off, but McCorley reached it in time.[30] Meanwhile RIC men commandeered a taxi and pursued the IRA. Fox recalled how their vehicle 'could not exceed 30 m.p.h. while the taxi with the police was much faster'. However, going at full tilt round a corner, two tyres came off the policemen's taxi and the IRA men escaped to Belfast.[31] Culhane and Murphy later took the Great Northern train to Dublin with first class tickets on the correct presumption that the police would never expect IRA men to travel first class. By the time they were on the train, three hours after their assassination of Swanzy, the consequences in Lisburn were already horrendous.

Within half an hour of the shooting a large angry mob had assembled in the town's Market Square intent on exacting retribution from the town's Catholic population. There were only fourteen police in the three RIC barracks in Lisburn, but those on duty nevertheless baton-charged the gathering mob, which quickly regrouped.[32] The Lisburn police phoned Belfast for reinforcements who duly arrived in a number of police cars but were too few to control the crowd which by 2.30 p.m. numbered thousands. The mob headed for the confectionery shop, Gilmore's, owned by one of two members of SF in the town and according to some sources he was also in the IRA.[33] The shop had been attacked in July but this time it was ransacked, the furniture thrown out of the upstairs windows and the building set on fire. Mrs Gilmore escaped by jumping out of a back window and running the gauntlet of 'a howling mob'. The mob then proceeded to attack and burn every Catholic-owned business in the vicinity, concentrating at first on public houses and spirit grocers. A detachment of troops from the 1st Battalion Somerset Light

Infantry arrived from Holywood. One lorry load of soldiers mounted guard at the large Sacred Heart of Mary convent which housed a community of twenty-eight nuns. The rioters burnt the lorry.

By evening the mob, fired up with plentiful supplies of alcohol, was roaming the centre of the town, looting and burning Catholic-owned shops. They interfered with the work of the fire brigade by cutting hoses and attacking their vehicles. As darkness fell, they vented their fury on Catholic-owned private houses. One of the first selected belonged to William Shaw, a member of Lisburn Urban District Council and the only SF councillor in Lisburn. The mob broke into his house, pulled him into the street and set about beating him viciously. He survived, making it to the local cottage hospital then discharging himself in case he was assaulted more seriously in hospital. Shaw was far from being the only victim. More than twenty other Catholics were hospitalized after grievous beatings; one publican who was shot and wounded spent months in hospital.[34]

Ironically, two of the men who had provoked this ferocious onslaught on the town's Catholics rolled through Lisburn shortly after 5.00 p.m. in first-class comfort on their way to Dublin. Culhane and Murphy were playing cards when they noticed 'a number of houses on fire, which we heard later were houses of Catholic sympathizers'.[35] So remote from the circumstances of the north were the Corkmen that even years later when they gave their statements to the BMH they had little idea of the cataclysmic consequences of their actions for the entire Catholic population of Lisburn.

Police reinforcements had arrived from Larne, more than thirty-five kilometres away, but still far too few to deal with the thousands on the streets. What seems to have been a whole company of the 1st Battalion, The Norfolk Regiment also arrived. However, all the troops in Lisburn were under the command of Hackett Pain and there was no question of him ordering them to fire on the rioters. Many of the rioters, especially those carrying weapons, were members of the UVF. Under Hackett Pain's orders, the troops adopted a passive role, throwing a cordon round the Catholic church and convent. Elsewhere, mobs had a free hand and the pillaging and burning continued into the night and the next morning. By Monday it was obvious to the local magistrates and council that the drunken rioters were inflicting serious damage on the economy of Lisburn and were also accidentally burning unionist-owned premises as well as those of nationalists. One of the Catholic-owned businesses destroyed was E. Donaghy & Sons boot factory that employed 100 workers, many of them unionist. It was estimated that £10,000 worth of stock went up in smoke.[36] Unionist residents and business owners hung union jacks from their buildings to keep arsonists away, but sometimes flames leapt across from adjacent buildings. Law and order had broken down. On Monday afternoon magistrates, councillors, police, army and Protestant clergy met. An 8.00

p.m. curfew was suggested and a local 'peace patrol' set up. The gas supply to the town was turned off to curtail the spread of fire. But the rioters ignored the curfew and jeered at the peace patrol, a mere twenty or so men, including local Protestant clergy. Burning and looting continued into the night. Still the military took no action. Only exhaustion brought the trauma of Lisburn's Catholics to an end on Tuesday as Swanzy's body was taken to the railway station for removal to Dublin and Harold's Cross cemetery.

Catholics had begun to flee the town on Monday, some by train, others on the backs of lorries or on horse-drawn carts. Many departed on foot for Belfast, some pushing hand carts carrying what little they could manage, or what little they had left. Scores were destitute, all their possessions having been thrown into the street and burnt. Many of those walking towards Belfast were set upon at Lambeg village, three kilometres east of Lisburn, and forced to divert to the mountain roads leading to Ligoniel and Ardoyne in north Belfast. Some ended up sleeping rough in Ardoyne, others sheltering along the wall of Flax Street mill in Ardoyne.[37] Eventually, a few hundred made it to St Mary's Hall where the St Vincent de Paul Society had set up a temporary relief centre to cope with Catholics dispossessed in the July riots in Belfast. No one knows how many fled Lisburn, but estimates suggest about 1,000.[38] In an obituary in 1943 of Canon O'Boyle, who was parish priest of Lisburn in 1920, the *Irish News* noted that there were normally three packed Sunday Masses in Lisburn in 1920. On Sunday 29 August nine people turned up.[39] Contrary to popular belief and folk memory, reinforced by a comment from Fred Crawford, the UVF's gunrunner, the entire nationalist population was not expelled.[40] The 1911 census shows 2,946 Catholics in Lisburn, 23.75 per cent of the town's 12,388 population.[41] The 1926 census has a figure of 3,730 Catholics, 30 per cent of a total of 12,406, so clearly for most Lisburn Catholics, the exodus in 1920 was not permanent, and even then only constituted about a third of the Catholic population.[42] Six years after the mob assaults, there were more Catholics living in Lisburn and they constituted a higher proportion of the town's population. Many returned to work in the town's textile mills, although how soon after the destructive rioting is not known. Those who did return to their homes in the town, desperate for work, were compelled to sign a humiliating undertaking before being re-employed, declaring: 'I [   ] hereby declare I am not a Sinn Féiner nor have any sympathy with Sinn Féin and do declare I am loyal to King and country.' For the majority of Catholic business owners, however, Lisburn was no longer a place where they could prosper. They headed mainly for Belfast, Newry or Dundalk; some went to Dublin. The loyalist mobs had cleansed the town of upwardly mobile Catholics.

The worst of the rioting was over, but trouble flared again on Tuesday evening 24 August and continued sporadically for the rest of the week. That night a mob concentrated on Chapel Hill where the Catholic church and parochial hall were located. These were defended by a cordon of soldiers. On the other side of town, the British officer in command advised the nuns to evacuate the Sacred Heart convent. Most went to Cushendall and Glenariffe. A dozen travelled to a sister convent in Bootle near Liverpool. The Norfolks repelled several attacks on St Patrick's church and St Joseph's parochial hall, but in the darkness did not notice a breakaway group of arsonists who outflanked them across fields and broke into the parochial house, which was empty, the three priests having fled. The mob ransacked the house and looted anything of value. Then they burned the parish records and torched the house. The intensity of attacks tailed off after Tuesday, partly because the rioters needed to go back to work, partly from exhaustion, but also because there were not many Catholic targets left to pillage and burn. Even so, there were sporadic attacks on individual Catholic-owned houses, not just that week, but for months thereafter. When the nuns returned to their convent in October, it was attacked and ultimately a permanent military guard was posted.

The most common reaction of unionist newspapers, visitors and observers was to lament the accidental damage done to unionist-owned businesses and homes. The damage caused was assessed by the RIC inspector general at over £810,000, the equivalent of £40 million today.[43] The RIC prosecuted a grand total of seven men for all the depredations in Lisburn in August. Five were convicted but appealed. In April 1921 they were given recorded sentences and walked free. Compensation claims against Antrim County Council and Down County Council by those who suffered material loss were heard in Belfast county court. Altogether, 278 houses and business premises had been destroyed and huge quantities of furniture, merchandise and goods had been lost. The total claims amounted to £806,538. Claimants found it impossible to prove what items they had lost and most businesses had had their ledgers burnt. The solicitors acting for the councils managed to reduce the value of claims in court to £233,952, still about £10 million in today's money.[44] It was to be paid out of the rates. The councils appealed and the cases dragged on into late 1921 when the new Northern Ireland government met the full costs of compensation. Thus, no one in Lisburn went to jail and no ratepayers had to pay for the deliberate destruction of their Catholic neighbours' property, even though many of them would have been in the rampaging mobs.

The killing of Swanzy also led to serious disturbances in Belfast. Many people were killed and gravely wounded and homes and businesses burnt to the ground, although in relative terms this was not on the same scale of systematic destruction as in Lisburn. There were a number of differences in the clashes in Belfast in August compared to those in July and also a range of political and security consequences which would set the pattern for Belfast until 1922. First, the IRA in Belfast took both defensive and offensive action, firing both at invading mobs and Crown forces. Second, Ulster Unionist leaders used the serious clashes, involving widespread discharging of firearms, causing many deaths and injury, as a pretext to lever the British government into giving them, in effect, control of law and order in the six counties that they correctly presumed would be partitioned under the Government of Ireland bill passing through Westminster.

Two days elapsed after Swanzy's assassination before intense loyalist assaults began on Catholic districts in Belfast. By 24 August attacks were in full swing. At first, it seemed that, as in July, only the usual places would be affected: the Short Strand and the flashpoints between Clonard and the Shankill. The Short Strand bore the brunt of attacks on the night of 24 August. Catholic-owned shops on the Newtownards Road and Mountpottinger Road that had been damaged in July, but resumed business, were targeted by arsonists. Attempts, some successful, were made to burn dwellings in front line streets. However, unlike in July, the inhabitants of the district were prepared and fought back with kidney pavers and broken flagstones. There were running battles.[45] The following day, workers, by now all unionist, heading past the Short Strand towards the shipyard and the Sirocco works, came under attack from those who had suffered the previous night. Large numbers of Catholics expelled from the shipyard and engineering works were now available both to defend the district and attack the men who had expelled them. Police and troops chased the attacking Catholics back into Short Strand's side streets. That night the loyalist mob appeared again, some carrying guns. Predictably, St Matthew's church was attacked. British troops guarding the building opened fire and killed two Protestants, one a woman, and seriously wounded another woman. Much the same sequence of events occurred in west Belfast. Mackies workers making their way home to the Shankill through Clonard were attacked. Others travelling from Mackies and the Albert Foundry in trams on the Springfield Road past Clonard were stoned by nationalists, many of whom would have lost their jobs in July. A hand grenade was also thrown at a tram but failed to explode.[46] Next day a detachment of soldiers provided protection for the Mackies men.

As the week went on, violence spread to previously untroubled parts of the city. On Saturday night, 28 August, loyalists launched a ferocious attack on the Marrowbone, a small, impoverished Catholic district of fewer than one thousand people adjacent to Ardoyne in north Belfast. The 'Bone' was surrounded by unionist districts. The attack seems to have been premeditated, well planned, and not just the usual headlong rush of a mob fortified with alcohol. Snipers positioned on a roof top, who had obviously military experience and good rifles, killed four Catholic men, two of whom were standing at their front doors. Eventually troops arrived and the snipers made off. So did the attacking crowd, but heading back to the Shankill, they turned their attention to a pub in Tennant Street off the Crumlin Road, which they torched. Again, troops chased them.

Over the weekend loyalist crowds tried to burn Catholic schools and churches. They also launched incursions across north and west Belfast into streets where nationalist inhabitants bordered loyalist districts. On Monday, 30 August, fighting broke out on York Street to the north of the city centre. Disturbances began early in the morning when expelled Catholic workers attacked trams carrying workers to Workman Clark in north Belfast. These workers alighted from the trams and mass pitched battles ensued all along York Street and in the maze of adjacent side streets. There was a lot of gunfire from the nationalist side, indicating an IRA presence. Four people were killed, including an 11-year-old Protestant boy. Only the arrival of troops, who fired bursts from a Lewis gun over the heads of the warring factions, brought the fighting to an end in York Street. However, the protagonists then took up new positions 300 metres nearer the city centre at North Street which is at the city end of the Shankill Road. Here, for the first time, clear evidence emerged of IRA organization in defence of a nationalist district, in this case Carrick Hill and the Old Lodge Road. A large loyalist mob, armed with a variety of weapons, including handguns, came down the Shankill Road into North Street led by a man carrying a union jack. They launched an attack into the warren of narrow, close-packed streets in the nationalist enclave but were met by a badly aimed volley of shots from Union Street and Winetavern Street. As the mob ran back towards the Shankill in disarray, they were ambushed by more gunfire at the junction of Peter's Hill and the nationalist Old Lodge Road. Many dropped their weapons and fled. RIC from nearby Smithfield barracks came to their rescue. Jim McDermott recounts that his grandfather's younger brother, Paddy McDermott, referred to this incident as the Carrick Hill ambush. McDermott's grandfather, Jimmy, organized and took part in it.[47] While this may have been the end of the disturbances that began at 8.00 a.m. in York Street, it was not the end of fighting on 30 August. Loyalists regrouped at the bottom of the Shankill and attacked Carrick Hill again. That night, a loyalist mob mounted another assault on the Bone and burned and looted Catholic-owned shops on the Oldpark Road, the main route through the Bone.

Violence reached an unprecedented intensity in Belfast during that last week of August. The RIC and army commanders settled on resolute action from 1 September. First, the army and police would escort workers to their place of employment in the mornings since that was when the daily fighting began as enraged nationalists, expelled from their jobs, sought retribution against the perpetrators. Second, a curfew was proclaimed from 10.30 p.m. to 5.00 a.m. and largely became the norm in Belfast until 1924. Even so, the

curfew did not stop sniping and speculative pistol fire into opposition streets
until the first week of September. The death toll for August in Belfast was
twenty-two, seventeen in the last weekend of the month alone. There were
169 seriously injured and an unknown number who suffered minor injuries,
but did not require hospital treatment.[48]

In the midst of this violence, Carson, Craig and other leading unionists
sought to take advance control of the six-county area that the Government of
Ireland bill going through Westminster in 1920 would designate as partitioned. Part of their plan was to establish a separate autonomous administration for the area, as well as to take control of security forces and law and
order, a plan well in hand before the outbreak of sectarian violence in Belfast.
The unionists used the frequency and intensity of the violence in Belfast and
Lisburn, and also in neighbouring towns in County Down, like Banbridge and
Dromore, to advance their demands for special constables to be sworn in to
maintain law and order. Their argument was strengthened by the obvious fact
that there were not enough troops and police to manage the scale of the widespread disturbances. The government in London either ignored, or did not
know, that unionist commanders like Hackett Pain prevented the army from
taking vigorous action against loyalist mobs. The British government was
faced with a rapidly deteriorating situation in the south and west of Ireland,
troop shortages that necessitated the deployment of the raggle-taggle Black
and Tan mercenaries – who had little effect except in many cases to make
matters worse – and widespread serious civil disturbances in Belfast and
Lisburn. In those circumstances, the availability of hundreds of local special
constables was attractive. Despite opposition from Dublin Castle, where officials were well aware that the special constables would all be from one community, London pressed ahead.[49] Already in Lisburn justices of the peace,
using an archaic power, had sworn in 800 special constables, many of whom
were former UVF, for three months' duty at a meeting on 30 August.[50]
Belfast would soon follow suit.

On 2 September, at a ministerial meeting in London, Craig presented an
eleven-point plan which developed the proposal he had made in July for a
special constabulary of 'men from the loyal population' and that the UVF be
the nucleus of that constabulary. He now added that the constabulary and
regular police should be controlled by an under-secretary based in Belfast, not
Dublin. His proposal was supported by a preposterous memorandum entitled:
'Appreciation of the situation in Ulster' in which he asserted that SF was 'the
predominant factor over a considerable portion of the province' and that 'loyalist leaders … find that their less restrained followers will not listen to them
unless they can give proof that the government is in earnest'.[51] This description was precisely the opposite of the case in Belfast and Lisburn, where 'the
loyalist rank and file' were the attackers, and the people under attack were the

Catholic population. The claim that the north-east was about to be overrun by the IRA and needed immediate armed reinforcements from the unionist population was entirely spurious. So too was the argument that permitting unionist leaders to transform rioters into special constables would mean a return to law and order because unionist leaders would be able to restrain the mobs once they were confident their leaders were in charge of resisting an imaginary IRA assault on the north-east. Only three ministers were present, all strong supporters of the Ulster Unionists. Bonar Law chaired the meeting and was accompanied by Balfour and Robert Horne, president of the Board of Trade.[52] Despite the entirely spurious arguments of Craig and Carson, the attraction of washing its hands of Ulster proved too strong to the Westminster government. Lloyd George, a prisoner of the Conservative Party, entirely dependent on its MPs to remain as prime minister, was in no position to refuse requests supported by the Ulster Unionists and the majority of Conservative MPs.

In another major success for Craig, the meeting approved an under-secretary for the six-county area who would be responsible to London. Lloyd George agreed to this on 6 September. Craig's proposals for a special constabulary and an under-secretary were formally approved on 8 September but remained confidential until 22 October. The new official, Sir Ernest Clark, arrived in Belfast on 17 September and began to set up the USC by using surviving UVF officers and structures. Fanning argues that Clark's appointment was 'a preliminary step towards partition'.[53] Basil Brooke, later prime minister of Northern Ireland, described Clark as 'midwife to the new province of Ulster'.[54] Colonel Wilfrid Spender, who had been the most effective staff officer in the pre-war UVF, had been instructed by Craig in July to start reconstituting the UVF. Now, liaising closely with Clark and his nascent northern administration, Spender worked to transfer UVF units and their commanders lock, stock and barrel into the USC. Spender sent a circular to all UVF battalions in Belfast in which he indicated that he saw the UVF being transformed into a new special constabulary comprising 10,000 men divided into three classes: A class were full-time and became the Royal Ulster Constabulary (RUC) in 1922, B class were part-time and C class comprised older men who could be called up in an emergency and were stood down in 1922.[55]

The arrangements were officially announced on 22 October to a reaction of amazement, incredulity and horror from northern nationalists. Three days later, Devlin asked the chief secretary

> whether this scheme has been undertaken by the Government, to arm
> the men who organized and carried out the pogrom against Belfast
> Catholic workmen, and who have expelled 4,000 Catholic workmen
> from their employment; whether Parliament will be given an opportu-

nity of discussing this organized conspiracy to place the lives, liberties,
and property of 500,000 Catholics at the mercy of their political opponents armed by the British Government?

Devlin went on to ask how unionist leaders knew five weeks before the
announcement of the government's intention to organize 'special constables to
exterminate the Catholics of Belfast'.[56] By the end of October it was obvious
in Belfast that circumstances had changed because, although fewer in number,
the men attacking Catholic districts were better organized and armed.
Furthermore, they were able to operate during the curfew because they were
members of the USC. Devlin pointed out in the Commons that a number of
special constables in Lisburn and Belfast had been arrested by the RIC and
charged with a series of offences, including looting. The character of the conflict in Belfast had changed radically.

 If one consequence of the major disturbances in Belfast and Lisburn in
July and August had been to enable unionists to take forward their plans to
develop a system of government and policing for the six counties before the
Government of Ireland Act became law in 1921, then another consequence
was better IRA organization within beleaguered Catholic districts. It was now
clear to the IRA that they were facing a better disciplined, armed, determined
and officially sanctioned attack, compared to the mass onslaughts of July and
August. In 1920 Manus O'Boyle was detailed by the Belfast Brigade to organize an IRA company to defend the Ballymacarrett district, which included the
Short Strand.[57] Thanks to the shipyard and factory expulsions there were
plenty of angry unemployed men ready to join; soon he had 120. O'Boyle
recalled that from July 1920 it 'was a continuous street fight in
Ballymacarrett'. The IRA used small arms and grenades, which were always
in short supply. They also had some rifles supplied by Roger McCorley, but
these were of little use in close-combat street fighting. O'Boyle's headquarters were the Cross and Passion convent in Bryson Street where he hid the
company's weapons and ammunition. The fighting continued through 1920
until the truce in July 1921 and after. There was sporadic fighting night and
day, regardless of the curfew. A group of IRA always stood outside the convent posing as a 'peace picket', but was ready to swing into action if the district was attacked. Despite the curfew, they were able to stay there late at
night inside the grounds of the convent.

 O'Boyle had some indispensable assets. First, there was his brother-in-law
Joe Clarke, an RIC man stationed in Brown Square barracks on the Shankill
Road. Clarke was one of the main intelligence sources for the IRA's Belfast
Brigade and passed much useful information to O'Boyle. He emigrated to
America after the truce but before he went Joe McKelvey presented him with
a gold watch on behalf of the 3rd Northern Division in gratitude for his work.

Perhaps more important for the immediate needs of the Short Strand was DI J.J. McConnell. The mother superior of the convent was always able to present O'Boyle with hundreds of rounds of .45 bullets supplied by McConnell. On one occasion McConnell came into the convent while a group of local IRA was sorting ammunition: 'He said nothing except "So this is the peace picket"', and walked away. McConnell was transferred to Cork after an attempt on his life in Belfast. He had paid one visit too many to the convent with ammunition. A Constable McNulty, based in the local Mountpottinger barracks, who later became harbour master in his native Ballina, also provided vital information about impending raids on the district by USC. He too provided ammunition.

In west Belfast, with its large nationalist population, the fighting was completely different from the beleaguered Short Strand. Better armed and equipped, with greater numbers and more support, the IRA was able to take the offensive at times. Thomas Flynn, who commanded the 1st Battalion active service unit (ASU) in 1921, recalled how the west Belfast districts defended themselves against night-time raids by British troops, RIC and USC murder gangs.[58] It took time for systems to evolve after July 1920. Again, as in east Belfast, there were plenty of unemployed men available to defend areas under attack. Eight men were selected from each of west Belfast's four companies and divided into two sixteen-man columns, one for day duty and one for night. By September 1920 there were also twenty-four unarmed pickets that kept watch at the perimeter of the district. For night duty they were supplied with torches with three different coloured filters for the lenses so that they could flash a colour to the armed columns to signify which type of attacker was trying to enter the district: British army, RIC, USC/murder gang. Once alerted, the armed IRA squads could engage the interlopers.

Flynn's account of defending west Belfast districts from summer 1920 onward is corroborated by Joseph Murray who was in 'D' company in the Falls Road.[59] By the summer of 1920, Murray was a full-time IRA volunteer and remained so throughout the next two years before moving to Dublin. As the IRA became more experienced and better organized in September and October 1920 at preventing incursions by USC into nationalist districts, the USC would call for assistance from the British army, claiming correctly that snipers were operating against them. The army would then arrive in large numbers of armoured cars, cordon off some streets and conduct house-to-house searches. That meant that weapons dumps had to be very carefully designed because rapid access to weapons was vital in the event of a murderous raid by USC. Murray recalled that the only way to prevent this military procedure was to dig trenches across streets to stop armoured cars entering the district, but that was seldom done because of the hardship caused to people living there. He conceded that generally the IRA was unable to deal with the military, but this problem ceased after the truce in July 1921.

Quick escape for the pickets, who gave early warning, and for the armed squads, was essential so that weapons could be safeguarded and arrests avoided. Murray revealed how passages between houses were created by knocking holes in partition walls, sometimes, tunnelling the entire length of a street. It took 'considerable time' for the IRA to persuade the residents of the necessity for these measures but the situation was so desperate that by

> the autumn and winter of 1920 and 1921 we seem to have settled down to semi-war conditions within the boundary of the city. The boundary of the nationalist areas resembled frontier posts where precautions had to be taken on entering and leaving these areas which were under constant watch by the specials and the military.[60]

When the expulsions from factories and shipyards in July 1920 were followed by the mass attacks on nationalist districts, and also by random attacks on individual Catholics going about their business, there was an upsurge in recruitment to the Belfast IRA, which changed the nature of the organization in the city. Séamus McKenna lamented the changes the influx brought.[61] He estimated that the total strength on paper of the Belfast IRA in July 1920 was about 300 men. When McKenna emerged from prison in January 1922, he reckons there were 'at least 1,000'. In his view between two-thirds and three quarters of the new recruits joined for sectarian reasons and were 'lacking in the ideals and principles which inspired the men who joined the movement in Belfast and remained in it between 1916 and 1920.'[62] Another criticism was that too many of the post-July 1920 recruits were ex-British army, who were quickly promoted, although they 'had not the slightest shred of national ideals or principles'. McKenna cited the example of two brothers who joined the IRA solely to avenge their father who had been shot dead by loyalists.[63]

It is true that McKenna had a bad taste in his mouth after his capture in Cavan and imprisonment, which he partly attributed to some ex-British army men who had joined after 1920 and against whom he harboured a grudge. Nevertheless, his observations are interesting in that he describes a divide in the Belfast IRA between late recruits, who joined in reaction to being expelled from workplaces, and the younger, more active men who had been Fianna Éireann members and Volunteers since before 1916 and who later constituted the ASU – Belfastmen like McCorley, Séamus Woods, Joe Murray, Thomas Flynn and McKenna himself.

In September 1920 the Belfast IRA went on the offensive in the limited way that was available to them, given lack of support in the city's nationalist community, intense hostility from the unionist community, and the arrival on the scene of the well-armed USC. Before the mass attacks on Catholic districts in Belfast in July, and Swanzy's killing in August 1920, there had been pressure from Devlin, T.P. O'Connor, IPP MP for the Liverpool Scotland constituency from 1885 to 1929, and from Catholic clergy, not to provoke retaliation from unionists who outnumbered nationalists three to one in the city as a whole, but by more than ten to one in exposed districts like the Short Strand. Senior Belfast IRA officers agreed. However, after the deaths and destruction in the final week of August 1920, the desire among the younger Belfast IRA members to take the offensive was untrammelled by such considerations.

A variety of motives drove Belfast's young IRA members in autumn 1920. They wanted to participate in the national struggle, which was intensifying, particularly in Dublin and in the south-west, where growing numbers of RIC men were being killed, many others resigning, and police barracks being vacated.[64] They felt the need to demonstrate that there was an IRA presence in Belfast, that the city was not composed exclusively of unionists and supporters of the discredited IPP. There was also the desire for revenge for the deaths, destruction and impoverishment visited on Catholics in the city by loyalist mobs allied with a desire to develop some kind of credibility among Belfast nationalists. The creation of the USC gave added impetus to the argument that IRA operations in Belfast were necessary. If nothing else, the USC provided a target other than indiscriminate shooting into loyalist mobs. However, in the event, the first offensive operation at the end of September resulted not in casualties among USC, but in the death of a Catholic RIC man and the wounding of two other policemen.

As elsewhere, the IRA in Belfast was chronically short of weapons. They stole them, bought them from British soldiers and UVF members and even made some matériel themselves.[65] But this was never enough and the shortage became acute in the autumn of 1920 as IRA numbers increased. On the night of Saturday 25 September, a battalion operation in west Belfast was planned to disarm RIC men on patrol and seize their weapons. Due to the heightened tension and the violence of the previous two months, all RIC patrols were armed and had been doubled and even trebled in size.[66] Therefore, a squad of IRA was needed to disarm the police. There were three attempts that night: one in Conway Street, one in Hamill Street near the city centre, and one at the junction of the Falls Road and Broadway. In Hamill Street there was an exchange of fire between the IRA and the police, one of whom was shot in the arm. The IRA escaped with the police guns. The attempt in Conway Street was aborted because police reinforcements had arrived on the Falls Road after the Hamill Street attack. On the main Falls Road, an IRA squad of four or five men from 'B' company attacked two police standing at the Beehive bar. The IRA ordered the police to put their hands up, but they drew their pistols and fired. Lieutenant Andy O'Hare was wounded. His comrades returned fire and killed Constable Thomas Leonard. Constable Farrell was wounded in the thigh and the IRA made off with the

policemen's weapons. For their safety, three members of B company –
Ignatius 'Wish' Fox, Paddy Byrne and the wounded O'Hare – left Belfast for
Dublin immediately after the operation.[67]

Leonard was the first policeman killed by the IRA in Belfast. Both police
were stationed in the nearby Springfield Road barracks and Leonard, a
Catholic, lived locally in Roden Street, 800 metres from the barracks.
Notably, the boycott against the RIC, which had been in operation since April
1919, was not implemented in Belfast and Antrim. Similarly, a general order
of 4 June 1920 for an intensification of the boycott was ignored because the
IRA could not enforce it and because the RIC in Belfast provided much-
needed protection from loyalist attacks.

No one anticipated the consequences of the attacks on the police, which
were immediate. That night, a dozen of Leonard's colleagues set out to
avenge his death and the other attacks on the police. Edward 'Ned' Trodden,
Seán Gaynor and Seán McFadden were shot dead. Police raided the homes
of two SF Belfast councillors, Denis McCullough and Denis Barnes, but they
were not at home. It is not known if it was the same police who killed the
other three.[68] The killing of the three men is well documented because it
induced profound shock among Belfast's Catholics.[69] The policy of reprisals
was already well under way in Munster but it was unknown in Belfast
because so far there had been no occasion to deploy such a policy. However,
the policy had been considered earlier that month by Craig who suggested to
the cabinet that 'organized reprisals against the rebels, mainly in order to
defeat them, but partly in order to restrain their own followers' be implemented.[70] Trodden and Gaynor were IRA men and lived close to Springfield
Road barracks. Trodden was also in the IRB and his barber shop was used
for IRB meetings. He was a member of the GAA and secretary of SF's local
Seán Mac Diarmada cumann. Gaynor was a member of B company, 1st
Battalion which, coincidentally, was responsible for the attack that killed
Constable Leonard. However, it is likely the RIC murder gang was looking
for his brother, Liam, a teacher who was a much more prominent IRA man
and the Ulster representative on the IRB's supreme council. He went on the
run after his brother's funeral.[71] McFadden's republican connections are not
as clear cut. He lived literally opposite the police barracks at 54 Springfield
Road and may have supplied intelligence to the IRA.[72] There were no military trappings for McFadden's funeral, unlike the other two.

From information given to Michael Collins's intelligence system by sym-
pathetic RIC men in Belfast, the names of the RIC murder gang and their
activities were soon known. The account sent to Collins read:

> At midnight a party of RIC under Chief Inspector Harrison left
> Springfield Road barracks, separated into three bands and proceeded

shooting up the Falls and Kashmir districts. Afterwards entering the house of the following men who were shot dead:

Edward Trodden, who was in bed when the party under Harrison entered, was pulled out of bed and dragged by the hair downstairs and shot in the yard. The party then proceeded to the Springfield Road, entered the house of John McFadden who met the party in the passage and was shot there in three places.

A second party led by Head Constable Giff forced an entrance into Gaynor's house and shot him in the bedroom. Giff, before leaving the room, drove a bayonet through Seán Gaynor's body, fired shots through the rooms in the house and threatened Gaynor's mother with the butt of his rifle for refusing to disclose the whereabouts of her elder son Liam.

The members of the gang were: Harrison who shot Trodden and McFadden; Giff who shot Gaynor, Sergeant C. Clarke, Sergeant Glover, Sgt. Hicks of College Square barracks and Constables Golding, Caldwell, Sterrit, Gordon, Cooke, Packenham (now H. Const.) and Norton.

The gang were given over to Nixon and became the reprisal outfit.[73]

These specifics were corroborated by family witnesses. The killings struck terror into the Catholic community partly because of the savagery and brutality (which was probably the intention) and partly because nothing like it had happened before. The names of the RIC men involved were passed to the Belfast IRA who began to target them for assassination, but not before some of the same policemen carried out other reprisal killings in Belfast.

The funerals of the three murder victims on 27 September were enormous with hundreds of men marching in military formation behind the hearses and thousands lining the Falls Road to the cemetery at Milltown on the outskirts of west Belfast. British troops in armoured cars hemmed in the cortège front and rear. The coffins of Trodden and Gaynor were draped with tricolours, which the British officer in command unsuccessfully demanded be removed. After the funerals, the tension and anger towards the police and army quickly turned to serious rioting that evening, which continued for several nights. The army shot dead four unarmed Catholics from west Belfast during these disturbances, which, as usual, rapidly developed into sectarian conflict in various predictable parts of Belfast. There was another upsurge of violence in October when the army shot dead two unionists near the Bone as a loyalist crowd returning from a football match launched an attack on the Sacred Heart church on 16 October. A third unionist was crushed by an armoured car there and a Protestant was shot dead that night in east Belfast, probably by the IRA.

The rapid and ruthless RIC reprisals produced a serious difference of opinion along familiar lines in the Belfast IRA. One view was that there should be immediate and equally ruthless retaliation against the police as the Belfast IRA knew from intelligence sources who was responsible. The argument was that if the IRA remained passive after the reprisals, then they would lose the struggle altogether and the police would win. On the other hand, those urging caution, mainly the Belfast Brigade staff, argued that retaliation would inevitably cause the deaths of many innocent Catholics, not only from police reprisals, but from indiscriminate loyalist mob attacks like those which had scarred the population in July and August. McCorley, unsurprisingly one of those arguing for immediate retaliation, recalled that a majority favoured executing the RIC responsible 'otherwise the policy of reprisals would be a complete success in Belfast as it was obviously designed to stop activities against the British forces for fear of the consequences which would follow such action'.[74] Plans were then made to draw up defence tactics for each company area in the event of reprisals after the RIC men were shot, an ambitious project given the IRA's limited resources. McCorley himself believed that the scheme was beyond the means of the Belfast IRA. In the event, the matter was postponed to the dismay of the rank and file.[75]

In the short term nothing came of the 'grave discontent' McCorley referred to, but dissent continued. The 1st Battalion, two of whose members were among those killed by the RIC, was obviously keen to retaliate. At the end of the year when O/C 1st Battalion, Joe McKelvey, was promoted, McCorley replaced him as O/C, despite the misgivings of the brigade staff who attempted to appoint their own more cautious commander. By that time the moment had passed and the three months after the end of September 1920 saw no IRA killings in Belfast.

Instead, the IRA concentrated on operations that were really nothing more than nuisance activities and caused no serious disruption to either the Crown forces or the economy of Belfast. These activities were marked by incompetence, poor planning, faulty intelligence and demonstrated the lack of capacity of the Belfast IRA. For example, in October the IRA raided the GPO sorting office to disrupt or steal mail being sent to Dublin from the new assistant under-secretary, Sir Ernest Clark, but the mail had already been sent and the mailboxes were empty. The squad was put at risk for nothing. At various times, the IRA cut telephone and telegraph wires which were repaired within a day. A mail van was held up to capture military correspondence being taken to the GNR station for transit to Dublin and England but it was the wrong van.

The biggest operation in the autumn of 1920 was a raid on a large garage and parking compound, Spence & Johnstone's, at the rear of the City Hall on 14 October. The intention was to burn 150 trucks and armoured cars that had just been delivered for the RIC and new USC. The complex extended over

CENTRAL ANTRIM REGIMENT.

Review by Sir Edward Carson, at Drumalis, of the Three Battalions on 11th-July, 1914.

1 Postcard of Sir Edward Carson reviewing three battalions of the UVF Central Antrim Regiment at Drumalis, County Antrim, 11 July 1914.

2 UVF parade at Balmoral Showgrounds, Belfast, 27 September 1913.

3 Joe Devlin, MP for West Belfast.
4 Parochial house, Lisburn, August 1920, with loyalists standing in the burnt-out shell.

5 Donaghy's Boot Factory, Lisburn, gutted in the anti–Catholic riots of August 1920.
6 Seán O'Neill, O/C Belfast Brigade IRA, 1920, later ADC to Michael Brennan, chief of staff, National army.

7 Funeral of riot victims, Leeson Street, Falls Road, Belfast, 1920.

8 Roger McCorley, O/C Belfast Brigade IRA, 1921 and Tom Fitzpatrick (alias Bob
O'Donnell), O/C Antrim Brigade IRA, 1921.

9 Staff members, 3rd Northern Division, 1921. *Left to right*: Séamus Woods, Tom McNally, Joe McKelvey, Frank Crummey.

10 'B' & 'C' companies, 1st Battalion, Belfast Brigade IRA, 1921, on Hannahstown Hill.
11 'D' company, 1st Battalion, Belfast Brigade IRA, 1921, on Black Mountain.

approximately two hectares of the old linen green off Linenhall Street. About twenty IRA were involved from different companies of the 1st Battalion. They held up men who were working overtime and poured petrol over the vehicles. As Joe Murray recalled, 'owing to a misunderstanding between company leaders and the pre-ignition of one of the fires of one of the buildings we failed to burn out the largest building which contained seventy-five cars.'[76] In fact, the IRA raiders were lucky to escape. Poor planning and lack of coordination were almost their undoing. They failed to cut all the telephone wires and, as a result, one of the employees was able to phone the police and fire brigade. The IRA did not know which buildings to concentrate on and had to retreat when they heard the fire brigade and police sirens approaching. According to the *Belfast Telegraph*, admittedly a unionist newspaper keen to minimize the effect of any IRA action, only three cars were burnt. There was nothing like the damage Murray claimed, either to buildings (which were really just sheds) or to a quarter of the vehicles.[77] A huge commitment in men had almost ended in disaster for the Belfast IRA.

Military activity in the autumn of 1920 was not the all-consuming interest of the Belfast IRA. Much of its members' energy was expended on the Belfast boycott, which was initiated in August in response to the expulsions of Catholics from the shipyards, engineering works, and textile mills. It seems to have been the brainchild of Joseph MacRory, Catholic bishop of Down and Connor, who was close to SF. He formed the boycott committee with Seán MacEntee, TD for Monaghan South and a native of Belfast, Denis McCullough, by then a SF Belfast city councillor, Frank Crummey, a teacher and the IRA's Belfast Brigade intelligence officer, and Fr John Hassan. The intention was to hurt unionists financially and economically, to try to compel them to re-admit the expelled Catholic workers. In that respect it was a complete failure. In some ways the boycott was a demonstration of the political and economic impotence of the nationalist minority in Belfast. The idea also showed a complete lack of awareness of the sources and structures of unionist business and money, much less the ability of nationalists to affect them. On 6 August MacEntee presented a petition to the Dáil signed by Belfast SF councillors and other citizens that pressed for a commercial boycott.[78] Ernest Blythe, SF TD for Monaghan North but born near Lisburn, County Antrim, and with strong Belfast connections, strenuously opposed the boycott plan both in the Dáil and outside. As an Ulster Protestant, Blythe had a keen insight into the society and economy of the north-east. He warned the Dáil that 'an economic blockade of Belfast would be the worst possible step to take. If it were taken it would destroy for ever the possibility of any union. Belfast could not be brought down through the banks.' He told TDs they were in the Dáil as a government, and they could not afford to range any section of the citizens against them.[79] Blythe was not alone. Constance

Markievicz, Arthur Griffith, Michael Collins and others agreed that such a boycott was divisive, ineffective, and, as Desmond FitzGerald argued, amounted to 'a vote for partition'.[80] Blythe unsuccessfully tried to amend MacEntee's motion but, after a short debate, it was carried.

As the attacks on Catholics in Belfast intensified throughout August, the Dáil adopted the boycott proposals more seriously and appointed Michael Staines TD, an important SF figure and later Garda commissioner, as director. He was given an initial budget of £2,500. In January 1921 this sum was increased dramatically to £35,000. Although the tactic was known as the Belfast boycott, in fact it extended to goods from Lisburn, Banbridge, Dromore and other towns where Catholics had been attacked. Trains and lorries travelling south were stopped and searched by the IRA and goods from boycotted towns and companies were seized or destroyed. The IRA in Belfast notified Dublin GHQ about goods arriving in the Belfast docks and being transported south. Belfast companies distributing goods or trading elsewhere in Ireland were listed for boycott. As time went on, some individuals in the rest of Ireland, including west of the Bann, took it upon themselves to boycott any goods from the north they thought might compete with their own business.

Liam Gaynor was appointed director of the boycott in east Ulster. His BMH statement detailed some of his actions. He had trains carrying Belfast goods raided in Tyrone and Monaghan, Richill station in County Armagh was burned and 'lists of Belfast business houses which were circulated throughout the country for blacklisting.'[81] Gaynor also had the circulation of northern banknotes throughout Ireland banned by the acting minister for labour Joseph MacDonagh, who became director of the Belfast boycott in January 1921, but this met with limited success. Gaynor travelled to England to try to stop Belfast goods being traded and asked Harry Boland to organize a boycott of Belfast linen in the US. Gaynor claimed that millions of pounds worth of business was lost to Belfast linen firms as a result. He also made the rather far-fetched claim that he managed to have some South American companies stop their orders for Belfast-built ships. David McGuinness, who was Frank Crummey's deputy intelligence officer in Belfast, gave a very sanguine opinion of the value of the boycott which he claimed 'brought the Northern Authorities to their senses'.[82]

There is no evidence to support this assertion or Gaynor's claims. The evidence points in the opposite direction. The campaign did hurt small and medium-sized businesses, but it had no effect on Belfast's major industries. Belfast's industrial might and prosperity were in effect extensions of Britain's industry and were integrated into Britain's financial and trading economy and its links to the British Empire. For example, most of the exports of machinery from Mackies factory on the Springfield Road went to India. No one in

Ireland bought liners built in Belfast's shipyards. If the aim of the boycott was to force these industries to take back expelled workers, it failed utterly. Not one was re-employed as a result. In fact, the boycott contributed to increased sectarianism, gave the opportunity for traders and businessmen in the rest of the country to take business from northern Protestants, not unionist big business, and, despite protestations to the contrary from the Dáil, produced violence against men transporting goods and men selling them, and, above all, it reinforced partition partly by provoking retaliation from northern businesses which refused to accept goods from the south after the Government of Ireland Act became law in 1921. The boycott limped on into 1922 and proved difficult to stop. The end came as part of the Craig–Collins pact in 1922.

Neither the IRA in Belfast, the Catholic Church, the nationalist community at large or the Dáil had any effect on unionism in Belfast in 1920–1, except to harden the attitudes of the majority population and make them all more determined to repress what they considered to be a disloyal and seditious people in their midst. Nothing republicans did had the slightest effect on altering the inexorable passage of the Government of Ireland bill through Westminster which was where the fate of northern nationalists was being decided, not on the streets of Belfast.

7 Belfast: operations and elections in spring 1921

Until January 1921 the Belfast IRA was oblivious to the prospect of British- or unionist-driven political developments at Westminster and continued their military campaign, believing themselves to be an integral part of the national struggle. Only when confronted with the imminent prospect of an election did northern nationalists ask Dublin for political guidance, although little was forthcoming owing to confusion about British intentions.[1] Would Lloyd George open negotiations with de Valera or press on regardless with repression before calling elections?[2] What should be the position of SF in the north in any elections? How to prevent partition becoming a reality?

In a new departure, from early 1921 Dublin GHQ took a greater interest in the north, especially Belfast, which GHQ had come to believe was being used both as a safe haven for RIC, British forces, regulars and Black and Tans, and as a transit point for incoming troops en route to the south and west. GHQ was also becoming better organized and more professional and as such wanted to exercise stronger central control over units in the provinces. While areas like Munster resented control from Dublin GHQ as interference, Belfast welcomed the attention, especially in the shape of full-time organizers, weapons and money. It was only during the early months of 1921 that the Belfast and Antrim IRA came into existence as properly constituted units.

References to Belfast and Antrim 'battalions' and 'brigades' in 1919–20 in the BMH are often post hoc. It was only after March 1921 that the north was organized into divisions following a meeting at Eskerboy, near Carrickmore in Tyrone.[3] Present were Eoin O'Duffy, who had travelled around the north since January gaining an impression of the state of the IRA, Joe McKelvey, O/C Belfast Brigade, and other northern officers.[4] By April GHQ had established the five northern and two southern divisions of the IRA. The 3rd Northern, set up formally in April, encompassed Belfast, Antrim, and North and East Down, although there was no IRA presence to speak of in those parts of Down. Lumping Antrim and part of Down in with Belfast indicated the IRA's weakness and small numbers in east Ulster. Seán Corr's account of O'Duffy's orders in Tyrone was indicative of GHQ's demand for increased activity everywhere in the north: 'some operation each week it didn't matter how simple it was, cutting of wires, trenching roads etc. Any opportunity of attacking Special patrols should be availed of'.[5] The rationale for this new interest in Ulster was laid out in unrealistic grandiose terms by GHQ in March:

> Ulster is the English lever for governing Ireland. The Military importance of Ulster has increased in proportion as Dublin has passed into

National hands. As a result, at the present time Ulster is becoming a bridgehead that the English cannot afford to lose and must spend lavishly to defend. Here then it is necessary to attack them with all the force that can be developed there. Military, Economic, Propaganda and the attack should be steady and persistent.[6]

As Robert Lynch points out, GHQ's objectives in ordering increased operations in the north in 1921 were first to prevent the north being a safe haven for British forces and, second, to take the heat off the south and west. Objections by senior northern figures like Seán MacEntee that these operations could cause reprisals and mass sectarian attacks in Belfast were overridden.[7] On the other hand, IRA figures like McCorley were delighted to be vindicated and encouraged in their activities.

The first major operation of 1921 by the Belfast IRA seems to have resulted from information supplied by GHQ in Dublin, although McCorley maintained it came from an RIC contact in Belfast.[8] The intelligence was so detailed and precise it is unlikely a low-ranking RIC man in the city would have had access to it. Roddy's Hotel, as the Railway View Hotel was known, was considered safe for troops and police because it was beside Musgrave Street barracks, RIC headquarters in Belfast. Its public bar was popular with police, especially since a side door leading to the bar faced the back door of the barracks. RIC, Black and Tans and Auxiliaries all stayed in the hotel while awaiting orders to move south. At least two of the barmen in Roddy's were IRA, one called Garvey and another, Vincent Watters, who was in 'C' company, 1st Battalion, Belfast Brigade. A third barman, Murdock, was a sympathizer.

In January Watters passed information to the Belfast IRA about three men the local head constable had booked into the hotel without supplying their names. The men did not mix with local police but were in contact with the Musgrave Street DI, Crown prosecution officials and military intelligence. Watters found out the trio comprised an RIC sergeant escorted by two constables. Later, information, which almost certainly came from Dublin, explained the mystery. Sergeant Patrick Fallon had been shot at Ballymote, County Sligo.[9] Sergeant Gilmartin, who was in Roddy's, escorted by two constables, Quinn and Heffron, was a witness for the prosecution of an IRA man accused of the killing. The trial was to be by court martial in Belfast. Not knowing how long the trio would stay in Roddy's, McCorley hastily gathered together eight men on the evening of 26 January. Four Volunteers under McKelvey provided cover outside while McCorley, Séamus Woods, Joe Murray and Séamus McKenna did the shooting after Watters pointed out the room occupied by the three RIC. McKenna recalled that the policemen were in bed and 'knew our purpose immediately. We threw open the door, switched on the light and they started screaming. It was a particularly ghastly business but we had to do it and it was done. We got away without difficulty, although we had less than half an hour before curfew time.'[10] The two constables were killed and Gilmartin, although seriously wounded, survived, but was invalided out of the force.

Probably because none of the police was from Belfast, or even from the north, there was no great hue and cry from the unionist population. However there were short- and long-term consequences. The barmen, Watters and Murdock, were arrested and taken to Victoria Barracks, a British army base in north Belfast. There, Watters was tortured by RIC Detective Sergeant Christy Clarke and crippled as a result, but said nothing. After Watters's treatment Murdock, who was not an IRA Volunteer, told the police Watters was in the IRA and that one of the shooting squad in Roddy's was called Murray and another Roger, but did not know his second name, presumably a reference to McCorley. After this, Murray went on the run.[11] That night DI Nixon's murder gang retaliated by killing a barman called McGarvey in his home at Bray Street off the Crumlin Road. He was probably targeted because his name was confused with Garvey, one of the barmen in Roddy's who, like the other barmen, was arrested and questioned about the IRA attack. RIC sources in Belfast reported to Dublin that Constable Gillen from Brown Square barracks had seen Nixon with Inspector Harrison and Head Constable Packenham driving down the Shankill Road minutes after the murder of McGarvey in a vehicle which matched the description of the one the killers drove off in.[12]

The long-term consequence of the operation at Roddy's was the establishment of the Belfast IRA ASU drawn from members of B and C companies.[13] McCorley and McKenna were well satisfied with the way events had gone that night and the spirit of the men involved. The ASU carried out exactly the type of operations GHQ had decided should be IRA policy in Belfast. McKenna described their aims and objectives as being to 'operate against visiting enemy agents or forces' using Belfast as 'a rest camp' while 'engaged in operations in other parts of the country'.[14] The ASU's base was above McDevitt's tailor's shop at 5 Rosemary Street, near the centre of Belfast. Walking through the shop and out of the back door gave access to an arms dump hidden in 8 North Street, which backed on to McDevitt's. The shop was also an important depot for dispatches. Maggie Fitzpatrick of Cumann na mBan was in charge of the whole operation. According to her, McDevitt's was one of the most important bases in the city.[15] West Belfast IRA scouts from McCorley's 1st Battalion patrolled the city centre streets daily, looking for Black and Tans or Auxiliaries and listening for men in plain clothes with English accents. They then reported their presence to the ASU. There were many fruitless patrols and some false alarms. Members of the

ASU also occasionally went on patrol. If they found targets, sometimes they opened fire on them there and then, or returned to McDevitt's if they needed a bigger squad.

The ASU's first killing was on 11 March 1921 when three Black and Tans were shot at close quarters in Victoria Square. A girl in the company of the Black and Tans was wounded in the hip and a civilian called Allen was shot dead, either by an IRA bullet or one fired by a Black and Tan, who managed to get up, open fire and run some distance before collapsing. He died of chest wounds next day.[16] Since the Black and Tans were neither from the north nor RIC men, but drivers based in Gormanston camp, there were no reprisals. However, that was not always the case.

A month later, on 23 April, McCorley and Woods shot dead two Auxiliaries in Donegall Place in the city centre. Chaos ensued as the gunmen fled through the Saturday evening crowds. An RIC detective in plain clothes near the scene fired after them but wounded two civilians, increasing the pandemonium. There were other armed IRA men covering the two shooters. These included Seán Keenan and Seán Montgomery, who also had to escape from the scene as motor vehicles full of Auxiliaries poured in from nearby city centre barracks and the Grand Central Hotel. Keenan ran up the narrow Castle Lane with McCorley and McKenna as did Murray, but Montgomery ran in the opposite direction into Queen's Arcade, a covered passageway of shops, only to find the arcade's iron gates at the end leading to west Belfast were locked. Turning back along the arcade, by a stroke of luck, he met a girl who knew his mother. She took his gun and he walked back out to Donegall Place. There he was stopped by an Auxiliary with his pistol drawn. The Auxiliary ordered a passer-by to search Montgomery while he covered him with his pistol, a search which, of course, drew a blank.[17] All IRA involved in the operation escaped to safety. The dead Auxiliaries were on escort duty from Sligo and due to return that day, but their train had been delayed.

Just before midnight, during the curfew, the RIC murder gang struck in reprisal in west Belfast.[18] The facts are not in dispute. There were six in the Duffin household in Clonard Gardens, a father and five sons. Thinking the knocking on the door was probably another military or police raid which had happened a few times before, John Duffin, who was upstairs, told his brother Pat to open the door. Three men came in and one shouted: 'Hands up!' John heard some talk at the door of the scullery, then muffled bangs and the three men ran out. Pat and Dan Duffin lay dead in pools of blood in the scullery. Dan, twenty-four, was an officer in 'B' company, 1st Battalion IRA and a playing member of St Gall's GAC. Pat was twenty-eight, a teacher in the nearby St Paul's National School in Cavendish Square. A dog had come in with the gang and was left in the house when they slammed the front door on the way out, not a stray, but, according to John Duffin, 'well-cared for'.

He kept it in the house whining to get out until the next day when DI Ferris from Springfield Road barracks arrived, surveyed the scene with the bodies of the two brothers still on the floor, took away two spent cartridges and the dog.[19] Ferris was received with intense hostility by a large crowd of locals in and around the house. Police accompanying him disregarded his orders to have the bodies removed to the morgue. Bishop MacRory also visited as did a large IRA contingent of up to twenty men led by McCorley. They intended to ambush the RIC when they came to remove the bodies on Ferris's orders but no police returned.

The IRA put on a show of strength at the funerals on 27 April which thousands attended. Draped with tricolours, the coffins were carried by relays of IRA across Belfast to the railway station at York Road for transfer to the cemetery at Martinstown in Glenravel in the Glens of Antrim, where the Duffin family came from. As the crowds made their way back from the station, a loyalist mob attacked them near the Old Lodge Road at the bottom of the Shankill and gunfire was exchanged without effect. The fear and horror felt by the nationalist community in west Belfast as a result of this swift and ruthless reprisal did nothing to deter the ASU. On the contrary, both McCorley and McKenna strongly believed that they should respond to any reprisal immediately, which they did. Their target was DI Ferris whom they were convinced was behind the killings of the Duffin brothers. Ferris was also believed to have been involved in the shooting of Tomás MacCurtain in 1920 and subsequently transferred north to the safer environment of Belfast. Indeed, McCorley claimed that Ferris was targeted on orders from GHQ, a claim corroborated by Séamus McKenna.[20] On Saturday 7 May, ten days after the Duffins' funeral, three members of the ASU, including McCorley, shot Ferris in the stomach, neck and head as he left St Paul's parochial house where he had met the parish priest. He was rushed to the Royal Victoria Hospital across the Falls Road and, to the disbelief of the IRA, survived.[21]

At that time, the Belfast ASU was severely depleted because some of its key members had been sent on a hare-brained excursion to Cavan to join an ASU in the county, probably on orders from Eoin O'Duffy, the reasons for which remain unclear. The embryonic ASU was betrayed by an informer in Cavan and surrounded on Lappinduff mountain where they fought a gun battle with British army, RIC and Black and Tans. Seán McCartney was killed and the rest were captured, including Tom Fox, Séamus McKenna and Séamus Finn of the Belfast ASU.[22] Lappinduff was disastrous in more ways than one. Joe McKelvey complained to Richard Mulcahy in GHQ that the operation had almost bankrupted the Belfast Brigade. Equipment and transport had cost £150 and McCartney's funeral £27. He asked if GHQ would pay.[23]

In Belfast, other IRA members continued the same sort of minor disruptions that O'Duffy had advocated in the new northern divisions. They cut telegraph and telephone wires, which were quickly repaired, they occasionally threw a hand grenade at a sentry post, they robbed banks and post offices, they raided private houses for weapons and ammunition. This escalation of IRA activity led to a corresponding increase in police patrols.[24] Furthermore, operating out of west Belfast, the IRA's activities tended to be largely restricted to the city centre which was conveniently close to districts where the IRA had members, namely the lower Falls Road, Carrick Hill and Smithfield. The IRA did not trouble the rest of Belfast – the greater part of the city. Elsewhere in west and north Belfast, and the Short Strand, IRA members concentrated their efforts on defending nationalist districts from sectarian attacks, opportunist sniping and incursions by USC during curfew hours.

Against this backdrop of sporadic IRA attacks in and around the city centre, what exercised the majority unionist population was the upcoming election on 24 May 1921 and its consequences for the north-east. For unionists the election was an opportunity to demonstrate the coherence of the north-east as a separate entity on the island of Ireland entitled to self-government and a chance to repudiate SF, to demonstrate that the six counties were different from the rest of Ireland. A solid vote of that nature would emphasize their right to establish their own administration.

Throughout 1920, as the Government of Ireland bill made its untroubled way through Westminster, northern republicans and nationalists alike remained in denial and disbelief that partition was coming, largely unaware of the British government's firm commitment to safeguard the unionists of the six counties before entering into any negotiations with SF. For anyone prepared to see it, the evidence was before their eyes. By November 1920, an embryonic northern administration was in place before the bill became law on 23 December. Lloyd George's appointment of Sir Ernest Clark on 8 September as under-secretary in Belfast had, in effect, established a separate government department for the north-east, although still nominally subordinate to Dublin Castle and the chief secretary. The USC had already been authorized in September which gave unionists their own police force, even if not officially operational until 1921.

The leaders of SF, Dáil Éireann and the IRA ignored these legislative and administrative developments. SF continued the consolidation of Dáil power and control over most of the island and the IRA intensified its military campaign through 1920 regardless. As a result of ignoring developments in Westminster and Belfast, the announcement, in January 1921 on foot of the Government of Ireland Act, of elections to two parliaments seemed to take the SF leadership in Dublin by surprise. When senior SF figures from the north went to Dublin for advice about how to respond to the election in the north, it was clear that the fight for the republic was the priority and, as usual, the plight of northern nationalists was not on the agenda. It took some time for the Dáil cabinet to come up with a political response to these developments, particularly in respect of the north-east. De Valera, who had returned to Ireland from the US on 23 December – by coincidence the same day the Government of Ireland Act became law – exchanged lengthy memoranda with Collins. On 13 January he agreed with Collins that SF should fight elections in the north as part of a national campaign to maintain 'the unity of Republican Ireland'. He believed that 'letting the elections go by default would seem to be the abandonment of the north as hopeless for us, and the acceptance of partition'.[25] For the leaders of SF, especially Collins, the elections were an opportunity for a national plebiscite to endorse the republic and the military campaign since 1919. The idea of participating in a northern partitionist assembly never occurred to de Valera or Collins.

However, to the exasperation of de Valera and Collins, Devlin and the remnants of the IPP in the north insisted on standing, thereby undermining any SF project for the elections to produce a single voice of Irish self-determination. De Valera and Collins worked hard to persuade Devlin to stand aside, but if he insisted on contesting the election in the north, at the very least they wanted him not to recognize the northern parliament. At a secret meeting in Dublin between de Valera, MacEntee and Devlin in February, no agreement was reached, although Devlin got more than he bargained for, being caught in an IRA ambush on British troops on Leeson Street bridge.[26] Devlin was in a very weak negotiating position. The 'unanimous opinion' of his closest advisers in Belfast opposed standing in the election and there was widespread disillusionment elsewhere in the north.[27] He had no money and no alternative but to submit to SF demands. In the end, MacEntee brokered a deal in March 1921 whereby Devlin would field candidates, support the SF line on self-determination, give second preferences to SF candidates and abstain from any institution. The deal with MacEntee allowed Devlin field twenty-one candidates. So low had the fortunes of the IPP sunk that Devlin was unable to find more than a dozen in the six counties, mainly for Belfast and Antrim seats; SF nominated twenty.[28] By 1921, the IPP was reduced to an extension of Devlin's local organization. The electoral pact with SF was ratified on 4 April at a nationalist convention in Belfast attended by 800 delegates from across the six counties, including Catholic clergy, councillors and businessmen. It was signed by Devlin, de Valera, Austin Stack and Joseph MacDonagh and endorsed by the Dáil cabinet on 6 April.[29]

A week later, on 14 April, the selection convention was held for Devlinite candidates for Belfast seats in the election scheduled for 24 May. Needless to say, Devlin was selected for the West Belfast constituency by the 500 delegates with his running mate, Belfast city councillor, Alderman Richard Byrne. Devlin also stood in County Antrim. The SF convention nominated Belfast councillor Denis McCullough and Seán MacEntee as candidates for West

Belfast, Councillor Archie Savage for East Belfast, Denis Barnes for South and Michael Carolan for North. Louis Walsh from Ballycastle, then imprisoned in Ballykinlar Camp, was nominated for North Antrim. The prospects after the elections did not look good for Belfast nationalists who were becoming sharply conscious that they would be trapped in an overwhelmingly unionist state with its own heavily armed police force. Rising sectarian tensions before the election led to street conflict. Sniper fire killed five Catholics in May in the run up to the election, again in the usual places: the Short Strand, Ardoyne, North Queen Street. The IRA killed a harbour policeman at the entrance to the docks near York Street.

The result of the election in Belfast was a foregone conclusion. On the nationalist side, in Belfast support for republicans had grown since 1918 and they did unexpectedly well, even in Devlin's West Belfast stronghold. Devlin polled 19.8 per cent of the vote in West Belfast and SF 17.2 per cent. Devlin was returned for West Belfast under the quota in a 92 per cent turnout with 10,621 votes on the first count. His votes were greater than the total of both SF candidates, McCullough (6,270) and MacEntee (2,954). There were virtually no transfers between the two camps, proof of the hostility between Belfast nationalists and republicans, but possibly also evidence of unfamiliarity with the new proportional representation (PR) system. McCullough picked up four transfers and MacEntee just one. Devlin got eleven transfers in his four counts.[30] However, in the other Belfast constituencies, North, South and East, the SF candidates outpolled Devlin's candidates; in East Belfast quite substantially. This may have been because the reputation of SF nationally had grown since the 1918 election, or because voters had nothing to lose by voting SF since there was no chance of electing a nationalist of any description in any of those constituencies. On the other hand, it may have been in gratitude for the work the IRA had done in defending the districts; there is no evidence either way. Overall, IPP candidates polled 16,502 votes (9.97 per cent) in Belfast, to SF's 18,751 (11.33 per cent). It was an indication of a lack of confidence in the former IPP, a significant swing to SF and confirmation that Devlin was now a one-man band.[31]

In County Antrim, which had seven seats, the dominant unionist majority prevailed. On a turnout of 85.5 per cent, six Ulster Unionists were elected. Devlin came in seventh under the quota with 9,448. Louis Walsh and John Connolly of SF polled 4,951 and 1,281 respectively. Walsh, along with other candidates, had been released from Ballykinlar a week earlier to show that the election was 'free and fair'.[32] On the face of it, Devlin queered the pitch for SF because had he not stood, there were enough nationalist votes to elect an MP. However, that ignores the hostility between SF voters and Devlinite supporters who may not have backed a SF candidate. Besides, had Walsh been elected he would have taken his seat in the second Dáil, not in

Belfast, so the balance in an overwhelmingly unionist northern parliament would not have been affected.

The results were also a demonstration of SF's failure to produce a political figure of standing in Belfast, or indeed anywhere else in the north. Louis Walsh was certainly popular and well known in north-east Antrim, particularly around Ballycastle, but not elsewhere. McCullough had been publicly active in republican politics since 1904 when he was involved with Bulmer Hobson in establishing the Dungannon Clubs, then as a member of SF, and later as a leading figure with the Belfast Volunteers in the abortive events at Easter 1916 in Coalisland. He had also been interned and jailed at various times. Despite this career, McCullough had never established a political profile in the city. It is true that life for a republican politician in Belfast was extremely difficult, constantly harassed by police, permanently under surveillance, always under physical threat, but, nevertheless, McCullough, as the public face of SF in Belfast, never exhibited any personal or political qualities to match the charisma of Devlin.

8 The IRA campaign in County Antrim, 1919–21

Outside Belfast, Antrim IRA membership and SF branches were restricted to the nationalist districts in the far north of the county. According to Feidhlim MacGuill, Antrim Brigade intelligence officer, these pockets included the coastal strip from Ballycastle to Glenarm and the inland districts of Armoy, Loughguile, Glenravel, Dunloy, Cloughmills, Portglenone and Toome.[1] However, in his opinion most people in these places were conservative 'Hibs' and conversion to SF was a 'tedious task'. Republicans were a minority in the nationalist population and a minuscule minority in the population of the county as a whole which, outside north Antrim, was over 80 per cent union-ist. Apart from the Glens and the north-east coastal strip, the only other dis-trict in the county, Lisburn, which had sizeable numbers of nationalists who worked in its textile mills, offered no prospect of any republican organization after the events of August 1920. There was also a small group of republicans near Lough Neagh around Toome, where a republican tradition had survived from 1798 and a vestigial IRB group existed at the turn of the twentieth cen-tury. There were few IRA volunteers in this group, but they tended to link with south Derry and east Tyrone rather than with the men in north Antrim.

The committee presenting the brigade activity report to the Military Service Pensions Board in 1937 described how 'More than any other area in Ulster we had to contend not only with a hostile civil population, but with armed yeomanry, who had been organized from 1913'.[2] Like Belfast, there was no IRA activity to speak of in Antrim until the spring of 1920, and even then operations were extremely limited. It could not have been otherwise. In total, there were fewer than fifty active IRA men in north Antrim until after the truce in July 1921; about twenty-five in and around Ballycastle and the rest scattered in Cushendall, Glenariffe, Glenravel and around Loughguile. MacGuill, from Glenariffe, indicated that his 'company strength never rose above fifteen men' and some 'were volunteers more in name than in the spirit of the organization'.[3] According to Tom Fitzpatrick, brigade O/C from April 1921, after the truce the numbers in the Antrim Brigade 'went up with a bound like every other brigade' to about 150.[4]

Paddy McLogan did much of the initial work to establish companies in north Antrim. He told Ernie O'Malley that the Belfast Brigade staff sent him to north Antrim in 1919 and then in 1920 he was attached to the organization department at Dublin GHQ. Later that year he was ordered to establish a new brigade covering Antrim and east Derry.[5] An IRB member, McLogan had fought in the GPO, had been interned in Frongoch, and was arrested fighting in Bray in 1917 under Desmond FitzGerald.[6] He led the north

Antrim men from autumn 1919 and gave firearms and tactics lectures with the men practising drill without weapons. By the time of his arrest in October 1920, four nominal battalions were operational on paper, but in reality each 'battalion' was about the size of a platoon – forty men – and most members were inactive. By July 1921 the total for the four County Antrim battalions had grown to 369.[7] Their geographical distribution confirms MacGuill's description of the locations of republican support. The 1st Battalion, with 59 men, based at Ballycastle had four companies: Ballycastle, Armoy, Glenshesk and Torr; although the latter two were notional companies, called 'outposts' until after the truce.[8] The 2nd Battalion of 91 men had three companies at Ballymena, Glenravel and Tannaghmore, north-west of Randalstown. The 3rd, with 85 men, had three companies at Cushendun, Glenann and Glenariffe and three 'outposts' at Carnlough, Glenarm and Feystown, a townland outside Glenarm. The 4th, with 54 men, had companies in Cloughmills, Dunloy, Loughguile and Magherahoney (a townland east of Loughguile). To put company numbers at the time of the truce in perspective, in the 3rd Battalion's three companies, there were twenty-one men on the roll in Cushendun, twenty-three in Glenann and fifteen in Glenariffe. Elsewhere, the average company number in battalions was twenty.[9]

These IRA squads were supported by Cumann na mBan units. A dozen County Antrim Cumann na mBan members claimed pensions in 1936.[10] The strongest units were those attached to the 4th Battalion and based in Cloughmills, Dunloy, Loughguile and nearby Corkey. There was also a Cumann na mBan branch in Ballycastle whose president was Lizzie Boyle. In her pension application in 1941, she summarized the role of the women well as

> Carrying arms to Volunteers. Conveying information and carrying dis-patches. Sheltering and guarding Volunteers while on the run ... Carrying and concealing arms. Providing transport and travelling with Volunteers while entering and leaving the district. Collecting informa-tion. Providing food, shelter, clothing etc.[11]

Two members of Cumann na mBan stand out: Lena Cunning, neé McCamphill, the wife of Brian Cunning, captain, B company, 4th Battalion, based in Loughguile; and Mary Fitzpatrick, neé O'Loan, from Martinstown in Glenravel, known locally as 'the tenth glen'. The reference from Willie John Lynn of Ballycastle supporting Cunning's pension application stated: 'this girl Cunning was about the best in Co. Antrim'.[12] She was based in Dunloy where she organized the Cumann na mBan branch. IRA men stayed in her house 'at all times of day and night'. She was the 'chief dispatch carrier to and from brigade HQ twenty-two miles away, twice weekly', and from 3rd Northern HQ in Belfast from 1919 to 1922. She brought in arms and ammunition to the district, hid weapons and documents and in summer 1922 helped IRA men escape. During the 1920s she emigrated to St Augustine, Florida where she died in 1994 aged ninety-nine.[13] As well as Lynn, Mary Fitzpatrick also testified to the Military Service Pensions Board in support of Cunning's application, verifying her activity during the War of Independence and adding that in the Civil War, Cunning had looked after wounded IRA men and was in charge of weapons. Cunning had claimed for service from 1 April 1916 to 30 September 1923, but, after much bureaucratic procrastination, only the period 1 April 1920 to 31 March 1923 was recognized. She received a pension from 1943.[14]

Mary Fitzpatrick seems to have been the senior Cumann na mBan officer in the county. Her pension application indicated that she was in charge of 100–150 women, almost certainly the total Cumann na mBan number in Antrim. She represented the 3rd Northern Division on the Cumann na mBan executive in Dublin and organized branches in Ballymena, Glenravel, Ballycastle and Cushendall. Her two brothers were IRA men and she was in charge of an arms dump on the family's land at Carrycowan, Martinstown, and other dumps in the hills nearby. Her home was headquarters for the Glenravel company; brigade and divisional meetings took place there. Raided on several occasions, two buildings belonging to the family were burned and during one raid the house came under fire from USC while Fitzpatrick was inside. Like other Cumann na mBan women she carried dispatches and smuggled weapons. She had a bicycle, which must have helped a lot. She stood by with bandages and first aid equipment during a major attack on Loughguile RIC barracks in February 1921 in case any of the attackers were injured. After the collapse of the abortive IRA offensive in May 1922, when the men took to the hills, she brought food to them and finally helped them escape to the Curragh. Although the growth of the Cumann na mBan organization seems to have been contemporaneous with McLogan's organization of the IRA in north Antrim in 1919, there is no mention of the role of women in his (or indeed any other) BMH account about Antrim. McLogan travelled by bicycle between the companies he had established in Glenariffe, Loughguile and Ballycastle (while women like Lizzie Boyle, Lena Cunning and Mary Fitzpatrick were organizing parallel branches of Cumann na mBan).

The first IRA operations were carried out in April 1920 as part of the nationwide exercise of burning RIC barracks, courthouses and tax offices. Men from the 2nd and 4th Battalions joined forces in an unsuccessful attempt to burn Loughguile RIC barracks, while others from the 3rd Battalion broke into the customs office in Larne and burned documentation. These men cycled forty kilometres in the dead of night from Cushendun and Glenariffe and back to carry out the attack. In a similar operation in May 1920, men from the same battalion burned the RIC house in Harbour Road, Carnlough, a thirty-two-kilometre round trip on bicycles at night. The premises, with accommodation for three policemen, were not a proper barracks and were not always manned. The cyclists were startled when a gunboat in Carnlough bay swept the Coast Road with its searchlight after its lookout spotted the flames from the house, but they escaped.[16] More hazardous was a lengthy cycle of twenty-five kilometres, also in May 1920, by men from the 2nd Battalion from Glenravel, brigade HQ, to burn the empty RIC barracks at Cullybackey. As the brigade report states, this trip was through 'an extremely hostile district', for Cullybackey is five kilometres from Ballymena, one of Antrim's five RIC district headquarters with two barracks at Henry Street and High Street in the town. Furthermore, the surrounding population was almost 90 per cent unionist. Cullybackey was a bigger barracks than Carnlough and normally housed a sergeant and five constables. The building seems to have been set ablaze but was not destroyed.[17] These exercises in April and May 1920 were rash in the extreme for IRA units with no explosives or firearms to speak of. They were more to make a point – that the Antrim men were part of a national campaign – rather than for their effect.

Taken together with the arson attacks in Belfast, the unexpected assaults on County Antrim RIC barracks at the same time can only have increased the alarm and dismay in the unionist population in spring 1920. The county was the safest for police in Ireland. Compared to the growing campaign against the RIC, particularly in the south and west of the country, relations in Antrim continued to be good. The strongly unionist population was supportive of the RIC. There was no boycott, and throughout the War of Independence no RIC man in Antrim resigned because of intimidation. No RIC man was killed in the county. No barracks were abandoned. In the latter respect, Antrim was not unique; the same was true for County Derry barracks.[18] The attacks in April and May 1920, like those in Belfast, demonstrated that there was an organized IRA in the county acting in concert with IRA GHQ. The ineffectual and small-scale nature of the attacks on isolated empty barracks also demonstrated the IRA's lack of capacity. Nevertheless, they contributed to the decision Carson and the UUC leadership took in June to resurrect the UVF to defend the north-east from an IRA onslaught which they convinced themselves was imminent.[19]

However, in Antrim no serious defensive preparations for any such IRA attack were made. Evidence for this lack of concern was the capture of Ballycastle RIC barracks in August 1920. The IRA company based in the town had the largest number of active men in the county. To avoid being conspicuous, soon after its formation in late 1919, the Ballycastle company moved activities such as meetings and drilling to hills a couple of kilometres south of the town at Ballyvoy in a district known as Cary. The first task was to acquire weapons because Liam McMullan, who led the Ballycastle company, recalled that in early 1920 they had a few shotguns and one of their members, Frank McCarry, had 'a very light type of Lee Enfield rifle', but no ammunition.[20] After a couple of false starts, the Ballycastle men managed in August 1920 to capture the RIC arms in the local barracks in a sort of light-hearted *Boys Own*-style adventure. Not having any weapons of their own, they had to devise a ruse to avoid a confrontation with the local RIC. This took the form of a sports day in a field outside the town, a novelty that attracted a large crowd, but also brought the police from the local barracks, partly to control the crowd, partly to gather intelligence because of the local republicans involved, but also probably to enjoy the competitions. The Ballycastle IRA brought in help from Loughguile and Glenravel as these men would not be known to the local police.[21]

The half-dozen local police attended the sports meeting unarmed and in plain clothes, obviously feeling confident of their congenial relations with the community. They left the barracks in New Market Street unmanned except for the orderly. A local IRA man, Willie John Lynn, knocked on the door and engaged the orderly in conversation, at which point two of the Loughguile men got out of a car they had parked nearby and held up the orderly at gun-point – and Lynn too, for appearances sake. Another car arrived and four men from it rushed into the barracks and seized everything they could lay their hands on: rifles, revolvers, ammunition, handcuffs and police uniforms. The raiding party made an unsuccessful attempt to burn the barracks, then drove off to where McMullan was waiting eleven kilometres south of Ballycastle on a hillside off the Cushendun Road near Loughareema. That night McMullan and the others hid their haul about ten kilometres away in a cave at Fair Head, a basalt cliff face rising a sheer 196 metres from the sea. While he waited on the hillside for help to move the weaponry, McMullan availed of refreshments left for him by Willie John Lynn and Frank McCarry; sweet biscuits and half a pint of Bushmills whiskey. As McMullan explained, 'At this time my principles were strictly teetotal, but because of the special circumstances and the exigencies of the time I took the liberty to deal with the whiskey.'[22] Altogether the IRA had captured half a dozen shotguns, nine rifles, four revolvers and several thousand rounds of .303 ammunition, not to mention RIC uniforms, caps, handcuffs and batons. They were never found.

Their only other major success in 1920 was an arms raid on Torr Head coastguard station on the remote north-eastern corner of Ireland in the second week in September. The station was to be closed and the coastguards trans-ferred to England.[23] The Ballycastle IRA waited until the furniture and equip-ment had been packed and everything made ready for the move. Led by McLogan, the whole company, about twenty-five men, marched from Ballycastle to Torr, thirteen kilometres, which took about three hours, arriving in the middle of the night. The raiders cut the telephone wires. The station consisted of five houses in a terrace with connecting doors. Five IRA men were detailed to each house with McLogan taking the officer's house. They knocked on the doors and told the occupants it was an arms raid. There was no resistance. The coastguards were handcuffed using those stolen from Ballycastle barracks, and the weapons and equipment in the station taken; it was already conveniently packed for moving.[24] The haul was substantial: seven Webley service revolvers, Verey pistols complete with rockets, several thousand rounds of .45 ammunition for the Webleys and two powerful telescopes. The IRA decided to hide the equipment that night, which meant carrying it all the way from Torr to their dump at Fair Head, several kilometres, 'over mountainous country which was devoid of roads of any description and it proved heavy and laborious work.'[25] Some weeks later, when they heard the building was to be used by Auxiliaries, a squad from Ballycastle travelled to Torr Head, soaked the vacant place in paraffin and burnt it. The ruins are still visible today.

Aside from these operations, IRA activity in north Antrim was mainly of nuisance value. They raided houses for arms, robbed postmen, post offices, post office vans and cut telephone wires. They fired Verey rockets in remote places having first blocked the roads so that police coming to investigate the distress signal were delayed. They took great pleasure in stamping, 'Passed by IRA Censor' on cheques, postal orders and bank notes that Black and Tans were sending to their wives in England. Then they returned the stolen financial paperwork, usually hanging it in a bag from the door of someone who opposed SF.[26] However, none of these activities advanced the IRA war effort or disrupted the British administration. For GHQ in Dublin, the intent seems to have been maintaining an IRA presence in all parts of the north-east of Ireland to destabilize unionists and spread alarm. Nevertheless, in 1921 these minor operations did fit in with what Townshend calls the 'third stage' of IRA tactics, 'small jobs robbing post offices … and grabbing headlines'.[27]

In October 1920 GHQ directed McLogan to organize a new brigade for Antrim and east Derry.[28] On 19 October he went to Gulladuff in south Derry to meet the officers of his new brigade. Séamus Dobbyn, as west Ulster representative on the IRB supreme council, was sent to south Derry to introduce McLogan as the new O/C. He told the BMH that after he and McLogan returned to Toomebridge in the early hours of the morning, the house was surrounded. Dobbyn's father, brother, himself and McLogan were arrested and sentenced to two years hard labour which they served in Mountjoy. They were released shortly after the Treaty was signed.[29] McLogan remembers them being arrested at Moneyglass on 20 October 1920. Despite this setback, GHQ in Dublin was determined to maintain an IRA organization in Antrim. Accordingly, Tom Glennon, a Belfast IRA officer, succeeded McLogan in November 1920 as a full-time organizer for Antrim, with an expenses allowance of £5 a week.[30] Unlike McLogan, who had been dividing his attention between the south Derry/Toome area and north Antrim, Glennon focussed exclusively on Antrim. However, although he did increase the pace of incidents, the nature of IRA operations in north Antrim did not change for some time. The only difference was that the attacks were more widespread, stretching south as far as Larne, and included holding up mail trains. It is difficult to see how it could have been otherwise. IRA membership and support were concentrated in the most remote, inhospitable districts of the north of the county. To strike at substantial targets would have required a long excursion to Ballymena or Ballymoney, towns with military and RIC barracks, but also places of overwhelming unionist support now bolstered by armed USC. After any attack in those places it was a long way back to safety and the IRA did not have many vehicles at their disposal.

The IRA therefore had to make do with what was available within striking distance of their bases. On 28 January 1921 men from the 4th Battalion, mainly Loughguile and Dunloy, attacked Rasharkin RIC barracks – only a lightly fortified house – unsuccessfully. The brigade activity report says the village was 'particularly hostile'.[31] A bomb designed to blow in the window of the sergeant's accommodation failed to explode. Half a dozen home-made grenades were similarly ineffective. The police responded to the IRA's fire with Mills bombs, rifles and Verey lights.[32] In his monthly report the CI described the attack as 'feeble', so much so that he thought it might have been a feint.[33]

The only success for the battalion in early 1921 was the burning of Loughguile RIC barracks, a house belonging to a local teacher called Daly taken over by the RIC to monitor the local IRA.[34] On 6 February the IRA attacked. In a tactic that had proved successful in the south-west of the country, one assailant climbed on the roof and dropped a grenade down the chimney. Its explosion set the building on fire. The brigade report stated that there were ten police in the barracks who retreated to the cellars where they held out all night until reinforcements, 'summoned by Verey lights', arrived at daylight. The IRA then retreated.[35] The RIC correctly deduced that the increased frequency and geographical spread of attacks indicated a new hand at work. In his February report the CI suggested 'there are probably agents from elsewhere working amongst them [the Antrim IRA]'.[36]

Surprisingly, concern about the number of IRA operations, albeit mainly of a minor nature, was not confined to the RIC. Liam McMullan recalled that in February 1921 Brigade HQ in Belfast sent orders, 'that we weren't to carry out any big ambushes or operations.'[37] As brigade O/C, Joe McKelvey had already fallen foul of the younger elements in the Belfast IRA in autumn 1920 for clamping down on operations, especially those likely to provoke reprisals. McKelvey was also concerned about reprisals in Belfast for operations causing police casualties in north Antrim. McMullan recalled the motive for instructing north Antrim to hold back was that 'any large concentration of police in the area ... would upset the good relationship which existed between the people generally and the Volunteers.'[38] Glennon seems to have paid no attention to McKelvey. In any case, he was accountable to Diarmuid O'Hegarty, IRA director of organization in GHQ. Glennon had increased the frequency of attacks in spring 1921, concentrating on burning buildings like courthouses and railway stations. He tried to organize as many simultaneous attacks as possible to stretch the resources of the police and USC.[39] For example, on 24 March one of Glennon's plans was to burn all the railway stations in north Antrim simultaneously. IRA squads burned eight stations, four of which were completely destroyed.[40] The stations were all in the far north of the county, four clustered near Cushendall, a clear indicator of the location of the IRA perpetrators.

As the number of IRA attacks grew, so did the police response. It was obvious from the locations of the attacks where the strength of the IRA in Antrim lay, so it was easy to concentrate patrols and searches in those areas. The major new factor in spring 1921 was the thousands of USC now available to the RIC across the north. From February 1921 the USC began to act more and more autonomously, operating from two RIC district headquarters in High Street, Ballymena, and Charlotte Street, Ballymoney. They drove north, searching farm buildings, arresting suspects and raiding houses. They had plenty of motorized transport and lorries that could carry up to twenty men. They knew the villages and towns where republican support was strongest like Ballycastle, Cushendall, Loughguile and Dunloy, and concentrated on them. By March, the leading IRA men, including Glennon and McMullan, were on the run.[41] McMullan, warned by a member of Cumann na mBan that the police had raided his house, went into hiding at Benvan, a remote spot high on a steep hill near Torr Head with no road leading to it.

In April, as a result of what seems to have been a decision of the newly established 3rd Northern Division, Glennon began to form an ASU for the Antrim brigade area, largely composed of men on the run who by then were full time. This decision was also likely to have been the result of efforts by Eoin O'Duffy to raise the level of activity in every brigade district in the north.[42] From April 1921 Antrim was part of the 3rd Northern Division, which included the Belfast Brigade and East Down. Technically, Glennon now reported to O/C 3rd Northern, McKelvey, instead of to GHQ. It was an academic point for Glennon's ASU never got off the ground. McMullan received orders from Belfast to go to Loughguile – the decision to form an ASU being a divisional one. He was to take weapons for himself from the Fair Head dump. However, no sooner had he received the orders than he was told the whole ASU had been arrested. He was the only one left.[43] Why Glennon chose Loughguile as the base to muster a county-wide unit raises questions about his tactical judgement. While there was strong support for the IRA in Loughguile, to bring men from elsewhere, especially Belfast, was asking for trouble given police reinforcements and large numbers of USC around Loughguile and Dunloy.

Loughguile was not easy to get to. Even today it is off the beaten track, twelve kilometres east of Ballymoney, 150 metres up on the Antrim plateau. Joseph O'Neill from Balkan Street in west Belfast was arrested near Glarryford on 9 April.[44] Almost certainly he was making his way on foot from Glarryford railway station towards Loughguile, seventeen kilometres away. Local police would have known immediately that he was a stranger. They hit the jackpot with his arrest. O'Neill was carrying a German automatic pistol and scores of bullets. He was clearly a candidate for the ASU, prepared for a campaign, for he wore two sets of clothes with leggings under his trousers. The *Belfast Newsletter*, reporting on the basis of information from the police, claimed that O'Neill had implicated a number of other men who were arrested within the next ten days, including Robert Dillon from nearby Cloughmills. What is more probable – for it would have been unlikely O'Neill would have known the names of local IRA men – is that local police knew which men in the district had disappeared from home and gone on the run and were looking for them. In the meantime, eight more members of the still-born ASU were captured at night on the outskirts of Belfast near Lisburn by USC from Dunmurry. The eight seem to have been planning an ambush, or perhaps an attack on the Dublin train, for they were surprised near the railway line. They were all armed with revolvers. Their arrests were fortuitous because a pair of B Specials had spotted two groups of four men on the Lisburn Road outside Belfast acting suspiciously. They followed them after telephoning Dunmurry RIC barracks for reinforcements. The IRA had failed to take the necessary elementary precautions. On 19 April Glennon and Joseph Smith from Belfast were arrested in a house near Corkey, a tiny, remote village two kilometres from Loughguile. The RIC seem to have scooped up the whole ASU by the end of that day after arresting four more men in Dunloy and Cloughmills.[45] Glennon was interned in the Curragh but escaped in September 1921 by hiding in a refuse cart. He later became adjutant 1st Northern Division and supported the Treaty in 1922 in Donegal.[46] Sixteen arrests did serious damage to the IRA in north Antrim, not only taking a lot of activists out of commission, but allowing the police to build up a very good intelligence picture of the IRA's structure and support network, which now had to be reorganized.

To replace Glennon, GHQ sent Tom Fitzpatrick, a formidably experienced IRA officer, to command the Antrim Brigade. He was told to use the name Robert McDonnell. Fitzpatrick was a valuable IRA asset. He had been commissioned as a lieutenant in the British army at the beginning of the First World War and left with the rank of acting major. He had served during the war in Gallipoli, Salonika and Palestine. Wounded twice, he was demobilized in February 1919. He joined both the IRA's 'C' company, 1st Battalion, in Belfast in August 1919, and the IRB. By October 1919, he was 'C' company's O/C. He then organized the 2nd Battalion in Belfast and became O/C.[47] Fitzpatrick found the Antrim Brigade in sorry shape, 'three skeleton battalions and a little company' near Toome; in reality not enough numbers for one proper company. Fitzpatrick set up his brigade headquarters at Glenravel. The available arms comprised about 18–20 serviceable rifles and a number of revolvers and small arms. 'The rest of the brigade armament consisted of shotguns.'[48] There was no system of communication between battalions so Fitzpatrick established a network of safe houses where members of Cumann na mBan could leave and collect messages. But after the losses in March and April, the IRA in Antrim was in no condition to carry out any major operations. Fitzpatrick records only one unsuccessful attack on Loughguile RIC barracks. Otherwise, the IRA continued with low-level activities as they had under Glennon, raiding post offices and mail vans and sending the proceeds to Belfast to help finance the Antrim and Belfast brigades. Even those operations were fraught with danger, as they were carried out in a universally hostile environment. Fitzpatrick says 'practically every house was connected with the B Specials', so several volunteers were wounded by gunfire in clashes with USC as they robbed post offices.

Gunfire was exchanged on a regular basis in Ballycastle and Loughguile, where Fitzpatrick recalled sniping at passing patrols was almost a weekly occurrence. In reprisal, the USC started burning nationalist houses, but Fitzpatrick, who had always agreed with McCorley's position on this matter, immediately ordered the burning of important premises belonging to local unionists, ideally somewhere 'at least ten times the value' of the destroyed nationalist home. He claimed that as a result, 'indiscriminate shootings and burnings were stopped because the bulk of the compensation which had to be paid fell on the unionists as they were in the majority.'[49]

Fitzpatrick provides an insight into the climate the IRA operated in. There were large-scale searches and sweeps by USC from their barracks in Ballymena, sometimes merely speculative, but always extremely intimidatory. On one occasion in May 1921, military and police in about forty lorries 'combed the area from Glenravel down to the sea coast and made a number of arrests but no IRA men were captured.' Fitzpatrick estimates that about 200 men were involved, a company-strength operation, an estimate, given his extensive military experience, which must be taken seriously.[50] Those arrested would be questioned about strangers in the district, unusual activity, groups of men moving around. Some would be threatened by USC, others knocked about. McKelvey had a valid point about the danger of alienating the local nationalist population by too many IRA actions. By the time of the truce, the police and USC were well on top of the IRA in County Antrim.

9 Election, truce and partition in Belfast and Antrim, 1921–2

The six months following the elections north and south on 24 May 1921 were a rollercoaster for both communities in the north-east as a series of events deeply affecting people's lives followed quickly one after another. The most profound impact was on the people of Belfast, where waves of sectarian murder ebbed and flowed in reaction to each event. First, one community, then the other, felt they had gained the upper hand, only to be cast down by a new turn of events. In Belfast the truce provided no respite from violence that continued intermittently throughout the summer of 1921 but returned to pre-truce ferocity in the autumn. The conflict grew overtly sectarian in winter 1921 when the IRA retaliated for USC and loyalist killings with indiscriminate bomb attacks on unionists. Following the truce there was a correlation, although not always exact, between events elsewhere and loyalist attacks in Belfast. For example, at the truce itself, at the beginning of negotiations between SF and the British government, and at the Treaty. From the truce in July onwards, the Unionist administration agitated ceaselessly to recover control of law and order and have the USC mobilized. Ultimately, with pressure on Lloyd George from ultra-Conservatives and Unionists in Westminster, they were successful in November. For their part, the Belfast IRA, no longer targeting Crown forces, was driven by September into the role of a Catholic defence force, though paradoxically better trained and armed than it had been during the War of Independence, but now devoid of any long-term strategic aim as it waited for the conclusion of negotiations between SF and the British.

Ulster Unionists won a comprehensive forty of the fifty-two seats in the May 1921 election to what was then called 'the northern parliament of Ireland'. In the immediate aftermath, they justifiably felt confident that they had achieved all their objectives. They had demonstrated the political and electoral separateness of the six counties that they had been given to govern under the Government of Ireland Act. They had control of law and order, had political control of their own heavily armed USC, and they were backed to the hilt by the British government. Unionists wasted no time consolidating their position. On 7 June 1921, a fortnight after the election, Sir James Craig as prime minister appointed the cabinet of the new Northern Ireland government at a meeting of northern MPs. This apparently assured position of unionists was confirmed on 22 June by the arrival of King George V to inaugurate the northern parliament in Belfast's ornate City Hall, there being no parliament building in which it could meet.

SF and IPP members boycotted the occasion. On their side of the political and national divide, the Belfast IRA carried on uninterrupted as if none of these momentous political developments had happened. They mounted attacks on RIC and USC, took pot shots at barracks, at passing tenders of police and USC, robbed post offices, raided shops for equipment, and performed acts of petty sabotage as before. Nationally, SF and the IRA were reassured by their endorsement in the popular vote in the election outside the north. SF won 124 out of 128 seats, which the party took as a complete vindication of the War of Independence. The Belfast IRA, the major component of the 3rd Northern Division, strongly felt it was part of that war and the electoral victory. The six SF MPs elected in the north naturally opted to take their seats in the Dáil. It never occurred to the IRA to do other than continue its campaign in the north as elsewhere in Ireland in the belief that the government of Northern Ireland would not last after inevitable negotiations between SF and the British government produced an all-Ireland settlement.

Sectarian tensions had been exacerbated in Belfast during the election campaign in May with provocative Orange marches and continued IRA operations. As usual, the isolated Short Strand was worst affected by Orange parades. On 18 May marchers in an Orange parade along the Newtownards Road fired fusillades into the streets of the Short Strand, killing John Smyth in Seaforde Street and wounding several others.[1] Elsewhere in May, loyalist snipers killed Catholics in Ardoyne and North Queen Street, including a 13-year-old girl. All six fatalities in May were Catholic.[2] The continuing IRA activity after the unionist electoral triumph only served to heighten tensions in the city and was certain to provoke retaliation from the ascendant unionist community.

The most ambitious IRA operation in the immediate aftermath of the election took place on 3 June when the Belfast Brigade mounted a carefully planned jail-break to rescue comrades arrested at the Lappinduff fiasco in County Cavan when thirteen members of the Belfast Brigade were captured. Four of those were valuable members of McCorley's Belfast ASU. The prisoners were to be court-martialled in Belfast's Victoria Barracks and, if convicted, would be sentenced to hang. They were being held in Crumlin Road Jail. McCorley claimed to have planned the prison break

The operation required a large number of men because immediately across from the jail was Belfast's grand Palladian-columned courthouse with armed guards. Running along one side of the courthouse that backed onto the Shankill district was Court Street where there was an RIC barracks housing many USC. McCorley posted three heavily armed squads to cover the jail entrance, the courthouse, and the mouth of Court Street that opened opposite the jail. Thomas Flynn, one of those covering the jail entrance, claimed each man had four grenades and two Webleys.[4] The jail-break was so dangerous that McCorley had asked only for volunteers because he considered some men would be killed. The plan started well. Séamus Woods and Thomas Murphy, both dressed as British officers, Seán O'Neill, O/C Belfast Brigade, himself a former British army officer, dressed as an RIC sergeant, and Pat McCarragher, in plain clothes, were let through the wicket gate in the main door of the jail into the guardroom as anticipated.[5] However, the warder inside instantly recognized O'Neill, who had been a prisoner in the jail, and started screaming for mercy so loudly that the army sentry in the exercise yard was alerted before he could be overpowered by IRA prisoners as planned. He immediately ran for the twenty-strong British army detachment in the jail. Realizing that the game was up, the four IRA men left, taking the warder's keys with them. They locked the main front door and walked out on to the Crumlin Road, returning the salute of a British soldier who happened to be walking past. From across the Crumlin Road, watching them depart, McCorley realized the plan had gone wrong and withdrew his covering parties. Eventually, the prison authorities had to phone the Belfast fire brigade who came with ladders to allow the soldiers and warders locked inside the jail to climb out over the wall.[6] Unionists were understandably outraged both at the audacity of the IRA and the humiliating shambles in the jail.

A week later, McCorley was in action again, this time with very serious repercussions. The IRA in west Belfast had long been intent on killing members of the RIC murder gang who had carried out reprisals after IRA killings. McCorley and a couple of other senior figures, like Séamus McKenna, were particularly eager to strike back against the police. They had always believed that shooting members of the murder gang would bring an end to reprisals and improve IRA morale. The main target was Constable John Glover who, their intelligence led them to believe, was involved in killing Gaynor, Trodden and McFadden in September 1920. On 10 June, as thousands of millworkers on the Falls Road made their way back to work after their lunch break, McCorley and his ASU struck. Sergeant James Sullivan and Constables Hugh Sharkey and John Glover, from Springfield Road barracks, were on the beat on the Falls Road. They were walking past the Diamond Picture House at the junction of Cupar Street when half a dozen men who had been lounging at the corner drew revolvers and opened fire. Glover was killed instantly; the other police and a passer-by were wounded before the IRA made their escape down side streets off the Falls Road.[7]

The unionist community was incensed. Glover, a 31-year-old Protestant from County Antrim, was a model Ulster unionist. He had been in the RIC since 1906, had volunteered for the Irish Guards at the outbreak of war in 1914, had been wounded twice and decorated. He re-joined the RIC in February 1919. His six brothers also served in the war, three in the British army and three in the US army.[8] Only three days before Glover was killed, the new government of Northern Ireland had been formally established on 7 June. Unionists, looking forward to controlling their own destiny, were furious that it made no difference on the streets of Belfast. Serious rioting broke out that evening at the Shankill/Falls interface at Cupar Street and Conway Street with enraged loyalist mobs attacking. There was stone throwing, then gunfire. The next day, Saturday, there were huge disturbances in the Dock area — Sailortown. A loyalist mob stormed into the district. There was fighting in Dock Street, Garmoyle Street, Nelson Street, along nearby York Street, Earl Street beside Gallahers tobacco factory and the ropeworks. A loyalist threw the first hand grenade of the Belfast troubles that exploded; it blew a hand off a nationalist in the crowd and injured others less grievously. The curfew at 10.30 p.m. had no effect. Police poured into the district from several barracks and fired over the heads of the rioters, but to no avail. According to the *Belfast Telegraph*, thirty people were seriously injured.

At the same time in west Belfast, there was a gun battle between the nationalist Kashmir Road and loyalist Lawnbrook Avenue, which continued into the night.[9] There is no specific evidence that local IRA squads were in action on 11 June, but given the amount of gunfire reportedly directed against loyalist attackers coming towards the Kashmir Road, and in the Sailortown district, it is likely the picket system with coloured lights, described by McCorley and Joseph Murray in their witness statements, was in operation.[10] That is most probable in the case of the Kashmir Road where the 1st Battalion, Belfast Brigade had many men available. Also, without some action from local IRA it is likely Sailortown would have been overrun and serious casualties inflicted there and in the Kashmir Road/Clonard district. Given that they did not usually fire indiscriminately into crowds, the IRA had only limited success in preventing large-scale incursions. Nevertheless, gunfire from nationalist districts aimed at snipers' positions had a mitigating effect on the mass onslaught.

However, the IRA was completely powerless to prevent reprisals. These took place unpredictably and, since the police were the assassins, in the dead of night during curfew hours. In the small hours of 12 June, RIC murder gangs avenged the death of Glover by killing three Catholic men. Given the distance separating the homes of that night's three reprisal victims, the time required to carry out the murders, and the locations where the bodies were dumped, three gangs seem to have been involved. In each case, uniformed RIC men arrived at the selected victim's house in a Crossley tender; there was no attempt to conceal their identity. Each victim was taken away and brutally killed, his body dumped unceremoniously on waste ground.[11] Alexander McBride was the only one of the three associated with the republican movement. The 32-year-old lived in Cardigan Drive, a comfortable middle-class district in north Belfast. McBride owned a pub in North Street at the city end of the Shankill Road and was a member of SF. A uniformed murder gang came for him at 1.00 a.m. claiming that he was needed for an identity parade. When McBride's wife appealed to them not to take her husband, the officer in charge said: 'You are alright. We are not the murder gang. We will be back in five minutes.' Mrs McBride later testified that DI Nixon, who visited her house the following day to express his condolences after her husband's body was found near Ballysillan Road two kilometres away, was the man who had reassured her in the early hours of that morning.

From the Old Lodge Road, a Catholic district near the city end of the Shankill, 26-year-old hairdresser William Kerr was dragged forcibly from his home, half-dressed, and thrown into a police tender. His sister ran screaming into the street after him, but one of the police put a revolver to her head and she was forced back inside. Kerr's body, with seven gunshot wounds, was found next morning lying in Dan O'Neill's Loney, off the Springfield Road, three kilometres away in west Belfast.[12] Kerr was a member of the AOH and the Foresters. A brother was a regimental sergeant-major in the Machine Gun Corps serving in Mesopotamia. The final victim was Malachy Halfpenny, a 22-year-old post office worker, also with no connection to republicanism. He lived in Herbert Street, Ardoyne. He and his four brothers had fought in the First World War; one was killed and Malachy, who served three-and-a-half years in the Royal Field Artillery, was wounded twice and had been gassed. When the police gang arrived, Halfpenny's mother would not open the door. It was broken in and Halfpenny was dragged to a Crossley tender. His body was dumped in Ligoniel, on the northern outskirts of the city. Like Kerr, he had also been shot seven times. Were there seven men in the police gang? Did each have to fire into the victim to ensure the complicity of all in the crime?

Despite questions in the House of Commons from Devlin and T.P. O'Connor and an assurance from Sir Hamar Greenwood that 'every effort would be made to trace the murderers', there is no evidence that anything was done.[13] On the contrary, it appears that James Craig, now Northern Ireland's prime minister, approved and supported the policy of reprisals, which was well under way in the rest of the country by June 1921.[14] In Belfast, republicans believed that RIC reprisals deliberately targeted supporters of Joe Devlin, rather than republicans, but members of the IRA and SF were also killed. Republicans believed that the authorities were hoping to so terrorize the general nationalist population that they would in the end appeal to the IRA to stop their campaign. These sentiments were expressed in the IRA intelligence report compiled on the Nixon murder gang in 1924.[15] The authors of the report claimed that two RIC men, Constables McDonald and Rogan, stopped a Crossley tender on the night in question near the Sacred Heart parish church in the Marrowbone, which, if true, means the occupants were most likely en route to kill Alexander McBride. McDonald and Rogan knew the RIC men in the tender and could list their names. The report suggested the murder gang targetted members of nationalist organizations such as the AOH in the hope that these bodies would denounce the IRA or name its members. Given the range of men killed in reprisals in Belfast in 1920–2, this assertion does not stand up to scrutiny. As well as respected middle-class nationalists murdered – most notably the McMahon family in March 1922 – large numbers of people, men and women, were shot at random by USC in retaliation for IRA actions and members of SF and the IRA were also targeted.

The aftermath of the serious disturbances in York Street and Sailortown over the weekend of 11–12 June illustrates the point about random killings. A gun battle began on the morning of Sunday 12 June after a lull during the early hours. A sniper shot dead Thomas Sturdy, an 'A' Special from Court Street barracks, as he sat in an armoured lorry at the junction of Dock Street and North Thomas Street. He was the first Special shot dead in Belfast.[16] There was an immediate and furious reaction from other USC in Belfast that afternoon, a reaction that continued spasmodically until the day after Sturdy's funeral on 14 June. Up to a dozen armed USC, leading a loyalist mob, attacked houses in the Dock district and shot two men dead on 12 June. The mob later wrecked houses from which Catholics had fled.[17] In west Belfast, at the Kashmir Road interface, firing from USC intensified on the afternoon of 12 June. There was also stone throwing between rioters. Hugh Jenkins, a 19-year-old Protestant from Emerson Street, was killed in gunfire from Kashmir Road. Later, USC rampaged along Cupar Street in Crossley tenders firing indiscriminately. They killed one woman, who was sitting in her house knitting, and wounded other people. Four tenders drove down the Springfield Road and turned left on to the Falls Road, their occupants blazing away at shops and houses. They had been unable to get into the Clonard district because of the defence put up by IRA squads, some firing rifles from behind sandbags, a new development.[18]

During an adjournment debate on 14 June, Greenwood rejected accusations by Devlin that Crown forces had carried out reprisal murders on 12 June. Instead, he read out a general report from the RIC Belfast City Commissioner Gelston about violence in Belfast since 10 June, including incidents that occurred earlier that day. The chief secretary's implication was that the killings Devlin had detailed were part of ongoing disturbances directed against the Crown forces. Failing to distinguish the killing of McBride, Kerr and Halfpenny from the others, Greenwood said six people had been killed since 10 June. He blamed the IRA for the violence and painted a picture of the RIC under attack in nationalist districts of Belfast for trying to maintain law and order. He claimed that police returning from the funeral of Special

Constable Sturdy had been fired on in the Falls Road, but made no mention of the undisciplined behaviour of the USC that afternoon, much less the people they had killed or injured as they fired into dwellings from their speeding tenders.[19] In a powerful forty-five minute speech, Devlin excoriated Greenwood and his policy in Ireland and ridiculed his accounts of events. T.P. O'Connor MP weighed in to support Devlin, as did Nenagh-born Jack Jones, Labour MP for Silvertown in West Ham. The Speaker threw Jones out of the House for repeatedly defying the chair.[20] In the end, after three hours debate Devlin's motion was overwhelmingly defeated by 192 votes to 64. Violence in Belfast continued unabated.

In the Sailortown district and streets off York Street, the heavily out-numbered nationalists had been unable to stop incursions by loyalist mobs and USC who had been attacking frequently since the end of May. Large numbers of Catholics had been driven out of their homes; others had decided it was too dangerous to stay. Figures vary, but the best estimate is that around 150 people left by the middle of June, a number provided by Kenna, who had excellent sources among his fellow clergy in the parishes of St Patrick's and St Joseph's who served that community.[21] Attempts were also made to expel Catholic workers from the nearby Gallahers tobacco factory and also to prevent them going to work. RIC officers protecting Catholic workers from the factory came under sniper fire from loyalists but no one was injured. In June fourteen people were killed, four Protestants and ten Catholics, and seventy-six seriously wounded.

The death toll rose markedly in the following weeks as political develop-ments threw the triumphant unionist population of Belfast and County Antrim into turmoil, confusion and anxiety. On 22 June King George V for-mally inaugurated the northern parliament, making a conciliatory speech intended to reach out to the SF leadership. Significantly, there was no con-demnation of the IRA in his remarks. The king had arrived in Belfast on the royal yacht *Victoria and Albert*, and proceeded with great pomp to Belfast City Hall, escorted by a cavalry detachment of the 10th Royal Hussars. As he sailed from Belfast the next day, his cavalry escort took the train to Dublin, but thanks to the widespread publicity surrounding the visit, the IRA in south Armagh, led by Frank Aiken, was lying in wait for the train. A small bomb between the sleepers on the track at Adavoyle, near Jonesborough, derailed the eighteen carriages which crashed down a five-metre embankment, killing the train guard, three soldiers and sixty-three horses.[22] It seemed that the king had received the republican response to his speech. Yet to the amazement and dismay of unionists, two days later it emerged that Lloyd George had invited de Valera to meet him to discuss an accommodation.[23] Craig and members of the new northern government were well aware, through their links with Walter Long MP and other Ulster Unionist supporters in cabinet, of clandestine contacts with the SF leadership that had been taking place for months, but the general unionist populace, which had been in the dark, was shocked and dismayed at the news. Rumours spread. A sense of paranoia and fear of betrayal pervaded the unionist community. What did it mean for their new government?

There was no easing of IRA activity in Belfast with robberies of post offices, various types of equipment stolen from hardware shops in broad daylight, and attacks on police. On Wednesday 6 July at 9.20 a.m., in their perpetual quest for guns, an IRA squad ambushed two RIC men from Glenravel Street barracks near Carrick Hill. The police were controlling traffic at the junction of Union Street and Little Donegall Street. The IRA men tried to overpower the policemen, but in the ensuing struggle Constable Timothy Galvin, a 26-year-old from County Limerick with eight years' service, was shot dead with his own revolver. The attackers shot and wounded Constable Henry Conway before he could draw his gun. Fortuitously, the bullet cut the lanyard attached to his weapon, which the IRA snatched, along with Galvin's gun, and ran off into Carrick Hill.[24] Nationalist districts expected reprisals and prepared to resist. Women were ready with whistles, bin lids to bang on the pavements, and metal rods to clatter against lamp posts to warn of the arrival of police. In the immediate aftermath there were police raids in the area and in the nearby Old Lodge Road. An IRA party arrived and there was a gun battle that continued on and off for two days until Friday night.[25]

Meanwhile, rumours of a truce swept Belfast. It was formally announced on Saturday 9 July that hostilities between the IRA and the Crown forces were to cease at noon on Monday 11 July 1921. If ever there was evidence of the disconnect between IRA GHQ and the north, and the absence of anyone from the north with any clout in SF or the Dáil, it was the timing of the truce. No one in Dublin had paused for a second to consider the effect on both nationalists and unionists in Belfast, in particular, of declaring a truce on the eve of the Twelfth of July, of all days in the year. The huge shipyards and factories in Belfast had closed on 9 July for the Twelfth holidays. Tens of thousands of workers from Harland & Wolff, Workman Clark, the Sirocco Works, the myriad foundries and engineering works and factories were now on holiday. Many began drinking their holiday pay on the Saturday night. Copious amounts of alcohol, which factory and shipyard workers imbibed during the weekend as they looked forward to the Twelfth of July holidays, fired up the frenzy of violence which gripped the city over the weekend before the truce. For the beleaguered nationalists of Belfast, it was the worst possible moment to call a truce. For unionists, the truce confirmed their worst fears; they were about to be sold out by the British government. The Unionist leaders knew perfectly well that nothing was further from the truth, but the loyalist mobs were not to be told. They knew who to blame and wasted no time taking out their fears and bitter disappointment on the Catholics of Belfast, even before the terms of the truce were known. A week-end of tremendous violence was inflicted on Catholic communities before the truce came into operation.

Tom Fitzpatrick, O/C Antrim Brigade, stated simply: 'The truce was not observed by either side in the north.'[26] According to McCorley, the truce in Belfast lasted six hours on 11 July.[27] It would be more accurate to say that there was a six-hour lull in the violence that had been at fever pitch in the city since 9 July. The frequency of attacks on Catholic districts had been increasing since the IRA killing of RIC Constable Galvin on 6 July. In addi-tion to the IRA killing of police, growing rage and apprehension among unionists about what the impending truce would involve, and what it meant for their newly established government, fuelled the violent onslaughts.

The spike in killings and burnings over the weekend occurred after the IRA ambushed police in Raglan Street in the lower Falls on the night of 9 July. The origins of the confrontation remain obscure. However, it is proba-ble that the local IRA acted on the assumption that an RIC murder gang, per-haps intent on reprisals for Constable Galvin's killing rather than an official raiding party or arrest party, was in action. What led them to believe that a reprisal attack was likely was the briefing that Tommy Flynn, O/C 'D' com-pany, had received from Frank Crummey that the notorious DI Nixon would be in temporary charge of Springfield Road barracks, pending the appoint-ment of a new DI.[28]

The most detailed and reliable account of that night's events is Seán Montgomery's.[29] On receipt of the information from Crummey, Flynn held a meeting of 'D' company. He ordered all fourteen members to report before curfew with weapons. The company also sent out its unarmed pickets with coloured lamps and waited. At 11.20 p.m. rattling bin lids and whistles sounded the alarm from the Pound Loney at the bottom of the Falls. It turned out to be a false alarm, but as 'D' company returned to Raglan Street, a warning lamp indicated the approach of police or USC. The company turned off into Peel Street, at right angles to Raglan Street, and waited. Flynn ordered everyone to hold fire until he gave the order. According to Montgomery, a scout reported that they 'were drunk with their faces black-ened – that it was a murder gang.' When the police tender was about ten feet from Peel Street, fire was opened. 'Jack Donaghy was using a Peter the Painter 12 rounder. He opened fire, three policemen fell, one killed and two wounded.'[30] The dead policeman was Thomas Conlon, a constable from Roscommon. Constable Edward Hogan and the driver, Special Constable Charles Dunn, were wounded. All were based in Springfield Road barracks.[31]

RIC reinforcements, including armoured cars, poured into the district and a gun battle ensued with the well-armed IRA company, but there were no further casualties. Outnumbered, the IRA beat a hasty retreat, running through houses, climbing over back yard walls, and escaping up passageways – known in Belfast as 'entries' – between the backs of rows of houses. Flynn fell and broke his wrist. Given the IRA operation that night and the killing of a policeman, he prudently decided to wait until the following afternoon before going to hospital.[32]

RIC reinforcements imposed a cordon round the streets of the lower Falls before raiding houses. They burnt the GAA club in Raglan Street where they claimed to have found weapons and 1,000 rounds of ammunition, something denied by the GAA.[33] Meanwhile, spurred on by rumours of the terms of the imminent truce and the noise of gunfire from the Falls, loyalist mobs, USC and some RIC, launched an enormous mass assault on the Clonard district and nearby streets, in an attempt to reach the main Falls Road. The shooting, fighting and burning lasted through the night and all next day into Sunday evening.

Clonard was not by any means the only district that suffered that Saturday night. A large crowd led by a number of armed USC attacked Carrick Hill. McCorley arrived at Brigade HQ in west Belfast at 2.00 a.m. on Sunday 10 July. Fortunately for Carrick Hill, McCorley was able to arrange a city-wide ceasefire by telephone through a local RIC Sergeant McGrath on the basis that, with less than twelve hours until the truce, there was nothing to be gained by killing each other. The RIC would withdraw the USC and McCorley would pull back the IRA.[34]

Some people have called 10 July Belfast's 'Bloody Sunday', one of several dates in twentieth-century Irish history competing for the title. By the Monday morning, the day of the truce, fifteen people – ten Catholics and five Protestants – had been killed and sixty-eight lay seriously injured in hospital. Large swathes of nationalist houses had been burnt out – 150 in total. Eleven houses of Protestants were also burnt.[35] USC continued to fire indiscriminately into the homes of Catholics and at pedestrians rash enough to venture out.[36] Among those killed was 13-year-old Mary McGowan, shot from an armoured car as she crossed Derby Street off the Falls Road with her mother who was wounded in the same incident. McCorley's ceasefire lasted until about an hour before the official truce when 'huge crowds of unionists surged in by back ways from the Shankill district' and began smashing their way into the homes of Catholics.[37]

McCorley recalled that, 'when the Angelus had rung at noon ... fighting died down immediately. The people in the Nationalist areas turned out in thousands and started to wave tablecloths and handkerchiefs.'[38] Hundreds, however, left destitute after fleeing their burning homes in what they were wearing, huddled in parochial halls, schools, GAA clubs, anywhere they could find space. Despite the initial jubilation among Catholics that the armed assaults by RIC and USC were over, that belief was misplaced. Sporadic shooting, skirmishing, and attacks on nationalist districts continued on Belfast's streets for the next few days during the emotionally charged high point of the Orange calendar. Inflammatory speeches from Orange platforms on the Twelfth incited attacks on nationalist districts, in particular the Short Strand, which was invaded by a mob on 13 July and again on 14 July when two Catholics were shot dead, twenty-eight taken to hospital, and many houses ransacked.[39] DI McConnell from Mountpottinger barracks was shot and seriously wounded and a sergeant with him shot in the wrist, as they confronted loyalist mobs in the district. Kenna alleged the mob was led by a Unionist MP, William Grant. There was yet another mass assault on 15 July.[40] By the end of the week twenty-three people, including Constable Conlon and IRA men Alexander Hamilton and Séamus Ledlie, had been killed, hundreds wounded and as many as a thousand people rendered homeless after about two hundred houses had been burnt.[41]

Unionists were indeed seething. Their leaders were shocked at the truce being extended to the north, which, following the election in May, they regarded as a separate political entity with its own recently established parliament and cabinet. They were also appalled at the terms of the truce which not only granted recognition to the IRA, but in effect suspended the Government of Ireland Act so that no further powers were to be transferred to Craig's regime. Worst of all, Craig lost his prized control of law and order when the USC was demobilized as part of the truce. Unionists were bewildered and horrified when IRA GHQ sent O/C 2nd Northern Division, Eoin O'Duffy, to Belfast as truce liaison officer to meet on equal terms with senior British army and RIC officers. O'Duffy set up his office in St Mary's Hall in the centre of Belfast. On 16 July he was able to announce that all IRA operations in the city, except in self-defence, would cease.[42]

Nationalists were cock-a-hoop. It seemed unionists had been stopped in their tracks: hope grew that partition would be abolished. The IRA in Belfast benefitted enormously from these rapid unexpected developments. Its role in defending Catholic districts from the recent onslaughts, albeit with very limited success, had greatly enhanced its reputation, but now that the British government had officially recognized the IRA, its credibility greatly increased. Senior figures in the IRA noted the change in attitude among the city's population. Séamus Woods told GHQ that 'With the signing of the Truce the Catholic population believing for the moment that we had been victorious and that the specials and UVF were beaten, practically all flocked to our standard'.[43] To add to unionist disquiet, the IRA in Belfast, following the truce, began openly to police and parade through the streets. New recruits, called derisively 'Trucileers', flocked to join the IRA. The Belfast Brigade grew from 367 members in June to 497 in July and 632 in August. The Antrim Brigade expanded from 111 in June to 260 in August.[44] By December 1921 the figures for the Belfast and Antrim Brigades were 835 and 302 respectively.[45]

Relieved of their duties to mount operations against the Crown forces and able to move freely, the IRA began to organize its forces and establish training camps for officers and the large number of new recruits. There was one at Hannahstown in the hills of west of Belfast.[46] By the beginning of August, officers from the 3rd Northern Division were sent to a camp at Ballyvoy, four kilometres east of Ballycastle, others to Dublin for training in technical and engineering skills.[47] Training sessions lasted a fortnight, then the newly trained officers were dispatched throughout their divisional area to train other batches of men.[48] Meanwhile, proper military structures were also established. Feidhlim MacGuill, Antrim Brigade intelligence officer, recalled how brigade staff officers and battalion O/Cs were appointed and a proper battalion structure created.[49]

Much the same was happening in Belfast. As new recruits flooded in, for the first time there were four battalions in the city, instead of paper units, but it should be emphasized that each battalion was not even the size of a true infantry company. The Brigade activity report stated the 3rd and 4th Battalions were non-existent before the truce.[50]

Some officers from Belfast were also sent to north Antrim for a much-needed period of rest and recuperation after weeks of sustained intense fighting. Thomas Flynn of 'D' company was 'in a state of extreme exhaustion.'[51] He, together with his wife and three other Volunteers, were dispatched to Rathlin Island for a holiday.[52] While there, Flynn and his comrades managed to lure the crew of a vessel, *The Bouncer*, to Ballycastle for a party. *The Bouncer* was engaged in salvaging HMS *Drake* which had sunk three kilometres off Rathlin. *The Bouncer* was carrying a substantial quantity of explosives which Flynn and his colleagues removed while the crew were ashore drinking in Ballycastle. They dispatched the explosives to Belfast next morning in a motor boat.[53] After another week Flynn, having successfully passed a written examination to select two officers from each of the Belfast Brigade's battalions, was sent to Glenasmole, County Wicklow, for training. After a fortnight there he was sent back as an instructor to the divisional training camp at Ballyvoy where they processed forty officers a week.[54]

It was not to last. By the end of August Flynn and the rest of the Belfast Brigade at Ballyvoy were recalled to Belfast as serious disturbances had erupted. With the IRA and British army off the streets under the terms of the truce, protection of the Catholic population from demobbed USC and freelance loyalist gunmen had fallen to the RIC. For a month after the truce these provisions seemed to be working, despite occasional sniping into Catholic streets. Eoin O'Duffy assiduously reported all incidents to the British, but as August wore on, he became more concerned at the provocations. 'Our people acting with wonderful restraint, refused to be drawn into acts of retaliation and ... the discipline shown by our people in Belfast has staggered our enemies.'[55] However, the operation of republican police in nationalist districts, IRA training camps, and the parading of armed IRA on the streets of Belfast, unnerved the unionist population and the newly elected northern parliament. On 10 August Craig met Sir Hamar Greenwood to ask for control of policing, using the usual argument that unionists were victims of IRA violence and he could not be responsible for the behaviour of loyalists if he could not show them that he was in charge of security. The request was refused, lest it be taken as a breach of the truce and cause negotiations with SF to break down. De Valera's rejection on 12 August of the British terms for negotiation further destabilized the Unionist administration whose leaders were fully aware of the standoff between Lloyd George and de Valera as the month drew to a close.[56]

The tension was reflected on the streets of Belfast. By 29 August serious gun battles had broken out in north Belfast, probably initiated by a bomb thrown into the house of a Catholic family.[57] That was followed by a heavy exchange of gunfire, which killed two Catholics in North Queen Street and New Lodge Road. After two days of shooting and bombing, on 31 August O'Duffy authorized the IRA to deploy to defend the district, though in fact IRA from west Belfast had already been involved. The situation was confused. The RIC was supposed to be maintaining the peace, but police were understandably reluctant to become caught in crossfire between the IRA and loyalists. Besides, there was a truce between the IRA and Crown forces, so firing on IRA men could lead to major complications. The same applied to the military who had remained confined in North Queen Street's large Victoria Barracks for those reasons.

There was consternation in the northern cabinet on 31 August as it became clear that the IRA's Belfast Brigade, released from constraints by O'Duffy's orders, was having an immediate effect on the streets. The more extreme members of the cabinet claimed that, given growing loyalist casualties, IRA sharpshooters must have been sent in by Dublin. Richard Dawson Bates, minister of home affairs, demanded the immediate mobilization of the USC and the introduction of internment. In response to urgent pleas from Unionist leaders, the assistant under-secretary, Andy Cope, and General Tudor went north post haste that evening to talk to the cabinet and steady the situation. Both men had recently been deeply involved in the negotiations at Gairloch in Scotland with senior figures in the British cabinet, including Lloyd George, to try to instigate talks between SF and the British.[58] They were most anxious that the truce Cope had helped set in place in July would be sustained and that violence in Belfast would not derail talks to be offered to SF within a week.

As well as meeting the Unionist cabinet Cope consulted O'Duffy and Catholic clergy separately to hear their version of events. They told him that loyalists had started the violence and that if the USC were mobilized, disturbances would intensify. Cope was concerned that IRA GHQ would indeed send reinforcements north to defend beleaguered Catholic districts in Belfast, perhaps causing a collapse of the truce. Cope seems to have been convinced by what he heard from O'Duffy and the clergy and disbelieving about the line taken by the Unionist cabinet and RIC Belfast City Commissioner Gelston.[59] When he met the Unionist cabinet again on 1 September, Cope indicated he had concluded that the violence was sectarian, not political. He refused to allow the USC to be deployed, but did promise to send more British troops north. He also said he would permit internment to be used, but only if both Catholics and Protestants were interned since both sides were shooting. He added that 'the arrest of Catholics only would undermine the confidence of that side in the Crown forces.'[60] For Dawson Bates, interning Protestants as well as Catholics was unconscionable; the cabinet dropped demands for internment. Cope was also aware that Craig was fully informed about the parlous state of recent contacts between the British government and de Valera and was perhaps even sceptical as to whether Craig wanted talks to happen.[61] Cope had already secured an agreement with O'Duffy that if British troops were deployed in Belfast it would not be regarded as a breach of the truce, and that the IRA would be withdrawn from the North Queen Street/York Road area. The emergence of British troops from Victoria Barracks brought calm after three bloody days in which fifteen people were killed and dozens badly injured. During August twenty-three people were killed, twelve Protestants and eleven Catholics, and 165 seriously injured.[62]

The sequence of events in August 1921 soon developed into a pattern that was repeated over the next six months and was often connected with events near the new border. Loyalist attacks were directed either at vulnerable Catholic districts like North Queen Street, York Road, the Docks, or the Marrowbone, all on the fringes of large concentrations of nationalists; or at the isolated Short Strand, cut off from any large nationalist population. West Belfast with its huge nationalist population and, by autumn 1921, its greatly expanded well-armed and trained IRA battalions, was left mainly alone. What had begun to happen after August was that following initial sniping or grenade attacks on small nationalist districts, units from nearby west Belfast rushed to the scene and opened fire with lethal effect using weapons supplied from IRA GHQ since the truce. The onslaught from the west Belfast IRA during 29–31 August clearly alarmed the Unionist cabinet and led them unsuccessfully to seek authority from Dublin to mobilize the USC. It was significant that in the gun battles at the end of August, for the first time since assaults on nationalist districts began in 1920, the death toll was equal; training and equipment counted.

The effectiveness of the Belfast IRA and the rebuff they had suffered from Andy Cope and General Tudor heightened the paranoia of the Unionist cabinet and northern MPs. With the British army confined to barracks, they had no confidence in Belfast RIC's ability to protect them from a fully operational, reinforced and equipped IRA, especially since the truce forbade engagement between the police and IRA. Furthermore, the truce had stripped the Unionist administration of its own security force, the USC, in their minds leaving them easy prey to an expanding, aggressive IRA controlled from Dublin and determined to destroy the new northern parliament and government. Various loyalists began to form vigilante groups, including the Ulster Protestant Association, to fill the gap in their defences, as they saw it, caused by the demobilization of the USC. They began to parade menacingly, copying the behaviour of the IRA in west Belfast. Throughout September Craig came under increasing pressure from members of his cabinet, from delegations of shipyard workers and the Orange Order. Dawson Bates told the cabinet on 10 September of 'widespread anxiety among loyalists ... which has found vent in the formation of Provisional Committees and the organization of armed loyalists to supply the protection which they consider is withheld by the authorities'.[63]

The northern parliament met for its first substantive session on 20 September. It was the occasion of repeated verbal attacks by Unionist MPs on the new administration for having no security powers and presiding over serious violence, not only in Belfast but in various locations throughout the six counties. The language of the Unionist MPs reported in Belfast newspapers raised tensions in the city, which duly boiled over at the Short Strand on 23 September. A London company, contracted to lay tramlines on the Newtownards Road, was operating a quota system of unemployed ex-servicemen, one third Catholic to two-thirds Protestant. A loyalist crowd, several hundred strong (the *Irish News* claimed two thousand), attacked the Catholics with sticks, iron bars and hammers, drove them into the Short Strand, and then followed up with a mass attack on the district.[64] The attacks continued and intensified the next day with a mob penetrating into the district. The invasion was pressed home mainly because IRA reinforcements from west Belfast and the Markets could not get across the Albert Bridge to the Short Strand due to Crown forces patrols. The Short Strand inhabitants were so exposed and unprotected that, as the *Irish News* reported, 'Orange gunmen, armed with rifles and wearing bandoliers and [gun]belts' were standing in the middle of Seaforde Street 'pouring shots into Catholic houses ... six or eight bullets are to be seen in window panes.' The onslaught was brought to an end when the IRA threw a bomb into the loyalist crowd, killing two and injuring thirty-four.[65]

The level of violence was such that Dublin Castle finally gave in to demands from Craig and allowed him mobilize the USC on 26 September, but on condition that the army commander control all forces in Belfast and that the

USC be confined to Protestant districts. Obviously, these constraints fell far short of Unionist demands. As a result, throughout October recruiting for unofficial unionist armed groups grew and was reported by IRA intelligence to Dublin. There was a revival of Cromwell Clubs based in UUC headquarters in the Old Town Hall led by an RIC man from nearby Musgrave Street barracks, and the emergence of a new body, the so-called Imperial Guards, an umbrella for a motley collection of loyalist organizations.[66] They were an amalgam of Ulster Ex-Servicemen's Associations, Cromwell Clubs, Ulster Unionist Labour Association shipyard workers, and ex-UVF, led by a provisional council chaired by R.H. Tregenna who had played a major role in expelling Catholics from the shipyards in 1920. By November the Imperial Guards were parading in east Belfast. The inevitable Fred Crawford appeared on the scene, agitating for the resurrection of the UVF to manage the alphabet soup of paramilitary groups. He met Craig on 15 October warning that 'societies were springing up with rash and irresponsible leaders who are either on the make or out for loot'.[67] The *Belfast Telegraph* reported on 19 October that the UVF was being revived.[68] This information was confirmed in parliament by none other than Lloyd George who went so far as to say that the UVF's reorganization was not in breach of the Government of Ireland Act, despite the act forbidding the establishment of any military body in the north.[69]

By October a bizarre situation had developed whereby Craig and his cabinet were demanding security powers over an armed force because of mounting incidents of IRA retaliation against sectarian onslaughts by loyalists often incited by some of their own Unionist MPs' speeches and loyalist street level activity. It is impossible to gauge to what extent the agitation was orchestrated by Unionist leaders, but the evidence is clear that unionist unrest was real and not confined to 'rash and irresponsible leaders'. On 13 November the Imperial Guards staged Sunday church service parades throughout Belfast. Twelve battalions comprising about 12,000 men participated, with Unionist backbenchers and two USC district commandants among the marchers.[70] This extra-parliamentary action took place in the context of intense pressure on Lloyd George from Conservative and Unionist backbenchers at Westminster, known as the 'Die-Hards'. They had tabled a censure motion on 31 October opposing talks with SF which Lloyd George easily defeated, but his room for manoeuvre was diminishing daily for Bonar Law and Balfour were also opposing concessions to SF.[71] Under this pressure from members of his own negotiating team as well as Conservatives in Westminster on whom he depended for his majority, Lloyd George gave in and agreed the transfer of executive powers to the Northern Ireland government by orders in council on 9 November, thereby completing partition.[72] He had no longer any leverage over Ulster Unionists; they were now masters in their own house.

Unionist control of law and order took effect on 22 November. The USC was now fully mobilized for the first time since 11 July. From this time on it becomes impossible to disentangle the motives or rationale behind the individual instances of increasing sectarian atrocities in Belfast. There was no longer any coherent IRA military strategy in the city; after all, there was still technically a truce, so against whom would a military strategy be directed? However, once he had powers restored, Craig had instructed that the truce be no longer observed and the truce liaison system be dismantled.[73] Craig also began expanding the USC along the lines of a notorious memo, the 'Wickham circular', sent to all USC commandants on 9 November.[74] In his circular, Colonel Wickham, the RIC commissioner, advocated subsuming 'the best elements' of burgeoning loyalist paramilitaries like the Imperial Guards into the USC as Class C, 'a military force to be called out in grave emergency'. The circular, leaked to SF probably by a friendly RIC source, caused uproar and had to be withdrawn on 23 November, but Craig proceeded to enrol and arm the C Class USC with UVF weapons held under British army guard in Tamar Street in east Belfast. He claimed they were police, not military, and therefore did not contravene the Government of Ireland Act. By the time the Treaty was signed, Craig's government had 3,453 A Specials, 15,944 B Specials and 1,084 C Specials.[75]

From mid-November the litany of horrendous sectarian attacks multiplied, reaching another crescendo on 22 November, the day the Unionist regime took control of law and order; in the words of Kenna, 'a terrible day'. A loyalist invasion of the Short Strand, this time concentrating on St Matthew's church and its grounds, where the sexton's house was burned, was halted by a bomb the IRA threw into the mob, killing one man and injuring forty-five. That evening the IRA threw another bomb in Corporation Street into a tram full of shipyard workers returning home from Workman Clark's north Belfast shipyard. It killed two men and injured many others. On 22 November fifteen people were killed, eighty-three badly injured, and an unknown number suffered minor wounds.[76] More shooting and IRA bomb attacks followed on trams full of workers passing through the Catholic district of Sailortown on the way home to east Belfast on 24 November. The following day a tram heading for the Shankill was bombed in Royal Avenue, killing two men and seriously wounding eight.[77] It was the shape of things to come. The Belfast IRA declined into a Catholic defence force defending Catholic districts as best it could against rampaging USC raids, but also retaliating against Protestant targets with ever-increasing indiscriminate ferocity in the futile hope that loyalists would desist from attacks for fear of immediate retribution. Naturally, far from stopping mass attacks on the Short Strand and repeated gunfire into North Queen Street and Sailortown, the IRA shootings and attacks on trams provoked instant reprisals. Three Catholic spirit grocers were shot dead in their premises and random sniping into Catholic streets killed several others.[78] The toll for November was thirty dead and 142 seriously injured.[79]

By the beginning of December republicans in Antrim and Belfast had new problems to consider. The Treaty was signed in London on 6 December. Unionist leaders did not wait for ratification by the Dáil. As far as they were concerned, the conflict was over and they would get on with establishing their own regime. Craig formally gave instructions that the truce was at an end and the following week abandoned the truce liaison system, neither of which the Unionist administration had been party to in the first place.[80] In Belfast there was no let-up in attacks on Catholic districts following the signing of the Treaty. Unionists seemed to regard everything, including the Treaty, as a threat. The release of internees and prisoners from Ballykinlar on 9 December – most from the south – provoked another onslaught.[81] So it continued until the end of the month with what the *Irish News* described as an assault of 'unparalleled ferocity' on the Short Strand on 17 December. The Marrowbone also suffered. Kenna described it as 'a wild weekend' with three killed and fifteen hospitalized. The assaults were exacerbated by destructive raiding of houses by the USC.[82] The year ended with the USC killing of David Morrison, an IRA volunteer, in his home in the Marrowbone on 27 December as he was preparing to go to 8.00 a.m. Mass.[83]

Should Antrim and Belfast republicans support the Treaty that clearly left them high and dry in a partitioned north? What should their attitude be to what unionists were determined would be a new state emerging in the north? Refuse to recognize the new state? Boycott its institutions? Engage in armed insurrection? Broadly speaking, the consensus in the 3rd Northern Division in January 1922 was to support the Treaty, not because they supported partition or because it offered any advantages, far from it, but because the only hope for them was that a government in Dublin would have the clout to be able to look after their interests by dealing with the new self-governing region on their behalf. Certainly, a Unionist administration would not. Unlike republicans west of the Bann and in south Armagh and south Down who entertained the possibility that a redrawing of the border after a boundary commission would allow them to join with the new state in the south, it was obvious to those in County Antrim, including Belfast, that there was going to be partition and that they would have to live under Unionist rule. Given the significant numbers in the USC and the weaponry they deployed, there was no prospect of an armed rebellion against Craig's regime successfully ending partition. Northern republicans had no alternative but to believe that Dublin would support them and intercede with the Unionist regime on their behalf. In the event, the intervention of the new Provisional government in Dublin, that Michael Collins masterminded, proved to be calamitous for nationalists in Antrim, but particularly those in Belfast.

10 Endgame: Belfast and Antrim in 1922

From the signing of the Treaty until his death in August 1922, Michael Collins held the fate of nationalist inhabitants in the north-east of the country in his hands. Almost without exception, he made matters worse for them. In the aftermath of the Dáil vote ratifying the Treaty and the establishment of the Provisional government on 14 January 1922, he moved swiftly to take personal control of policy towards the newly partitioned six counties. What emerged was a confused mixture of duplicity, double-dealing and aggression that some have dignified with the description 'conspiracy', as if it were planned. Based on the outcomes, a more accurate description of Collins's actions is that he was thrashing around trying to find some way, or ways, to resolve several disparate problems. How to keep northern republicans united; how to prevent objections to the Treaty among republicans in the rest of Ireland from descending into armed conflict that would extend to northern border counties, especially Tyrone and Fermanagh; how to find a way to mitigate the impact of partition on northern nationalists; how to relate to the new Unionist government. Should he encourage non-recognition, undermine it, negotiate with it on behalf of the beleaguered Belfast Catholics, or encourage an armed uprising to overthrow it? Collins tried all these approaches, some of them simultaneously in different parts of the six counties, but all failed in the end.

Each of his approaches proved disastrous in greater or lesser degrees for Belfast Catholics in general, but for the IRA's 3rd Northern Division, in particular. Aggression at the border in Fermanagh and Monaghan in January and February produced immediate and terrible retribution for Belfast's Catholic population with indiscriminate murderous shooting and bomb attacks on men, women and children. Bishop MacRory of Down and Connor, in a pastoral letter in February 1922, said that 'the people of Belfast are being punished for the sins of their brethren elsewhere ... the doctrine of vicarious punishment'.[1] Attempts to broker an end to the blood-letting failed in January and March 1922. The nadir was May 1922 when the IRA in Belfast and Antrim launched an abortive uprising, instigated by Collins, without the support they had been promised from other IRA divisions. The new Unionist government responded fiercely, unleashing its new police force and the USC on Catholic districts. Killings reached a climax in May 1922. By the end of June 1922, following the introduction of internment, the blood-letting and internecine street conflicts of the previous two years were over, the Unionist government emerged on top, running the new Northern Ireland region. The IRA, defeated in Belfast, overwhelmed in County Antrim, left high and dry by the outbreak of the Civil War, departed the scene, many heading south to join the National army, others to the US. According to McCorley, 'When Collins was killed the northern element [of the IRA] gave up all hope.'² Partition had been copper fastened and the Irish Revolution was over in the north.

It is always speculative to explain the motivation for Collins's actions, partly because he was by nature secretive and conspiratorial, partly because he liked to operate through the structures of the IRB, of which he was Supreme Council president, but also because he was inclined to act without taking advice. As a senior SF figure, Kevin O'Shiel, put it, he was prone 'to come to quick decisions without consulting many'.³ In this context, no clearly defined motive can be discerned for his establishment of the 'Ulster Council' or 'Northern Command' in January to direct IRA operations in the six counties and border area. Was it an attempt to keep IRA men opposed to the Treaty united by convincing them that he was going to render the new northern state unworkable? Was it genuinely a coordinating body for the northern IRA divisions? Or was it an attempt to keep Frank Aiken's powerful 4th Northern Division onside? Or a badly reasoned combination of some of these reasons? Ernie O'Malley later recorded that Aiken, whom Collins made director of operations of the Ulster Council, told him that in December 1921 in Clones, Eoin O'Duffy had addressed a meeting of all the senior officers in the north, including Joe McKelvey, O/C 3rd Northern Division, and Seán Mac Eoin, O/C of the Midland Division. O'Duffy said, 'speaking with great vehemence that the signing of the Treaty was only a trick; that he would never take that oath and that no one would [be] asked to take it. He told us that it has been signed with the approval of GHQ in order to get arms to continue the fight.'⁴

This meeting, with O'Duffy's assurances, led to the formation of the Ulster Council in early January with Collins, O'Duffy and Richard Mulcahy at its head. They directed IRA activity in the six counties. If Aiken believed O'Duffy in January 1922, he later claimed he had been traduced. He told O'Malley that, as it turned out, 'From that night to the attack on the Four Courts, he [O'Duffy] worked like a fiend for the success of the Pro-Treaty party … without him and Mulcahy and [Eoin] MacNeill the Civil War, I believe, would not have occurred.'⁵ Aiken is far from an unbiased observer. By the time he spoke to O'Malley there was a lot of bad blood between him and O'Duffy and Mulcahy. Nevertheless, Aiken's actions or inaction later in 1922 indicate that he did not believe the Ulster Council had been established for the benefit of the northern IRA or to render the six counties unworkable. Instead, he came to believe that those in the leadership in Dublin, advocating the Treaty in January, were well aware of the sentiments at play in the northeast and had acted quickly to bring all factions onside in a common purpose, especially since serious splits were opening in Derry, Tyrone and Fermanagh.⁶

It would be February 1922, however, before the activities of the newly created Ulster Council became apparent.

Meanwhile in Belfast events continued in their normal horrendous pattern.
January was a month of unremitting loyalist violence: relentless sniping, sometimes at British troops who had been called out to quell rioting and defend
nationalist districts; hand grenades flung into the houses of Catholics; people
shot dead or wounded in the streets, in their homes, in shops, in their workplaces. In York Street disturbances were daily so that the curfew was advanced
to 8.00 p.m., but to no avail. Crown forces fired hundreds of rounds over the
heads of rioting mobs. In east Belfast St Matthew's parish church was raked
with rifle fire.[7] Eight people were killed in the city between 1 and 5 January.
The USC, A, B and C Specials, were out of control, so much so that in
Ardoyne, the rector of Holy Cross parish, Fr Sebastian, brokered a deal on 4
January with the British GOC General Cameron and RIC Commissioner
Gelston that the USC would be kept out of Ardoyne and the Bone where they
had been shooting, beating and carrying out of destructive raiding at will. DI
Nixon, whose RIC district was affected by this ruling, complained bitterly.[8]
The arrangement did not stop USC incursions, or the violence. A week later,
loyalists threw a hand grenade at a group of school children in Herbert Street
in Ardoyne, injuring six of them. The IRA shot dead two Protestants, husband
and wife, Mr and Mrs Anderson, in nearby Hooker Street, Ardoyne, the next
day in retaliation.[9] These killings were in turn followed by loyalist retaliation
against Catholics in Clonard, and so on it went.

What seems to have produced the intensification of loyalist attacks was
anxiety about the potential consequences for the north-east of a series of
events unsettling for unionists: the ratification of the Treaty, followed by the
announced departure of Crown forces from Ireland after the establishment of
the Provisional government, even though there would be no evacuation from
the six counties. Unionists were particularly disturbed by the announcement
of an amnesty for 'political crimes' on 14 January, the day the Provisional
government was declared. Hezlet wrote that 'the situation was made worse
when the British government ... released another thousand prisoners who
were not just internees but men who had actually been convicted, including
96 from Belfast and 37 from Derry gaols.'[10] Churchill, for his part, called the
amnesty 'an act of oblivion'.[11]

Churchill, then colonial secretary, had since 21 December chaired the cabinet committee dealing with Irish affairs. He was, as Fanning says, in effect,
'minister for Irish affairs South and North'.[12] Churchill was anxious to adhere
to the Treaty to encourage support in Ireland for Collins and the Provisional
government so that in turn he could have the Treaty given the force of law
in the Irish Free State (Agreement) bill going through parliament which was
hotly contested by Conservative die-hards. Therefore, he moved swiftly to

implement the provisions of the Treaty so as not 'to get ourselves back into that hideous bog of reprisals from which we have saved ourselves'.[13] To that end, as soon as the Provisional government was established with Collins as chairman, prisoners amnestied, and powers formally transferred on 16 January, Churchill wanted a meeting between Collins and Craig to tie up loose ends, especially the Boundary Commission, and find some way to halt the bloodshed in Belfast.

The three met in London on 21 January for three hours; the outcome was the first Craig–Collins pact, which demonstrated complete divergence on the main item at issue, the Boundary Commission, though they did agree on dispensing with a British nominated chairman. However, what was of greater concern to nationalists in Belfast was what Collins agreed about their plight. Typically, Collins went on a solo run, not consulting northern nationalists at all about what line he should take. The pact agreed that Catholics expelled from the shipyards would be taken back, 'subject to the revival of trade'; the Belfast boycott would end, and a 'system of relief on a large scale' would be devised to alleviate the hardship of those rendered unemployed by expulsion from their employment and affected by the communal strife. In fact, Collins had his eye wiped. Craig had not the ability to return Catholics to the shipyards even if he had wanted to, much less to protect them if any did manage to return. Besides, there was no timescale in the pact and by 1922 there had been a serious downturn in demand for shipping; men were being laid off since 1920. There was no means of enforcing any of the provisions of the pact. One observer, Joseph Connolly, later a Stormont senator, said the pact, 'showed a complete lack of appreciation on Collins's part for the realities of Belfast.' Connolly continued that, as for giving Catholics their jobs back, Craig has as much power 'to give visas to take them [Belfast Catholics] past St Peter into heaven.'[14]

Nationalists, particularly the expelled workers in Belfast, were annoyed that Collins had given up the Belfast boycott. Although it had not had any substantial impact on unionist big business, which was intimately interwoven with Britain's economy, and was largely counter-productive in its effects, nationalists clung to the erroneous belief that it had been effective, but perhaps more importantly, it was also symbolic recognition by Dublin of injustice done to them.[15] They were disappointed that Collins had taken it upon himself to abandon it, but had obtained nothing concrete in return. Furthermore, in making the pact with Craig, Collins had officially recognized the northern government, yet the IRA in Belfast and Antrim did not and still saw themselves as members of the army of the Republic. Had they now been abandoned to the new regime? In the event, nothing came of the pact. It collapsed after a fractious meeting between Craig and Collins in Dublin on 2 February showed they had been talking at cross purposes, particularly about the Boundary Commission. All the issues had to be revisited at another meeting in the colonial office on 29–30 March.

As it turned out, the failed Craig–Collins pact was a sideshow to the rapidly deteriorating circumstances in Belfast, an inevitable consequence of events in Fermanagh and Tyrone. On the very day the Provisional government was established, 14 January, five officers of the 5th Northern Division, including O/C Dan Hogan, were arrested by A Specials at Dromore, County Tyrone and remanded in custody, charged with possessing firearms. Their cover story, that they were Monaghan footballers on their way to play in the Ulster championship final, cut no ice. In reality they were going to Derry to reconnoitre the jail with a view to springing three IRA prisoners due to be executed on 9 February.[16] The sequence of events that followed had serious consequences for relations between London and Dublin, but fatal consequences for many in Belfast.

Despite representations made to the British through Andy Cope, the northern administration refused to release the 5th Northern Division prisoners. Eoin O'Duffy, now chief of staff of the developing National army, but with strong links to Hogan, determined to retaliate. Collins was fully aware of the rising tensions in the IRA about the imminent executions in Derry and indeed had sent men to assassinate the hangmen. He also knew about O'Duffy's intentions, but held back from any action pending his negotiations with Craig on 21 January.[17] Immediately afterwards, however, as the pact headed towards failure over serious differences about the Boundary Commission, Collins agreed to O'Duffy's plan to kidnap 'one hundred prominent Orangemen in Counties Fermanagh and Tyrone'.[18] On the night of 7–8 February, in a large IRA operation with men from Monaghan, Armagh, Longford, Leitrim and as far away as Mayo, squads seized dozens of unionists. In the border town of Aughnacloy alone they kidnapped twenty-one. The operation did not go well. Some intended victims were shot and wounded, one killed; IRA units soon became bogged down in fire fights with urgently mobilized USC at checkpoints and border crossings. Some were pinned down, others arrested. Skirmishing, gun battles and sniping continued for weeks into March. It seemed like an invasion to unionists.[19] Matters took a very serious turn for the worse on 11 February at the railway station in Clones, County Monaghan, with an exchange of gunfire between the local IRA and a party of nineteen uniformed USC heading by train to Enniskillen. The resultant gun battle left four of them dead along with the local IRA commandant.[20] The incident became known as the 'Clones Affray' and helped exacerbate the outraged feelings of unionists in Tyrone and Fermanagh already shocked by the assaults of 7–8 February.

The unionist reaction was entirely predictable. Craig immediately demanded reinforcements of British troops, an invasion of the south to free kidnapped unionists, the occupation of a cordon sanitaire along the border and much more, including the recruitment of thousands more USC.[21] Churchill rejected all his demands. In Belfast, of course, unionists took matters into their own hands with intense attacks on Catholic districts. From 6 to 25 February forty-three people were killed, twenty-seven Catholics and sixteen Protestants. Ninety-five were badly wounded and many more hurt less seriously. The most intense spell of killing was 13–15 February, in the immediate aftermath of the Clones Affray. Thirty-one were killed, ten on 15 February alone, and it was during this period that one of the worst atrocities of the years 1920–2 occurred.

Weaver Street was a cul-de-sac in a tiny Catholic enclave off the Shore Road on the outskirts of north Belfast. It was entirely surrounded by strongly loyalist streets. On 13 February loyalists threw a bomb into a group of children playing in the street. Most were gathered at a lamp post taking turns at swinging round it on a rope. The bomb killed two children instantly and four others died later in hospital. Twenty-two other people were injured. The *Belfast Telegraph* said the bomb 'was one of the largest ever used in the city' and the blast was heard over a wide area.[22] In the Commons Churchill described the incident as 'the worst thing that has happened in Ireland in the last three years'. Bishop MacRory had telegrammed Lloyd George the day before asking for protection: 'No adequate protection here for Catholics. Military urgently needed on the streets.'[23]

Nothing was done. Neither the bishop nor nationalists in Belfast knew anything about the internal workings of the British government, much less the politics of the Conservative Party. Senior Unionist MPs met on social terms regularly with government ministers, giving them influence and personal relationships no nationalist could compete with. For example, at dinner one night in March Churchill assured Craig's wife about the Boundary Commission, that 'none of the ministers would stand for more than the mere rectification of boundaries'. He added that 'Ulster would come out on top'.[24] It was pointless for MacRory to appeal to Lloyd George. By January 1922 he had practically opted out of dealing with Irish affairs. His political position at the head of the Conservative-dominated coalition was parlous by February. Many Tory die-hards were objecting on principle to the Treaty and the Irish Free State (Agreement) bill which gave the Treaty legal force. Once enacted it would enable formal recognition of the Irish Provisional government, the dissolution of the 'southern parliament' elected in 1921, the calling of elections, and the establishment of a constitution. At the same time, the die-hards were backing Craig to the hilt. On 27 February Lloyd George actually threatened to resign if he could not be guaranteed Conservative support.[25] Churchill was the key figure, who, for his own political advancement, was giving total support to Craig to retain the backing of the Tory die-hards in the short term to get the Free State bill through parliament.

One consequence of the appalling Belfast death toll over that February weekend was that it prompted Devlin to take his seat in Westminster to raise the murderous events. He made a typically powerful speech on 16 February, but received no sympathy for the plight of Belfast Catholics. Devlin acknowledged what support nationalists had received in Westminster, which amounted to four MPs, Oswald Mosley, Sir Donald MacClean, Lieutenant Commander Kenworthy and Lord Cavendish-Bentinck; men, Devlin said, who had 'faced unpopularity and lost influence in their constituencies ... by espousing this cause', but at least they had raised the consciences of people in Britain. Devlin said he was the sole voice representing a quarter of the Belfast population, who

> have been hunted; they have been persecuted; they have been murdered; they have been attacked by assassins, some of them uniformed and the liveried servants of this very government. Life for a Catholic in Belfast for the last twelve months has been practically impossible ... a series of attacks has been made upon them unparalleled in the story of barbarity of any country in the world.[26]

Despite a barrage of heckling and interruptions, Devlin proceeded to present a catalogue of murders of Catholics perpetrated in Belfast, concluding with the bomb in Weaver Street three days before. As it transpired, just before he rose in Westminster to speak about the horrendous events of the weekend of 13–15 February, Churchill had made a lengthy speech in favour of the Irish Free State bill, which received several hostile interjections from Tory diehards. Given the parliamentary arithmetic, telegrams from Bishop MacRory, letters and telegrams from Collins, and speeches by Devlin, no matter how eloquent, would fall on deaf ears. Craig was untouchable: violence would continue. The British government would not intervene.

As for the Belfast IRA, since November 1921 when security powers were returned to Craig's administration, it had become a Catholic defence organization, but by the end of 1921 many members indulged in sectarian retaliation, a feature of its activities that increased in early 1922 and became common in the bloodletting of February. IRA snipers killed individual Protestants going about their work, including the caretaker of Clifton Street Orange Hall, William Waring, on the same day as the Weaver Street bomb. Clifton Street is the most important Orange hall in Belfast, situated at Carlisle Circus, the location of the largest Presbyterian church in the world, the starting point for the annual 12 July parades and of great symbolic significance to northern Protestants. A sniper went down on one knee to fire the carefully aimed shot that killed Waring.[27] Also that day in Divis Street in west Belfast, about a dozen men stopped some workers at Hughes & Dickson's mill, asked their religion (Protestant), and opened fire, killing one and wounding another.[28] Several other Protestants were deliberately selected as random targets and shot that day. The *Belfast Telegraph* was in no doubt that the cause of the surge in recent shootings was 'the cowardly murder of the Ulster Special Police at Clones'.[29]

On 15 February, after Waring's funeral, an infuriated mob from the Shankill gathered at Denmark Street near Clifton Street Orange hall and launched an attack on the nationalist Old Lodge Road, backed by loyalist gunmen in buildings overlooking that district. Soldiers from the Norfolk Regiment took up positions guarding the nationalist district, but loyalists continued shooting so the troops returned fire. The assault on the Old Lodge Road ebbed and flowed all day until the afternoon when, in what must surely have been a unique event in any city in Britain or Ireland, the Norfolks fixed bayonets and under covering fire charged the Shankill mob, and ended the rioting for the day.[30]

By this stage no one could remember who was retaliating for what: it was open season. Morale in the Belfast IRA was at rock bottom, there was no strategy, and discipline was ragged with men independently carrying out reprisals. Some Volunteers, including McKelvey, were questioning the commitment of the Provisional government to their future welfare and moving to oppose the Treaty as a disaster for the north-east. To stop the rot, Collins stepped in on 22 February by establishing the Belfast City Guard, a full-time paid unit of 60 men, plus 4 Belfast Brigade officers and 8 battalion officers, 2 from each of the four Belfast battalions. They would be paid £3 a week, which was good money, especially for IRA men in Belfast who were mostly unemployed.[31] Ernest Blythe wrote that the reasoning behind the creation of the unit was 'mainly economic' because Volunteers could not carry on daily work and had no means of support.[32] However, there was much more to it than that. The timing was important; it was in the middle of the SF ard fheis when there were mutterings of dissent from the north about the Treaty. Denis McCullough, the most senior SF figure in Belfast and lifelong member of the IRB, told the ard fheis that while people were 'making their minds up about the Treaty their people in the North were being murdered day by day … They could not stand up to terror in Ulster unless they had a united organization behind them.'[33] The ard fheis agreed to set up a SF advisory committee on the north with representatives from both de Valera and Collins on it to counsel the leadership in Dublin on matters northern. At its first meeting on 7 March, the committee agreed to support the Treaty, just as conflict was erupting between opposing factions in the south.[34] About this time Charles Daly, O/C 2nd Northern Division, was relieved of his command. Collins could not afford to lose Belfast and the 3rd Northern Division. His support of the Belfast IRA at the end of February proved successful in securing its allegiance for GHQ at Beggars Bush, but by the end of March, after the anti-Treaty executive was established, that support was wavering again.[35]

There may have been another reason for intervening to bolster the organization and fighting capacity of the Belfast IRA. Collins had adopted a much more aggressive policy towards the north by late February and through the Ulster Council was planning a series of major attacks coordinated and directed by O'Duffy which began on 19 March in Pomeroy, County Tyrone.[36] There are indications that early in March Collins, operating through his IRB organization, which was a conduit for dealing with anti-Treaty IRA members, was planning major operations in the six counties, including Belfast, to try to bring down the Unionist government.[37] He, therefore, could not allow the IRA in Belfast to go under. The City Guard of picked men would be the vanguard of the Belfast IRA when the planned operation took place in May. Before that, however, the IRA in Belfast had to weather a twofold crisis.

First was the inevitable unionist reaction in Belfast to the assault launched in March on Tyrone, Fermanagh and County Derry, then extending right along the border. In Belfast the USC increased their searches, raids and arrests in response. Freelance loyalists attacked Catholic districts and individual Catholics with bombs and bullets. If February was a bad month for deaths and injuries, March was the worst month since concerted attacks on Catholics had begun in July 1920: 59 people were killed, 37 of them Catholic. Even the police shared in the passions aroused as a result of the IRA border campaign. The RIC report for February–March 1922 stated: 'The patience of the 'B' men is almost exhausted and it will be very difficult to exercise restraint if this state of affairs continues'.[38] Not only were the IRA active in western counties and along the border in Armagh and Down, but their comrades in Belfast continued to attack members of the USC whenever possible. Others carried out sectarian reprisals including throwing bombs at trams full of Protestant workers.

The second element of the crisis came when, as part of the intensification of searches and arrests, on 18 March a platoon of USC raided St Mary's Hall and uncovered a trove of documents. This struck a hammer blow to the Belfast IRA who had been living in cloud cuckoo land since the Treaty was signed. Its leaders still considered themselves part of a national army of the republic maintaining a truce with Crown forces, and they acted as such. The leaders of the 3rd Northern Division remained in denial of the reality that there was a government in the north growing in strength which did not recognize a truce and regarded the IRA (correctly) as a subversive organization determined to overthrow the new government. As the IFS bill moved towards the statute book and the Treaty was given legal force in the UK, and Northern Ireland's opt out of the IFS came closer, Craig's government correspondingly grew in confidence and began a resolute process of annihilating the IRA. Preposterously, the Belfast IRA still considered St Mary's Hall the headquarters of the truce liaison office and that they still enjoyed some sort of immunity or official status. Incredibly, this misapprehension was sustained despite Craig's government passing the draconian Civil Authorities (Special Powers) Act in March, which would come into force on 7 April, making the IRA, IRB and Cumann na mBan illegal, and despite a speech on 15 March by the minister of home affairs, the rabidly anti-Catholic Dawson Bates, declaring that the northern government was 'at war' with the IRA.[39]

The St Mary's Hall raid ended any illusions the IRA still held about its role in the north. The USC uncovered a vast cornucopia of documents containing names, addresses and ranks of IRA men, not only in Belfast but across the north, locations of safe houses in Belfast, of bomb-making workshops, and letters and memos unmistakably implicating Collins, Mulcahy, O'Duffy and GHQ in IRA operations in the north during 1922.[40] The cache gave Craig's government a huge propaganda coup and helped to justify the role of the USC as a bulwark against subversion and the assault which was in progress along the border. Craig now had ample proof that he could publicize of the IRA's malevolent intent towards his regime; the discoveries provided irrefutable justification for eradicating the IRA. The mass of information would be put to good use when the Special Powers Act came into operation the following month: the RIC and USC set out to search every premises and arrest every man named in the copious documents unearthed.

Undeterred, the IRA carried on as before. On 23 March the IRA shot dead two 'A' Specials in Belfast at 12.15 p.m., Special Constables Chermside from Portaferry, County Down and Cunningham from County Cavan.[41] At 1.20 a.m. the following morning in reprisal, DI Nixon's police murder gang struck in one of the worst atrocities of the period. Five men, four in uniform, some wearing police caps, sledgehammered down the door of a substantial house in Kinnaird Terrace off the Antrim Road, rushed upstairs, ordered Owen McMahon, a prominent Catholic publican, his five sons and a barman employed by McMahon, downstairs. Mrs McMahon, begging for the lives of her family, was knocked to the floor. The intruders lined the men up against a wall 'and fired volley after volley'. One of McMahon's sons, 11-year-old John, survived and was able to report the details of the murders. McMahon, a close friend of Joe Devlin, owned the Capstan Bar in Belfast. He was a director of Glentoran FC. An estimated 10,000 people attended the funerals.[42] The horrific nature of the murder of the family in the dead of night, during curfew, and the fact that there were witnesses who could describe the uniformed killers, attracted widespread attention and universal condemnation, including by British newspapers attacking the regime in Northern Ireland.[43]

Devlin raised the murders in the Commons on 28 March, describing Owen McMahon as 'a very close and intimate personal friend'. He quoted with approval the *Belfast Telegraph*, 'a leading unionist paper', as he called it, stating that the murders were 'the most terrible assassination that has ever stained the name of Belfast'.[44] He pointed out that the British government funded the USC, 'malefactors in uniform' (which was why the Speaker permitted him to raise the matter at Westminster) and therefore the British government was responsible for their actions. Devlin maintained that the men who had been killed in recent days – not just the McMahons – had as little to do with SF as the colonial secretary (Churchill). Devlin told the House that his supporters in business said: 'You the constitutionalist, you the man that looks to Parliament for the redress of public grievances, this is how your constituents are treated and there is no redress'. He added, 'so long as the British government chooses to pay to maintain these special constables, so long will these things go on.'[45] In a lengthy and equally eloquent reply, Churchill said 'one would have to search all over Europe to find instances of equal atrocity, barbarity, cold-blooded, inhuman, cannibal vengeance – cannibal in all except the act of devouring the flesh of the victim – which will equal this particular event.'[46] However, to the annoyance of Devlin, Churchill went on to compare the murders with the IRA onslaught in the border counties in the previous month. He expressed his hope that the conference he had called between Craig and Collins, four ministers of the Provisional government and five from the northern cabinet for the following day, 29 March, would find 'some method of modifying the appalling horrors'. That did not set the bar for success very high.

The McMahon murders had a profound effect on Belfast's Catholic middle-class business community. Catholic publicans – by far the majority of owners in the city – had often been targeted in their premises for random killing, and so had barmen, but for a police murder gang to seek out an innocent family in their home added an entirely different dimension. Would Catholics be able to carry on business at all? Was this a warning for Catholic businessmen to get out of the city? Devlin told the Commons that 'two hundred shops belonging to Catholics have been burnt to the ground, and nearly a hundred of these men or their shopmen or assistants have been murdered. One of my greatest friends in business in Belfast told me the other day … that he had not slept in his house for six months.'[47] As a result of these fears, a group of Catholic businessmen, mainly Devlin supporters, proposed to Craig a series of measures to end the violence. The leading figures, Raymond Burke, a ship broker and Hugh Dougal, owner of a transport company, liaised with Bishop MacRory to produce a blueprint which became the basis for what was agreed between Craig and Collins on 30 March and became known as the second Craig–Collins pact.[48]

On this occasion, unlike with the first failed pact, Collins took advice from northerners, including Bishop MacRory, and brought with him to London Dr Russell McNabb of Belfast SF, but he pointedly excluded Devlin. At the heart of the pact was the reorganization of policing. There was to be recruitment of Catholics for a mixed special police force in Belfast which would extend 'as speedily as possible' across the north. An advisory committee of Catholics would recommend Catholic recruits. Police would wear numbered uniform on duty and deposit weapons in an armoury when off duty. Searches for weapons would be carried out by units half Catholic, half Protestant. If the prospect of some of those provisions working was delusional, other clauses were pure fantasy. For example, despite the simultaneously portentous and laughable introduction, 'Peace is today declared', the idea that IRA activity would cease, as clause VI stated, was nonsensical since the IRA had split into pro and anti-Treaty factions at the Army Convention in Dublin on 26 March. The anti-Treaty IRA rejected the pact. De Valera called the pact 'a scrap of paper'.[49] Furthermore, Unionist ministers and police authorities were outraged at what they saw as the dismantling of the USC by unworkable proposals and attacked Craig in the Northern Ireland House of Commons for making the deal with Collins.[50] The only people who were to any extent content were middle-class nationalist supporters of Devlin. However, any chance of success was quickly damaged fatally by the anti-Treaty IRA who ignited large fires in Belfast premises on the day after the pact, announced a resumption of the Belfast boycott, and gave justification to hard-line unionists by mounting sectarian attacks on Protestants in Belfast as soon as the provisions of the pact were published. Unionists did not distinguish between pro- and anti-Treaty IRA attacks.

The IRA, RIC and USC in Belfast gave their answers before the ink was dry on the pact. On 31 March two Specials in plain clothes were shot while walking to their barracks in the Short Strand; Constable Hall died in the early hours of 1 April.[51] Later that day a bomb was thrown into the house of a Protestant family in Brown Street off Millfield and shots fired through the front window. A father and two children were killed.[52] That night RIC Constable Turner, on patrol with members of the USC from nearby Brown Square barracks, was shot dead by a sniper from Stanhope Street.[53] The IRA denied shooting Turner and Catholic residents claimed the shot was impossible from Stanhope Street. However, there were now two IRA factions in Belfast and it is a stretch to claim, as the IRA report in the Nixon file did, that fellow police shot Turner as an excuse for reprisals.[54] The police reprisal was immediate and horrendous. It became known variously as the Arnon Street Murders, or, most commonly in Belfast, the Arnon Street Massacre. Police from Turner's barracks took a sledgehammer, and a party of them in an armoured Lancia drove into nearby Arnon Street, directing automatic fire into houses, then alighted and assaulted anyone they encountered, men, women and children. More lorry-loads of USC followed, rampaging through the district. They smashed doors and killed five people, including a 7-year-old boy in the most savage fashion imaginable, graphically described in all its grisly detail by Fr Hassan, a local priest who was on the scene shortly afterwards. One victim, Joseph Walsh, literally had his brains knocked out with a sledgehammer. Children were shot and wounded while three men were shot dead.[55] Sectarian killings continued in the following days, exacerbated by anti-Treaty elements in the Belfast IRA behaving in an undisciplined fashion.

The Belfast IRA used the events in Arnon Street and other USC assaults as a negotiating tool with GHQ in Dublin. Only a minority supported the anti-Treaty IRA. Joe McKelvey, O/C 3rd Northern Division, defected immediately after the Army Convention and never returned to Belfast. He was under a cloud after the catastrophic damage to the IRA caused by the St Mary's Hall raid that many brigade officers blamed on his naivety and poor sense of organization and security. Séamus Woods, adjutant, 3rd Northern Division, who succeeded McKelvey, claimed that McKelvey had originally said he would remain loyal to GHQ but defected when he heard there was going to be an inquiry into his role as O/C.[56] Woods reported to Mulcahy that McKelvey's departure had a serious effect on morale, that many 'Trucileers' opted out of the IRA as a result and that two Belfast battalions had to be dissolved.[57] However, there were more complex matters at play than the loss of McKelvey. Other important Belfast activists wanted to know whether, and to what extent, GHQ would support them with weapons and money, and went to Dublin to negotiate as the Army Convention approached.

The most crucial figure was McCorley who provided a lengthy account of his visit to Dublin and meetings with Eoin O'Duffy. He was accompanied by Thomas Fitzpatrick. They informed O'Duffy that they would back the anti-Treaty executive if they did not receive satisfactory assurances from GHQ. For Collins, O'Duffy and Mulcahy, that would have been a disastrous outcome. Losing Belfast and Antrim, effectively the whole 3rd Northern Division, would probably tip the balance in the north, with Aiken's 4th Division unreliable and dissension in Daly's 2nd Northern Division that necessitated Daly's removal. McCorley made clear that 'unless GHQ would make at least as good an offer of supplies as had been made by the Executive', he and Fitzpatrick 'would have no option but to advise the Belfast Brigade that they should support the Executive.'[58]

McCorley told O'Duffy that his support 'would go to the people who would help us honour our obligations to the nationalists in Belfast. I said I would not allow my personal opinions as to the rights and wrongs of the quarrel between GHQ and the Executive to influence me in this matter.'

O'Duffy then made 'a definite promise that GHQ would provide all the supplies necessary within a short space of time. I told him that if that were so I would be in a position to advise the Belfast Brigade to support GHQ with whom my personal sympathies lay.'[59] In short, it was McCorley and Fitzpatrick who held the 3rd Northern Division for GHQ, despite senior figures like McKelvey and Seán O'Neill, O/C Belfast Brigade, defecting. O'Duffy appointed Séamus Woods, his aide-de-camp, to replace McKelvey and McCorley to replace O'Neill.[60] As an added incentive, O'Duffy integrated the officer corps of the 3rd Northern Division into the new National army establishment, an arrangement then extended to others to retain their loyalty. In the 3rd Northern Division, forty-five officers were paid by, and took orders from, Beggar's Bush from 1 April, although they were not in the National army.[61]

However, while acquiring the wherewithal to defend Belfast nationalists was McCorley's priority, he was merely a pawn in a much bigger political game. Collins, Mulcahy and O'Duffy attempted to use the fate of northerners as a way to unify the ever-widening split in the rest of the country between the pro- and anti-Treaty IRA. GHQ had managed to hold together most of the northern divisions, apart from the 4th, despite the misgivings of many rank-and-file volunteers. Now the immediate objective was to try to bring together both sides of the IRA in a military campaign to end the desperate position of northern nationalists, especially in Belfast. Indeed, many northerners were calling for such a campaign.[62] While Collins may have been personally committed to the support of northerners, even to ending partition, he was also determined to avoid a military assault by anti-Treaty IRA on the Provisional government and to satisfy Britain's requirements to honour the Treaty he had signed. In the end, he could manage only one – to honour the Treaty.

Florence O'Donoghue claimed that even while Collins was negotiating with Craig at the end of March, he was planning an offensive against the north with his IRB comrades which would involve the anti-Treaty IRA.[63] At least it would provide them with a target other than the Provisional government. The planning and organization of the offensive have been well documented elsewhere.[64] In the event, neither the planning nor the organization was carried out as envisaged, with terminal consequences for the IRA in Belfast and Antrim, both organizationally and for the lives of some volunteers. The scheme involved elaborate subterfuge to disguise the fact that the Provisional government was sponsoring the attack on the north. Northern IRA men would do the fighting and armaments were transported north, largely from Cork. British weapons supplied to Collins's government that were to be used in the north were swapped for IRA weapons. British rifles had their serial numbers filed off in case they were captured.[65]

Meanwhile, throughout April the death toll in Belfast mounted, reaching a peak from 17 to 21 April after a mass attack on the Bone when a football crowd invaded the enclave on their way home to the Shankill after a match. They fired indiscriminately into streets in the Bone but were driven off by RIC firing from a Lancia. Later that night, ignoring curfew, the mob returned, pouring gunfire into the district, killing three and wounding sixteen, but this time setting fire to houses in Antigua Street, burning fifteen and making forty families homeless. Police and military stood by.[66] Loyalist incursions became widespread across the city during the following days with, inevitably, killings in the Short Strand and even shooting at streets in the Falls Road. In the three weeks since the second Craig–Collins pact, 22 people had been shot dead and 39 seriously wounded, while 75 houses had been burned and 89 families evicted.[67] With the IRA divided and in disarray after the army convention and several men on the run following the St Mary's Hall raid, it was unable to respond in any meaningful way to the attacks, more so because they were carried out across so many different districts simultaneously.

It was also the case that some leading figures in the City Guard – in effect now the only disciplined IRA unit in the city – were engaged in preparations for the major assault on the six counties planned for May. It was to begin with an audacious attack on Musgrave Street barracks, Belfast RIC HQ, to seize weapons, but more importantly to drive off eight Lancias and four armoured cars (known colloquially as 'Whippets') with machine-guns mounted. Men were sent to Dublin to learn how to drive the vehicles.[68] Meanwhile, rifles and explosives were being transported north in oil tankers and some by boat to Down and Antrim. McCorley claimed that each of the three brigades in the 3rd Northern Division were 'to receive 150 rifles, plus 150 revolvers for the Belfast Brigade together with supplies of bombs, explosives and ammunition.'[69] The offensive was to begin on 2 May, but, as McCorley explained, 'It was unfortunate that the date was fixed before the supplies had arrived ... We were now faced with the difficulty of having the whole operation postponed since Belfast would be short of its supplies.' The Antrim Brigade had also not received anything.[70] There was no alternative but to ask for a postponement. Organizational chaos then ensued. The 2nd Northern Division could not postpone as orders had already been issued and their assault was in train. Woods, O/C 3rd Division, then asked for a further postponement of a fortnight which O'Duffy granted.[71]

The consequences of the failure to coordinate should have been obvious. The USC was able to deal with each IRA offensive separately instead of having to face a combined attack simultaneously across the north, though in the event, only the 2nd and 3rd mounted any kind of serious attack, a source of subsequent recriminations.[72] By the time the Belfast Brigade was ready on

18 May, the 2nd had been overwhelmed in Tyrone and Derry by the ferocious reaction of hundreds of USC, and the 1st, 4th and 5th Divisions did not move.[73] Nevertheless, the Belfast and Antrim Brigades pressed on. Initially, the Belfast attack on Musgrave Street barracks went well, twenty-one men being admitted to the barracks by a RIC sympathizer at 3.00 a.m. They divided into three groups. One began trussing up rifles in bundles of six to take away, but another led by McCorley and Joe Murray, O/C 3rd Battalion, Belfast Brigade, ran into trouble in the guard room. Special Constable McKeown tried to draw his revolver but McCorley pistol-whipped him causing 'terrible loss of blood'. At this sight, the other policeman, Constable Collins, began shouting, which woke the whole barracks and a machine-gunner on the roof opened up at the figures near the vehicles in the barracks compound.[74] The two police apparently tried to draw small automatics from their pockets but McCorley shot and wounded McKeown while Murray shot Collins dead. Woods's party was trying to get the Lancias started when the commotion erupted and he ordered his men to run for their lives; they all escaped under heavy gunfire to the lower Falls.[75] The area was cordoned off and searches conducted until 5.00 a.m., but no one was apprehended.

USC poured into Belfast from elsewhere in the north. McCorley says they came in train loads.[76] Killings of innocent Catholics as well as republicans and known IRA members increased dramatically from Friday 19 May over the weekend. Republicans in turn took savage revenge for loyalist attacks; in one instance, in a cooperage in the Docks nine men entered and asked for 'the Micks'. When the Catholics were picked out, the intruders shot four Protestants dead.[77] Meanwhile, an IRA arson campaign began, with businesses and mansions of wealthy unionists being targeted: eleven substantial businesses, including warehouses, mills and department stores, were destroyed in one day which provoked a violent unionist response.[78] Over the weekend twelve Catholics and two Protestants were killed.[79]

The 3rd Northern Division's 2nd Brigade based in County Antrim, which had been inactive since it was routed in June 1921, was busy too, starting on the same night as the attack on Musgrave Street barracks. Men rowed across Lough Neagh, from Toome, and burned Shane's Castle, the stately home of Lord and Lady O'Neill. At Cushendun, the home of Ronald O'Neill MP, later Lord Cushendun, was burnt. A party led by Felim MacGuill burned Crebilly Castle near Ballymena and another group burnt Ballymena railway station. Further north, men from Dunloy blew up the railway bridge linking Belfast to Derry at Killagan.[80] Led by Tom Fitzpatrick, the brigade headquarters company mounted a well-planned attack on Martinstown RIC barracks on 19 May, beginning with grenades and fusillades of rifle fire. A sergeant, two RIC constables and four USC held off the attackers. The defenders launched Verey lights, which alerted USC at Ballymena who went to investigate. The IRA had expected this outcome and ambushed the USC reinforcements on their way to Martinstown. By the time the USC arrived at the barracks, the IRA had fled.[81] Various other raids took place that night with an unsuccessful attack on the RIC barracks in Cushendun, while on the Coast Road bridges were blown up. Tom Fitzpatrick maintained they did 'considerable damage' to Ballycastle barracks with a bomb thrown down the chimney.[82] The attackers then withdrew to their bases as USC from Ballymena and Ballymoney mobilized and reinforced all barracks.

The USC obviously decided it was pointless dividing up to chase small groups of IRA who had gone to ground in the Glens. Instead, they spent some time planning a large-scale operation against the Antrim Brigade. Once organized, large numbers of USC conducted a major sweep through republican districts in north-east Antrim with A and B Specials searching, raiding and arresting men under the Special Powers Act in operation since 22 May. Fitzpatrick recalled that 'the brigade was forced into the hills'. He estimated there were about 4,000 USC and British troops involved in the operation.[83] The brigade disintegrated. Those men who could go home without fear of arrest did so. The others hid in dugouts in the Glens or went on the run, heading eventually through Belfast to the Curragh. The men in hiding were supplied with food by members of Cumann na mBan like Mary Fitzpatrick and Lena Cunning until it was safe to move south.[84] As MacGuill recounted,

> It soon became evident to us after our Rising had failed that to remain in County Antrim was almost an impossibility for those who had taken part in the Rising. Round-ups and mass raids were the order of the day, not only for those who took an active part in the operations during the Rising, but also for all those known to have republican tendencies.[85]

As MacGuill put it bluntly, 'As far as the six counties as a whole were concerned the general Rising was a flop.'[86] Only the Belfast IRA remained a serious problem for Craig's government, but with the defeat of all other republican assaults, unionists could now concentrate on the Belfast Brigade. The obviously coordinated attacks in Belfast and Antrim from 19 May unnerved the northern cabinet. Coming at the same time as the Collins–de Valera pact of 20 May to permit pro- and anti-Treaty SF wings to fight the coming elections as a national coalition panel, the IRA offensive against the north destabilized unionists who feared that the whole Treaty was in jeopardy. Churchill was also alarmed that if Collins was successful in uniting SF in the south, there would be a major attack on the north.[87] On 22 May the Belfast IRA went one provocation too far and gave the Unionist government the opportunity its hard-liners had been waiting for. At least two men shot

Unionist MP William Twaddell dead in broad daylight in the centre of Belfast. Twaddell had been noted for his speeches inciting loyalists and was rumoured to be a leading figure in the Imperial Guards, but he was a unionist political hero in Belfast. Craig immediately introduced internment; the same day 200 republicans were arrested, the IRA was proscribed and a curfew extended across the north, although it must be said that initially most of those arrested were SF members and the IRA in Belfast was able to continue its arson campaign and engage in gun battles for some weeks to come.

However, internment was the beginning of the end for the 3rd Northern Division. Its concerted attack from 19 May, combined with shootings of USC members and extensive fire-bombing of unionist businesses and mansions, provoked a frenzied response from Craig's government which unleashed the full strength of the USC in Belfast, a city which now descended into anarchy in republican districts with the thump of explosions and gunfire crackling up and down streets as Crown forces battled it out with both pro- and anti-Treaty IRA. The 3rd Northern Division faced a force with 5,500 A Specials, 4,215 B Specials and 946 C Specials, all full-time, but a total of 19,000 B Specials when part-timers were included. From 1 June there were also 1,000 of the new unionist police force, the RUC.[88] The IRA had launched an offensive whose avowed purpose was, in McCorley's words, 'to bring about the downfall of the six-county government by military means'. Craig's government responded accordingly.[89] With the 2nd Northern and the Antrim Brigade out of the reckoning, the full force of the Unionist government's paramilitary strength could be concentrated on the Belfast Brigade. It was now only a matter of time before the strength of numbers and massive firepower prevailed.

In the week following the assassination of Twaddell, the fire-bombing campaign and attacks on USC members by both wings of the IRA continued, despite internment and USC raids. On 25 May Special Constable James Murphy from Ballymena was shot dead on the Falls Road. Later that day Special Constable George Connor from Lisburn was shot in the Markets and died next day.[90] Nine civilians were shot dead in tit-for-tat killings between 25 and 28 May, five Catholics and four Protestants, as well as several people wounded and houses burned. On 29 May the IRA shot dead RIC Constable Henry O'Brien, a 23-year-old from Leitrim, as he and a colleague talked to a civilian outside their barracks on the Cullingtree Road off Divis Street near the lower Falls Road.[91] This killing initiated a series of violent repercussions that produced the worst two days of mayhem in two years, culminating on 31 May in what Kenna called 'the most hideous date in the two years of horrors in Belfast.'[92]

After O'Brien was shot, police mounted raids in the street from where the IRA men had run away and an armoured car raked the street with a machine-gun. The IRA returned fire with a variety of weapons, killing 20-year-old A

Special John Megarity from Armagh.[93] In response to these killings, USC men poured into the lower Falls, driving round for most of the afternoon in Lancias and armoured cars, firing indiscriminately into houses, wounding many people. The *Irish News* called it 'an unparalleled reign of terror'.[94] After a lull on 30 May, the anti-Treaty IRA shot two Specials at Millfield: Constable Andrew Roulston, from Strabane, was killed and Constable William Campbell, from Ahoghill, was wounded and died in June 1924.[95] The response was immediate and deadly. The USC ran amok in Millfield and Carrick Hill. Many people were killed and many more wounded when, apart from blazing away at random, USC on foot broke doors down and shot people in their homes. A loyalist mob followed the USC into the district carrying biscuit tins full of petrol. As the *Irish News* reported, 'Entire blocks of houses were burned to the ground and as the conflagration raged, machine-gun, rifle and revolver fire added terror'.[96] That evening USC members returned, firing into houses. They broke into a pub in nearby King Street, looted it, then, 'in a pretty drunken state', according to Kenna, riddled the nearby presbytery of St Mary's parish church with three priests and house-keepers inside.[97] At the same time, loyalists from the Shankill again invaded Millfield and the Old Lodge Road firing at random and burning Catholics' homes.

One notable IRA casualty of USC indiscriminate gunfire was McCorley who emerged from an IRA meeting near King Street to seek an explanation for the intense gunfire. He was hit by a round from a Lewis gun and seriously wounded. He was brought on a handcart to an ambulance, which contained two or three corpses and made it through a USC road block by playing dead when Specials opened the ambulance doors. McCorley was taken to St John of God's nursing home opposite the Mater Hospital where, by coincidence, he was in a private ward beside O/C Antrim Brigade, Thomas Fitzpatrick, who had been wounded in the knee in north Antrim. Fitzpatrick stated McCorley was still unconscious when admitted. McCorley recuperated in the home of Eoin MacNeill near Glenarm, then made it to Dublin via Glasgow. He never returned to Belfast.[98] Fitzpatrick succeeded McCorley as O/C Belfast Brigade, a largely meaningless position by June.

Fighting in Millfield and Carrick Hill continued into the night as the USC carried out arrests, including Frank Crummey, intelligence officer 3rd Northern Division, and one of Collins's nominees to the joint advisory committee established under the Craig–Collins pact. The IRA's attempts to ward off USC incursions by throwing grenades at armoured cars and firing at patrols as marauding gangs burned houses were largely unsuccessful. The death toll for 31 May was eleven, nine Catholics and two Protestants, with sixteen seriously wounded.[99] Séamus Woods later reported that 31 May was 'the hardest blow that the civil population received'.[100] The Belfast IRA was now leaderless, many of its best operators interned or on the run. Seán McGouran, adjutant 3rd Northern Division, reported to Mulcahy that

> The morale of the civilian population as a result of this raiding and the enemy's display of such numerically superior forces, has been considerably weakened ... B Specials with their local knowledge ... have played a very prominent part in these raids and have made it very difficult for our men to escape.[101]

The USC now began to occupy west Belfast. They took over strategic buildings on the Falls Road, gave the owners notice to quit, and turned them into strong points fortified with sandbags and barbed wire. First was the Beehive Bar at the junction of Falls Road and Broadway on which they flew a large union jack.[102] Then followed the Carnegie library, two hundred metres away, then the Falls public baths, one hundred metres from the library. Sporadic IRA activity continued throughout June, but it was purposeless and only provoked more raids and arrests. IRA volunteers were penniless and in hiding. The actions of the remnants of both IRA wings, particularly in robberies and arson of work places, were antagonizing the nationalist community, some of whom began to pass information to the RUC and USC. Loyalist sectarian killings went unanswered. There were twenty-four killings in June, six Protestants, including a baby, and eighteen Catholics.

By the end of the month the political picture had changed completely. On 16 June in the general election, the pro-Treaty faction defeated the anti-Treaty wing by 58 seats to 36, strengthening Collins's hand, but the following week, 22 June, Field Marshal Sir Henry Wilson, former chief of the Imperial General Staff, Unionist MP for North Down and Craig's security adviser in 1922, was shot dead on his own doorstep in London by two IRA men.[103] The assassination provoked an enormous reaction from London and also in Belfast. The House of Commons was adjourned; the cabinet met and initially issued instructions for retaliation against the Four Courts garrison whom they believed responsible. In the event, they decided to exert unanswerable pressure on Collins to act against the anti-Treaty IRA, which led him to bombard the Four Courts on 28 June, inaugurating the Civil War.

In Belfast there was rioting as a result of Wilson's killing, although nothing on the scale of previous disturbances. It was mainly between the Falls Road and Sandy Row on the Grosvenor Road where one of the houses burnt was the home of Denis McCullough's mother; four people were killed, one by the Crown forces.[104] However, the most egregious response was in Cushendall. On 23 June a party of A Specials from Ballymena in Crossley tenders and lorries, accompanied by British troops, drove into the north Antrim village, having picked up on their way a youth, James McAllister, who was cycling home to Glenariffe from Cushendall. In the village they jumped out of the lorry and immediately opened fire on people in the main street. They then dragged McAllister, along with another they had grabbed, off the main street into an alley near stables and shot them both dead. They killed a third person who had hidden in a shop, after he stood up and raised his arms above his head, one of the killers saying: 'This is for what you did to Wilson', or words to that effect.[105] Although four people were killed in July, in reality the blood-letting was over after two years. The IRA in Belfast was beaten. Those not interned headed south where many joined the National army and a minority the anti-Treaty IRA. Others emigrated. As soon as the Civil War erupted unionist anxiety dissipated, the IRA was out of the equation and the British government was satisfied that the Treaty was honoured with the oath of allegiance included in the new constitution.

What was known as the Belfast Pogrom was over as abruptly as it had begun. Jonathan Bardon provides an overview:

> Between July 1920 and July 1922, the death toll for Belfast was 453 – 257 Catholics, 157 Protestants, two of unknown religion and 37 members of the security forces. Catholic relief organizations estimated that between 8,700 and 11,000 Catholics had lost their jobs, that 23,000 Catholics had been forced out of their homes and about 500 Catholic owned businesses had been destroyed.[106]

Robert Lynch divides the figures for deaths slightly differently: 452 dead of whom 267 were Catholic and 185 Protestant; he includes the religion of police and British army. Lynch counted over 1,100 wounded and 650 homes and businesses destroyed, but gives a figure of approximately 8,000 for the number put out of their homes. Charles Townshend broadly agrees with these figures.[107]

A detailed contemporaneous tally of the names of the dead was kept by Fr John Hassan, a curate in St Mary's, the oldest Catholic church in Belfast, located in Chapel Lane at the city end of the Falls district. He published his account in *Facts and figures of the Belfast pogrom, 1920–22* under the nom de plume of G.B. Kenna. It was many years before Hassan's book saw the light of day because its details were so shocking and his indictment of the Unionists leading the new government in the north so damning that, on its scheduled day of publication, 1 August 1922, the Dublin government and Catholic Church had it withdrawn and pulped for fear of provoking more mayhem in Belfast after the violence appeared to have ended in July.[108]

While the overall scale of the violence is not in dispute, there has been much academic argument about what the breakdown of casualties signifies. Most of the effort in recent years centred on refuting nationalist interpretations that what happened was a pogrom. Townshend suggests that nationalists labelled the events a pogrom, 'to show the outside world that the real problem was not the attitude of loyalists but the machinations of the British government and the unionist employers.' He concludes that 'the republican response was visceral rather than logical'.[109] Alan Parkinson and Peter Hart, and to a lesser extent Tony Hepburn, questioned whether the events of those two years in Belfast technically constituted a 'pogrom' and, second, whether IRA actions both in Belfast and elsewhere in Ireland provoked retaliatory attacks on Catholic nationalist districts. Finally, there is the question of to what extent the IRA was successful in defending nationalists from indiscriminate attack.

Hassan's use of the term 'pogrom' in 1922 was the common contemporary description, and as such must be respected. The word had only recently come into English from Yiddish, borrowed from Russian meaning 'storm' or 'devastation'.[110] Its first recorded use was in 1891.[111] By 1906 'pogrom' was being used to mean 'an organized, officially tolerated attack on any community or group'.[112] This meaning was clearly the one Hassan had in mind. The *Irish News* was using the term freely by September 1920. Perhaps more significantly, given that its editorial position was less partisan, the London *Daily News* on 1 September 1920 described 'five weeks of ruthless persecutions by boycott, fire, plunder and assault, culminating in a week's wholesale violence, probably unmatched outside the area of the Russian or Polish pogroms.'[113] Devlin was using the word with that meaning in the Commons in October 1920 when he spoke of how 'the pogrom against Belfast Catholic workmen … expelled 4,000 Catholic workmen from their employment'. He asked whether 'Parliament will be given an opportunity of discussing this organized conspiracy to place the lives, liberties, and property of 500,000 Catholics at the mercy of their political opponents armed by the British Government?'[114] Obviously, it was Devlin's conviction at the time that the attacks of July 1920 and thereafter were organized in such a way as to meet the definition of pogrom.

Since the Second World War the literature in various disciplines has expanded the definition of pogrom considerably so that there is now no single agreed definition, though all have certain common characteristics. Pogroms have to be organized attacks on an identifiable minority group, ethnic or religious. Also, state authorities either instigate, control, participate or condone the attacks, or at least remain passive or inactive. It is also assumed that considerable numbers of deaths, certainly hundreds, but often thousands, occur. The word 'massacre' usually applies. Perhaps the best modern definition is that of Werner Bergman, which does not require state involvement:

> A unilateral, nongovernmental form of collective violence initiated by the majority population against a largely defenceless ethnic group, and

occurring when the majority expect the state to provide them with no assistance in overcoming a (perceived) threat from the minority.[115]

That definition certainly applies to many occasions in Belfast during the period 1920–2 (and in Lisburn, Dromore and Banbridge in July and August 1920). However, it is notable that in 1920–2 there were almost no deadly mob incursions deep into homogenous nationalist districts because the Catholic population was not 'a largely defenceless ethnic group', given the presence of armed IRA squads. By 1922 however, the IRA was so heavily outnumbered and outgunned that there were occasions that did qualify as pogroms when out-of-control USC men rampaged with impunity through districts, firing wildly, killing, wounding and beating residents. Generally, streets on the periphery of the tightly segregated districts were most dangerous because they were open to spontaneous attacks from enraged loyalist mobs which were usually beaten back by the residents and or IRA gunmen. It is also important for the criteria of pogrom definitions that the violence was not continuous over two years. There were sporadic outbursts of varying intensity, the worst period being the first six months of 1922 when violence was most intense in the Short Strand, North Queen Street, York Street, Carrick Hill and the Old Lodge Road, a densely populated Catholic slum near the city end of the Shankill Road. Over the whole period the worst affected areas were four electoral wards to the west and north of the city centre stretching from Smithfield through Carrick Hill to York Street and the Docks and an outlier, the Short Strand, cut off on the 'wrong' side of the River Lagan. Most people were killed in streets in those places.

The most detailed recent work on the spatial distribution of the violence and the age and religion of the victims shows that they were disproportionately Catholic men.[116] Catholics comprised 24 per cent of the Belfast population but suffered 56 per cent of the deaths. However, to meet one of the criteria for a definition of a pogrom there should be indiscriminate killing of the ethnic or religious victims, but normally that was not the case in Belfast. Over 80 percent of all Catholic victims were men, mainly aged 20–45.[117] It is likely, therefore, given the age and gender profile, that most of those Catholics killed were men either engaged in the defence of their district or in attacks on a neighbouring district who fell victim to a sniper's bullet or general gunfire, or were felled by a missile thrown from the opposition. The Military Service Pensions Collection shows that, contrary to the previous belief that no IRA died in the street violence between 1920 and 1922, in fact sixteen members of the Belfast Brigade were killed in action, plus five Fianna Éireann as well as five others in reprisals by the RIC 'murder gang'.[118] Although most of the dead were Catholic and it was Catholic districts that came under attack, the violence was not completely one-sided, another criterion for a pogrom. Belfast Catholics were not passive, defenceless victims. About 160 Protestants or 39 per cent of the death toll were killed over the period. There were also thirty-five police killed, twenty-eight of them certainly by the IRA.[119]

To what extent was the state involved either through organization, instigation or connivance? The evidence is incontrovertible that after the (unofficial) establishment of the USC in September 1920 many participated in riots and attacks on nationalist districts, but if the authorities organized or instigated the attacks, they did a poor job.[120] The fact is that they did not need to. Many of the attacks met the criterion of Bergman, namely 'collective violence initiated by the majority population against a largely defenceless ethnic group, and occurring when the majority expect the state to provide them with no assistance in overcoming a (perceived) threat from the minority'. They were ethnic riots as described by Donald Horowitz, the release of pent-up passions driven by hostile impulses towards Catholics and in the belief that violence would go unpunished.[121] Among the Unionist population of Belfast there was a conviction, encouraged and inflamed by unionist politicians, particularly during and after July 1920, and later in May 1922, that the northeast of Ireland was under threat from the IRA, and that if they did not take matters in hand themselves (as Carson threatened on 12 July 1920) then the IRA would prevail. That the vast majority of the nationalist population of Belfast did not support SF, let alone the IRA, had no effect on the actions of the unionist majority who, thanks to the inflammatory language of their political leaders, had come to see all Catholics as 'disloyal' and as a threat to their livelihood and way of life.

As described above, there is a correlation, particularly, but not exclusively, in 1922, between IRA operations elsewhere (for example the killings of Smyth and Swanzy) and assaults on Catholic districts. Belfast Catholics at large, regardless of any political adherence or convictions, were treated as hostages for the behaviour of republicans. Loyalist mobs made no distinction between Catholic supporters of Devlin and the IPP, Labour, or SF supporters or exservicemen. Catholics were the targets. As well as individuals, unionist rioters targeted Catholic institutions such as convents in Lisburn and Belfast, presbyteries, schools, churches like St Matthew's in the Short Strand and businesses, such as a Catholic-owned boot factory in Lisburn, and commercial premises like pubs. They took revenge as they saw it for IRA behaviour anywhere in the six counties. As Bishop MacRory put it in his pastoral letter in February 1922, 'the people of Belfast were being punished for the sins of their brethren elsewhere'. Loyalist mobs were confident they would not be punished for their actions.

Far from instigating the violence when it erupted in 1920, the Crown forces, especially the British army, tried to stop it. They fired disproportionately into Catholic crowds during various disturbances, but they did kill people on both sides of the political divide. After the Government of Ireland Act became law in January 1921, the posture and activity of the USC became overtly anti-Catholic, and, following the Treaty, it was hostile to the Catholic population as a whole, participating in organized murderous assaults on vulnerable Catholic enclaves which qualified as pogroms. Rather than organizing and coordinating such attacks, senior Unionist politicians (though not all of them) were anxious to prevent indiscriminate attacks, first in 1921 in case such attacks would damage the case for a six-county administration, and then in 1922 in case it appeared the new Unionist administration had lost control of law and order. Indeed, pressure from Westminster precisely because of the escalating anti-Catholic violence in spring 1922 led to the abortive Craig–Collins pacts that year. Rather than one continuous pogrom lasting two years then, Brendan O'Leary describes the period as 'characterized by pogroms, deadly ethnic riots, inter-communal street fighting, sniping and assassinations'.[122]

The Irish Revolution in the north-east, best exemplified by events in Belfast, was not the overthrow of British government but the substitution of national control from Dublin by the reimposition of British state power in that part of Ireland in the shape of a Belfast client administration run exclusively by Ulster Unionists.

Notes

CHAPTER ONE *Belfast and County Antrim in 1912*

1 William P. Kelly & John Young (eds), *Scotland and the Ulster plantation: explorations in the settlement of Stuart Ireland* (Dublin, 2009).

2 The 1911 census recorded the largest number of Irish speakers in the Ballycastle district which covered the northern glens and Rathlin Island where 1,139 people spoke Irish and English. Rathlin had a population of 351 and 122 of the census returns were in Irish. Some native speakers survived in the glens until the 1970s. The last native speaker on Rathlin died in 1985. Next most numerous was the Larne district which covered the coast and southern glens with 434 Irish speakers. Report of the 1911 Census, Province of Ulster, County Antrim [www.census.nationalarchives.ie].

3 Nisra.gov.uk/archive/census. The statistics that follow are taken from Census of Ireland, Area, houses, and population. Also, the ages, civil or conjugal condition, occupations, birthplaces, religion, and education of the people. Province of Ulster, County Antrim. www.cso.ie census reports 1821–2006.

4 Pat McCarthy, *Waterford: the Irish Revolution, 1912–23* (Dublin, 2018), p. 2.

5 Census of Ireland 1911. www.census.nationalarchives.ie.

6 Ibid.; Jonathan Bardon, *Belfast: a century* (Belfast, 1999).

7 For a discussion of the effects of 'city-regions' in Europe see A.C. Hepburn, *A past apart: studies in the history of Catholic Belfast, 1850–1950* (Belfast, 1996).

8 Grace's Guide to British Industrial History. www.gracesguide.co.uk; John Lynch, *An unlikely success story: the Belfast shipbuilding industry, 1880–1935* (Belfast, 2001). Workman Clark had actually two shipyards, one on each side of the Lough.

9 Province of Ulster, City of Belfast. www.cso.ie census reports 1821–2006.

10 Bardon, *Belfast*.

11 www.belfastcity.gov.uk. The city hall cost £369,000. Charles Brett, *Buildings of Belfast, 1700–1914* (Belfast, 1985), p. 67.

12 The 1911 census shows the Catholic population of Belfast was 24.1 per cent.

13 Marianne Elliott, *The Catholics of Ulster: a history* (London, 2000), p. 322.

14 Jonathan Bardon, *A history of Ulster* (2nd ed., Belfast, 2005), pp 381–2.

15 For example, Derry had a ratio of 1:728, though the numbers stationed in the city were second only to Belfast's ratio, while County Down had 1:732; see Adrian Grant, *Derry: the Irish Revolution, 1912–23* (Dublin, 2018), pp 7–8.

16 *Royal Irish Constabulary and Dublin Metropolitan Police. Appendix to the Report of the Committee of Inquiry, 1914* (Cd. 7637), p. 93.

17 These figures for barrack strengths are from the Census of Ireland, 1911, Report, Province of Ulster, city of Belfast.

18 Ibid.

19 www.winters-online.net., www.irishconstabulary.com. Nationalarchives.ie census of Ireland 1911.

20 Ibid.   21 Hepburn, *Past apart*, p. 8.

22 Province of Ulster, City of Belfast. www.cso.ie census reports 1821–2006.

23 Census of Ireland 1911. The census report for the county shows Presbyterians were most literate, in some districts 99 per cent. Catholics had twice the average percentage of illiteracy for the county. The same was true in Belfast where Catholic illiteracy was 6 per cent but 8 per cent in west Belfast with pockets like the Falls district very bad: 2,326 illiterates

in 1911. Interestingly, 2 per cent of the Belfast population – 7,595 – clustered in Catholic districts could speak Irish. There were only four in the city whose sole language was Irish; all of them were under the age of three.

24 Brian Feeney, *Seán Mac Diarmada* (Dublin, 2015), pp 58–9.
25 Oldbelfastpicturehouses.rushlightmagazine.com.
26 Ambrose Macaulay, *Patrick McAlister, bishop of Down and Connor, 1886–95* (Dublin, 2006).
27 Eamon Phoenix, The *Irish News* Centenary Supplement, part 1, p. 6 (Belfast, Nov. 1991).
28 Danny Kennedy, 'History of the *Belfast Newsletter*', *Newsletter*, 24 Aug. 2011.
29 Ed Curran, 'History ingrained in the walls of *Belfast Telegraph*', *Belfast Telegraph*, 6 Oct. 2015.

CHAPTER TWO *Unionism in Belfast and County Antrim, 1910–14*

1 Alvin Jackson, *Home rule: an Irish history, 1800–2000* (London, 2003), p. 83.
2 Patrick Maume, 'T.H. Sloan 1870–1941' in James Quinn & Patrick Maume (eds), *Ulster political lives* (Dublin, 2009), pp 285–91.
3 Walker, *Parliamentary election results*, p. 137
4 Henry Patterson, 'William Walker', *ODNB*; Ramsay MacDonald was his election agent in the 1905 by election. Ivan Gibbons, *The British Labour Party and the establishment of the Irish Free State, 1918–24* (London, 2015), p. 39; Henry Patterson, 'Independent Orangeism and class conflict in Edwardian Belfast', *Proceedings of the Royal Irish Academy*, 80, Sect. C, 1 (1980), 1–27; Bob Purdie, 'William Walker, Belfast trade unionist, socialist, and Irish unionist' in Keith Gildart & David Howell (eds), *Dictionary of Labour biography, XII* (Basingstoke, 2005), pp 283–92.
5 Patrick Buckland, *Irish unionism II: Ulster unionism and the origins of Northern Ireland, 1886–1922* (Dublin, 1973).
6 Ibid.   7 Walker, *Parliamentary election results*.
8 www.arc.ac.uk, Westminster elections in the future Northern Ireland.
9 Ibid.   10 Jackson, *Home rule*, pp 106–8.
11 Nicholas Mansergh, *The unresolved question: the Anglo-Irish settlement and its undoing, 1912–72* (New Haven, CT, 1991), p. 50.
12 Young Ulster was a secret society. A membership requirement was ownership of one of three types of gun: a Martini rifle, an American Winchester or a .45 revolver plus 100 rounds of ammunition, see Keith Haines, *Fred Crawford: Carson's gunrunner* (Donaghadee, 2009), p. 125. Some drilling had begun in 1910 before the December election and the arms committee of the UUC began piecemeal importation of weapons. Jackson, *Home Rule*, p. 116.
13 Jackson, *Home Rule*, p. 116. Special meetings, 15 Dec. 1911, 23 Aug. 1912.
14 Timothy Bowman, *Carson's army: the Ulster Volunteer Force, 1910–1922* (Manchester, 2007), p. 20.
15 Diane Urquhart, *Belfast Telegraph: Covenant centenary supplement*, 25 Sept. 2012; P. O'Kane, 'The UWUC and the Ulster crisis 1912–4: "no idle sightseers"'. www.academia.edu., accessed 10 Oct. 2019.
16 Margaret Ward, *Unmanageable revolutionaries: women and Irish nationalism* (London, 1983); eadem, *The women of Belfast and Cumann na mBan: Easter Week and after* (Belfast City Council publication, 2016).
17 Rachel E. Finley Bowman, 'An ideal Unionist: the political career of Theresa, marchioness of Londonderry, 1911–19', *Journal of International Women's Studies*, 4:3 (2003), 15–29.
18 Bowman, *Carson's army*, pp 143–4.
19 R.J. Adgey, *Arming the Ulster Volunteers, 1914* (Belfast, 1952), p. 20.
20 Haines, *Crawford*, p. 143.

21 A.T.Q. Stewart, *The Ulster crisis* (London, 1967), p. 197.
22 D. George Boyce, 'Craig, James, 1st Viscount Craigavon', *ODNB*.
23 Mark Radford, '"Closely akin to actual warfare": the Belfast riots of 1886 and the RIC', *History Ireland*, 7:4 (1999), 27–31. In 1886 32 people were killed, hundreds injured and £90,000 of damage caused, about £10 million in today's money. The rioting went on sporadically from June until September. See also, Andrew Boyd, *Holy war in Belfast* (Tralee, 1969); Ian Budge & Cornelius O'Leary, *Belfast: approach to crisis, a study of Belfast politics, 1613–1970* (London, 1973).
24 *Hansard (Commons)*, 14 May 1912, vol. 38, cols 960–1.
25 Bowman, *Carson's army*, pp 18–19.   26 Grant, *Derry*, p. 27.
27 *Times*, 1 Aug. 1912.   28 *Hansard (Commons)*, 31 July 1912, vol. 41, cols 2111–17.
29 Grant, *Derry*, pp 26–9.
30 Michael Foy, 'Ulster unionist propaganda against home rule, 1912–14', *History Ireland*, 4:1 (Spring 1996), 51.
31 *Hansard (Commons)*, 31 July 1912, vol. 41, cols 2088–149.
32 The troops patrolled the Queens Road outside the shipyards for some weeks to prevent disturbances but inside the shipyard gates mob rule prevailed.
33 *Hansard (Commons)*, 30 July 1912, vol. 41, col. 1867.
34 For a detailed account of the background to the Covenant and its signing see Jonathan Bardon, 'Perspective on the Ulster Covenant', lecture at Stormont, reference SO 01/12/13. www.niassembly.gov.uk.
35 RIC Crime Special Branch, 'Importation of arms and secret drilling in Ulster, 8 Sept. 1911' (TNA, CO 904/182).
36 Report to the under secretary, Dublin Castle, 13 July 1912 (TNA CO 904/28/2).
37 Minute by N. Chamberlain, 1 Sept. 1912 (TNA CO 904/28/2).
38 Bowman, *Carson's army*, p. 34.   39 Ibid., pp 53–80.
40 Ibid., pp 142–3.   41 *Irish News*, 30 Sept. 1912.
42 Haines, *Crawford*, p. 132.
43 McCammon was killed in action in April 1917 commanding the 2nd Hampshire Regiment, see Bowman, *Carson's army*, p. 81.
44 Timothy Bowman, 'The Ulster Volunteers 1913–14: force or farce', *History Ireland*, 1:10 (2002), 43–7.
45 Haines, *Crawford*, p. 160.
46 The Mid-Antrim and East Antrim Regiments were subsumed into Central which drew its strength mainly from the towns of Larne and Carrickfergus. Its CO was Robert McCalmont, MP for East Antrim, a brigadier-general in the Guards. The Central Antrim Regiment played a crucial role in the Larne gunrunning.
47 www.36thulster.com/north-antrim-uvf.html. accessed 20 Apr. 2019.
48 For details of numbers and organization of the UVF in Belfast and County Antrim see www.quincey.info. accessed 20 Apr. 2019.
49 Cited in Bowman, *Carson's army*, pp 89, 101–2.

CHAPTER THREE *Nationalist politics in Belfast and County Antrim before 1914*

1 Thomas Bartlett, 'Defence, counter-insurgency and rebellion: Ireland, 1793–1835' in Thomas Bartlett & Keith Jeffrey (eds), *A military history of Ireland* (Cambridge, 1996), pp 270–80.
2 Peter Brooke, *Ulster Presbyterianism: the historical perspective* (Dublin, 1987).
3 Eamon Phoenix, *Feis na nGleann* (Belfast, 2005).

4 J.R.B. McMinn (ed.), *Against the tide: a calendar of the papers of Rev. J.B. Armour, Irish Presbyterian and home ruler, 1869–1914* (Belfast, 1985).

5 Ian Cawood, *The Liberal Unionist Party: a history* (London, 2012).

6 Conor Morrissey, '"Rotten Prods": Protestant home rulers and the Ulster Liberal Association 1906–18', *History Journal* (online 24 July 2017), 1–23.

7 Tom Garvin, *The evolution of Irish nationalist politics* (Dublin, 2005 [1981]).

8 *Hansard (Commons)*, 16 Jan. 1913, vol. 46, col. 2255.

9 Phoenix, *Northern nationalism*, p. 5.

10 Brian O'Neill, 'Irishman's Diary', *Irish Times*, 23 Oct. 2000.

11 Séamus Dobbyn (BMH WS 279, p. 1). Boyle and Dobbyn's father were refused the sacraments of the Catholic Church for their IRB activities. The Temple of Liberty, Learning and Select Amusement, to give it its full title, was designed and built by Revd John Carey, a Presbyterian minister. Built in 1866, this remarkable edifice could seat 1,500, had an organ and a fifty-candle chandelier. It boasted a library with 5,000 books. It was burnt in 1910.

12 NAI, DICS files, carton 6 (Northern Division), DI Gambell.

13 Feeney, *Mac Diarmada*, pp 56–61; Dobbyn (BMH WS 279, p. 2).

14 Denis McCullough (BMH WS 914, pp 1–2).

15 Feeney, *Mac Diarmada*, pp 56–61.

16 Bulmer Hobson, *Yesterday, today and tomorrow* (Tralee, 1968).

17 Hobson (BMH WS 30, p. 2).   18 Ibid.

19 Liam Gaynor (BMH WS 183, p. 3).

20 Earnán de Blaghd, 'An outstanding leader of genuine nationalism', *Irish Times*, 13 Sept. 1968.

21 Blythe (BMH, WS 939, p. 4a).   22 Feeney, *Mac Diarmada*, pp 93–4.

23 Feeney, *Sinn Féin, a hundred turbulent years* (Dublin, 2002), p. 54.

24 Feeney, *Mac Diarmada*, pp 139–46.

25 Gerry McKeever (ed.), *Up The Falls* (Belfast, 1988). Both Dobbyn and Gaynor were later members of the IRB Supreme Council representing Ulster, west and east, see Séamus Dobbyn (BMH WS 279, p. 13), Liam Gaynor (BMH WS 183, p. 14) and Rory Haskins (BMH WS 223, p. 3).

26 Blythe (BMH WS 939, p. 4a).   27 Ibid., p. 5.

28 Jim McDermott, *Northern divisions: the old IRA and the Belfast pogroms, 1920–22* (Belfast, 2001), p. 4.

29 St. John Ervine, *Craigavon: Ulsterman* (London, 1949), p. 191.

30 Stewart, *Ulster crisis*, pp 73–8.

31 Ibid.   32 Feeney, *Mac Diarmada*, p. 154.

33 Ibid., pp 152–4.   34 Ibid.   35 Grant, *Derry*, p. 45.

36 Ibid., p. 46.   37 McCluskey, *Tyrone*, p. 46.

38 Seán Cusack (BMH WS 9, p. 7).   39 Ibid., p 3.

40 Liam McMullan (BMH WS 762, pp 4–5). McMullan is spelt McMullen in the BMH witness statement but his signature is clearly McMullan.

41 Denis McCullough (BMH WS 915, pp 7–8). The RIC believed there were 3,250 in the Volunteers in Belfast, CI report, Aug. 1914 (TNA, CO 904/94).

42 Ibid., Seán Cusack (BMH WS 9, p. 3).

43 For Redmond's speech and the politics behind it see Ronan Fanning, *Fatal path: British government and Irish revolution, 1910–1922* (London, 2013), pp 134–6.

44 This account is based on Seán Cusack (BMH, WS 9, pp 10–11).

45 Séamus Dobbyn (BMH WS 279, p. 5); Liam Gaynor (BMH WS 183, p. 8).

46 *Irish News*, 26 Oct. 1914; Eric Mercer, 'For King, country and a shilling a day: Belfast recruiting patterns in the Great War', *History Ireland*, 11:4 (2003), 29–33.

47 IG Report, Aug.–Sept. 1914 (TNA CO 904/94).
48 Mercer, 'King, country & a shilling a day'.
49 Richard Grayson, *Belfast Boys: how unionists and nationalists fought and died together in the First World War* (London, 2009), p. 10. The Power Loom Manufacturers' Association on 7 August cut their hours to 28 per week substantially reducing wages. (Ibid.)
50 McCluskey, *Tyrone*, p. 52.
51 Denis McCullough (BMH WS 915, p. 9).
52 Mercer, 'King, country & a shilling a day', 29–33.

CHAPTER FOUR *The Easter Rising and the split in northern nationalism*

1 Grayson, *Belfast Boys*, p. 196. There were over 500 Belfast men in the Royal Irish Rifles and 349 in the Inniskillings. In 2nd RIR there were 102 dead by the end of 1915, see ibid., p. 197.
2 Fanning, *Fatal path*, pp 136–7.
3 Frank Callinan, *T.M. Healy* (Cork, 1996), p. 510.
4 Fanning, *Fatal path*, p. 138.
5 Denis McCullough (BMH WS 916, p. 11).
6 Ibid., p. 12.
7 Ibid.
8 Feeney, *Mac Diarmada*, pp 222–5.
9 McCullough (BMH WS 916, p. 15).
10 Ibid.
11 Six Belfast Cumann na mBan women travelled to Coalisland: Elizabeth and Nell Corr, Ina and Nora Connolly, Kathleen Murphy and Eilis Woods (BMH WS 179, p. 2).
12 The RIC estimated there were 517 Volunteers in Tyrone at the end of 1914, McCluskey, *Tyrone*, p. 55.
13 Grant, *Derry*, p. 60.
14 On events in Tyrone, see McCluskey, *Tyrone*, pp 55–61; see also Denis McCullough's account, 'The events in Belfast', *Capuchin Annual* (1966).
15 Seán O'Mahoney, *Frongoch: university of revolution* (Dublin, 1987), pp 170–1.
16 *Irish News*, 1 May 1916.
17 Executive committee minutes Belfast National Volunteers, 26 Apr. 1916 (UCDA, Belfast Volunteer Minute Book, P11/a).
18 Report for Belfast, RIC: 'Reports on state of the counties', 1916 (TNA, CO 904/120/3).
19 Phoenix, *Northern nationalism*, p. 22.
20 Ibid.; George Dangerfield, *The damnable question: a study in Anglo-Irish relations* (London, 1977), p. 215.
21 For a detailed account of the negotiations see Phoenix, *Northern nationalism*, pp 21–35.
22 Grant, *Derry*, pp 55, 73.
23 Phoenix, *Northern nationalism*, p. 23.
24 *Irish News*, 13, 14 June 1916.
25 Ibid., 17 June 1916.
26 Grant, *Derry*, pp 71–3.
27 Phoenix, *Northern nationalism*, p. 34; F.S.L. Lyons, *John Dillon: a biography* (London, 1965), pp 400–1.

CHAPTER FIVE *Belfast and Antrim, 1917–20: unionist redoubt*

1 Michael Laffan, 'The unification of Sinn Féin in 1917', *IHS*, 17 (1971), 353–79.
2 McCluskey, *Tyrone*, pp 69–74.
3 Ibid., pp 71–7; Grant, *Derry*, pp 84–6.
4 Padraig Yeates, 'Dublin' in John Crowley, Donal Ó Drisceoil & Michael Murphy (eds), *Atlas of the Irish Revolution* (Cork, 2017), p. 591.
5 Seán Culhane (BMH, WS 746, p. 1).
6 RIC Inspector-General report, Sept. 1917 (TNA, CO 904/104).

7 *Irish News*, 23 Nov. 1917.

8 RIC Inspector-General report, Dec. 1917 (TNA, CO 904/104).

9 David McGuinness, 'Memoir', p. 8. In most respects the memoir is a copy of McGuinness's testimony to the Bureau of Military History, WS 417.

10 Roger McCorley (BMH WS 389, pp 2–4). Seán Cusack, a British army veteran who became O/C Antrim and East Down brigade, maintains that at the end of 1917 there were only two companies in Belfast, A and B, and that Peter Burns, a 1916 internee, formed C company from the Seán McDermott cumann (BMH WS 402, pp 6–7).

11 Thomas Fitzpatrick (BMH WS 395, pp 1–2).

12 Ibid., p. 2.

13 Séamus McKenna (BMH WS 1016, p. 1).

14 Padraig Yeates, '"Have you in Ireland all gone mad", the 1918 General Strike against conscription' (Century Ireland 1918). An abridged version appears in *Saothar*, 43 (2018), 47–53.

15 Charles Townshend, *The Republic: the fight for Irish independence* (London, 2013), p. 175.

16 Ibid., p. 3. Johnson was sacked for 'disloyalty to the Crown' by Day & Co. where he was a commercial traveller. Curiously, in his detailed BMH account of the conscription crisis he makes no mention of his activities in Belfast (BMH WS 1755, pp 17–27).

17 Yeates, 'Have you in Ireland all gone mad', p. 6.

18 Séamus McKenna (BMH WS 1016, p. 1).

19 Laffan, 'Unification of Sinn Féin', 378.

20 RIC Inspector's report, Sept. 1918 (PRONI, MIC 448/72).

21 She was sworn into the republican movement by Mac Diarmada and Hobson on Cavehill, probably in 1914: see pension application by Nellie Neeson (IMA, MSPC, 34REF11037).

22 Ibid.; pension application by Winifred Carney (IMA, MSPC, 34REF56077); pension application by Elizabeth Delaney (IMA, MSPC, 34REF26212). Ward and McCullough did not submit pension claims but their roles are mentioned by many other claimants.

23 David McCullagh, *De Valera: rise, 1882–1932* (Dublin, 2017), p. 152.

24 McDermott, *Northern divisions*, p. 16.

25 *Irish News*, 28 Nov. 1918. The headline was 'Sinn Féiners v Mill Girls on the Falls'.

26 Ibid., 29 Nov. 1918.

27 Jack McNally, *Morally good: politically bad* (Andersonstown, 1987), p. 5. McNally was an eyewitness. He had joined the Fianna in 1917 and later graduated to the IRA.

28 McCullagh, *De Valera*, p. 152.

29 Ronaldo Munck, 'Class and religion in Belfast – a historical perspective', *Journal of Contemporary History*, 20:2 (1985), 241–59; Padraig Yeates, 'Hidden history: an Irishman's diary on the Belfast engineering strike of January 1919', *Irish Times*, 21 Jan. 2019.

30 Ibid.   31 Ibid.

32 Yeates, 'Hidden history'.

33 Liam McMullan (BMH WS 762, p. 4).   34 Ibid., p. 5.

35 *Irish News*, 21 Apr. 1918.

36 From Clady in County Armagh, McLogan joined the IRB in 1913 aged 14. He fought in the GPO and was interned in Frongoch. In 1917 he went to Belfast to do IRB work, then returned to Dublin, was arrested and was on hunger strike in Mountjoy with Thomas Ashe. In 1918 he returned to Belfast and became O/C of 'D' company, 1st Battalion. He later became chairman of SF in 1950.

37 Liam McMullan (BMH WS 762, p. 7).   38 Feidhlim MacGuill (BMH WS 609, p. 3).

39 Roger McCorley (BMH WS 389, pp 2–3).

40 A letter from Seámus O'Neill to the Military Service Pensions board supports Carney's application including the information about her role in 1920 (IMA MSPC, 34REF56077).

41 Séamus McKenna (BMH WS 1016, p. 2).

42 Síobhra Aiken, Fearghal Mac Bhloscaidh, Liam Ó Duibhir & Diarmuid Ó Tuama (eds), *The men will talk to me: Ernie O'Malley's interviews with the Northern Divisions* (Kildare, 2018), pp 1–11.
43 Joseph Murray (BMH WS 412, p. 3).
44 Aiken et al., *The men will talk to me*, pp 1–11.
45 Roger McCorley (BMH WS 389, pp 3–4, 13); Thomas Fitzpatrick (BMH WS 395), p. 2.
46 Townshend, *Republic*, pp 115–16.
47 Townshend suggests that the attacks on the tax offices in Belfast triggered Carson's revival of the UVF in July, ibid., p. 175.
48 Grant, *Derry*, p. 94.   49 Townshend, *Republic*, pp 122–4.
50 Ibid., 13 July 1920.
51 Michael Farrell, *Arming the Protestants* (London, 1983), pp 21–9.
52 PoliceHistory.com; Garda Síochána Historical Society; J. Anthony Gaughan, *The memoirs of Constable Jeremiah Mee RIC* (Cork, 2012 [1975]), pp 95 and 125ff.
53 Seán Culhane (BMH WS 746, pp 5–6).
54 Pearse Lawlor, *The burnings 1920* (Cork, 2009), p. 61.
55 *Irish News*, 22 July 1920.

CHAPTER SIX *The 'Belfast Pogrom', 1920–2*

1 Joseph Murray (BMH WS 412, pp 5–6).
2 Farrell, *Arming the Protestants*, p. 32; Fanning, *Fatal path*, pp 231–5 for details of the cabinet meeting of 23 July.
3 See, for example, *Northern Whig*, 23 July 1920.
4 Farrell, *Arming the Protestants*, p. 32.
5 'Prinkipo policy triumphant', *Times*, 27 July 1920.
6 Timothy Bowman, 'Policing in History', *Belfast Telegraph*, 9 Sept. 1999.
7 Farrell, *Arming the Protestants*, pp 13–14.   8 Ibid.
9 The figures that follow are taken from William Sheehan, 'The British army in Ireland' in Crowley et al. (eds), *Atlas of the Irish Revolution*, pp 363–70.
10 *Irish News*, 22 July 1920.
11 G.B. Kenna, *Facts and figures of the Belfast pogrom* (Dublin, 1922), pp 18–20. Belfast newspapers 22–9 July 1920. The details that follow of events 21–24 July 1920 are taken mainly from the *Irish News* which provided the most reliable reports of the communal violence of those days. Unionist newspapers like the *Newsletter* and *Northern Whig* and English newspapers like the *Daily Mail* published clearly partisan accounts of the events. In the case of the *Irish News* while its editorials were partisan, its reports were usually factual.
12 *Irish News*, 23 July 1920.   13 Kenna, *Facts and figures*, p. 23.
14 Ibid.   15 Séamus McKenna (BMH WS 1016, p. 3).
16 Ibid.   17 Roger McCorley (BMH WS 389, p. 11).
18 Séamus McKenna (BMH WS 1016, Addendum, pp 1–2).
19 Ibid., p. 16 and Addendum, p. 2.   20 McDermott, *Northern divisions*, p. 42.
21 Roger McCorley (BMH WS 389, p. 3).   22 Ibid., p. 12.
23 Lawlor, *Burnings*, p. 37.   24 Seán Culhane (BMH WS 746, pp 8–9).
25 McCarthy had access to RIC codes and reported to Collins through Frank Thornton at IRA GHQ. J.B.E. Hittle, *Michael Collins and the Anglo-Irish War: Britain's counterinsurgency failure* (Washington, DC, 2011). McCarthy later became a Garda chief superintendent.
26 Seán Culhane (BMH WS 746, pp 9–10).
27 John Borgonovo, *Florence and Josephine O'Donoghue's War of Independence* (Dublin & Portland, 2006), p. 136.

28 Tom Fox (BMH WS 365, pp 4–5). Fox, like McCorley, later became a colonel in the National army.
29 The most comprehensive recent account of the killing of DI Swanzy is provided by Lawlor, *Burnings*, pp 102–114.
30 Tom Fox (BMH WS 365, pp 5–6). 31 Ibid., p. 6.
32 Lawlor, *Burnings*, p. 116. The account that follows of the destruction in Lisburn is largely based on Lawlor.
33 Tom Fox (BMH WS 365, p. 6). 34 Lawlor, *Burnings*, p. 118.
35 Seán Culhane (BMH WS 746, p. 13).
36 *Belfast Telegraph*, 24 Aug. 1920. 37 McDermott, *Northern divisions*, p. 52.
38 Lawlor, *Burnings*, p. 135. 39 *Irish News*, 2 Apr. 1943.
40 Patrick Buckland, *Irish unionism: the Anglo-Irish and the new Ireland, 1885–1923: a documentary history* (Dublin, 1972), p. 445.
41 Census of Ireland 1911 nationalarchives.ie.
42 Census of Northern Ireland 1926, County Antrim, nisra.gov.uk. There was no census in Ireland in 1921 such was the disturbed state of the country.
43 Inflation.iamkate.com; Lawlor, *Burnings*, p. 152.
44 Lawlor, *Burnings*, p. 210. 45 *Irish News*, 25 Aug. 1920.
46 Detailed reports of these incidents are provided in the *Irish News* for 25 Aug.–2 Sept. 1920. The following account relies on *Irish News* reports unless otherwise footnoted.
47 McDermott, *Northern divisions*, p. 56, n. 41.
48 *Belfast Telegraph*, 31 Aug. 1920. 49 Townshend, *Republic*, p. 180.
50 Lawlor, *Burnings*, pp 160–1; Farrell, *Arming the Protestants*, p. 35.
51 Farrell, *Arming the Protestants*, p. 37.
52 For a detailed account of the meeting see Fanning, *Fatal path*, pp 234–5.
53 Ibid., p. 236.
54 John McColgan, *British policy and the Irish administration, 1920–22* (London, 1983), pp 26–31.
55 Farrell, *Arming the Protestants*, pp 40–54.
56 *Hansard (Commons)*, 25 Oct. 1920, vol. 133, cols 1328–30.
57 Manus O'Boyle (BMH WS 289, pp 5–7).
58 Thomas Flynn (BMH WS 429, pp 2–3).
59 Joseph Murray (BMH WS 412, pp 5–6). 60 Ibid., p. 6.
61 Séamus McKenna (BMH WS 1016, pp 38–9). 62 Ibid., p. 39.
63 Ibid. 64 Fanning, *Fatal path*, pp 181–8.
65 Roger McCorley (BMH WS 389, p. 12); Joseph Murray (BMH WS 412, p.7); Aiken et al., *The men will talk to me*, p. 107.
66 Joseph Murray (BMH WS 412, p. 8).
67 Séamus McKenna (BMH WS 1016, p. 4). 68 *Irish News*, 27 Sept. 1920.
69 *Antrim's patriot dead, 1797–1953* (Belfast, 1966), pp 32–7. The details that follow about the three men killed and their funerals are taken from this publication which is online. www.treasonfelony.wordpress.com.
70 Austen Morgan, *Labour and partition: the Belfast working class, 1905–23* (London, 1990), p. 289.
71 Liam Gaynor (BMH WS 183, p. 19).
72 McDermott, *Northern divisions*, p. 61 n. 10.
73 Nixon file 20 Feb. 1924 (UCDA, Blythe papers, P24/176). Street Massacre (NAI, DT, S1801).
74 Roger McCorley (BMH WS 389, pp 12–13). 75 Ibid.
76 Joseph Murray (BMH WS 412, p. 7).
77 *Belfast Telegraph*, 15 Oct. 1920. 78 *Dáil Debates*, 6 Aug. 1920.
79 Ibid. 80 Fanning, *Fatal path*, p. 177.
81 Liam Gaynor (BMH WS 183, p. 19). 82 Ibid.

CHAPTER SEVEN *Belfast: operations and elections in spring 1921*

1 Phoenix, *Northern nationalism*, pp 104–12.
2 For a detailed discussion of British political manoeuvring Dec. 1920–Jan. 1921 see Fanning, *Fatal path*, pp 245–55.
3 Seán Corr (BMH WS 458, p. 12).   4 Ibid.
5 Ibid. O'Duffy taking command of the 2nd Northern Division produced an increase in activity in Derry and Tyrone from March 1921. Grant, *Derry*, p. 115.
6 Memorandum by GHQ, 24 Mar. 1921 (UCDA, Mulcahy papers, P7/A/17) cited in Robert Lynch, *The Northern IRA and the early years of partition* (Dublin, 2006), p. 75.
7 Ibid., pp 78–9.   8 Ibid.
9 McCorley was under the mistaken impression that the case was about the killing of a DI Hunt in Tipperary. Michael Grey was convicted and sentenced to death for the killing of Fallon but was spared by the truce. See Aiken et al., *The men will talk to me*, p. 88, n. 12; Richard Abbott, *Police casualties*, pp 239–40.
10 Séamus McKenna (BMH WS 1,016, p. 7).
11 Joseph Murray (BMH WS 412, p. 14).
12 Nixon file (UCDA, Blythe papers, P24/276); Séamus McKenna (BMH WS 1,016, p. 8).
13 Roger McCorley (BMH WS 389, p. 41).
14 Séamus McKenna (BMH WS 1,016, p. 8).
15 Maggie Fitzpatrick's affidavit and references for military pension claim (IMA, MSPC, 34REF26214).
16 Séamus McKenna (BMH WS 1016, pp 8–10); *Irish News*, 12 Mar. 1921. McKenna maintained he was told years later that Allen was accidentally shot by the dying Black and Tan.
17 By coincidence the passer-by was a member of 'D' company, 1st Battalion, called Michael McLaverty from Clowney Street in Beechmount.
18 *Antrim's patriot dead*, pp 39–41; *Belfast Telegraph*, 25 Apr. 1921.
19 Intelligence from the RIC in Belfast to Collins in Dublin named the murder gang as Sergeants Hicks and Clarke, Constables Caldwell and Golding, and that Hicks fired the fatal shots using a silencer on his weapon (Nixon file, NAI, DT, S1801) Confidential report on DI Nixon, 20 Feb. 1924 (UCDA, Blythe papers, P24/277).
20 Roger McCorley (BMH WS 389, p. 45); Séamus McKenna (BMH WS 1,016, p. 16).
21 Ibid.
22 For a detailed and very jaundiced account of events at Lappinduff, see Séamus McKenna (BMH, WS 1,016, pp 18–28).
23 Lynch, *The northern IRA*, p. 102.   24 *Irish News*, 27 Jan. 1921.
25 Phoenix, *Northern nationalism*, p. 108. For an account of the negotiations between northern nationalists and the Dáil cabinet see Phoenix, *Northern nationalism*, pp 106–20.
26 Maeve McGarry (BMH WS 826, pp 16–17).
27 Phoenix, *Northern nationalism*, p. 116.
28 Sydney Elliott, *Northern Ireland parliamentary election results, 1921–1972* (Chichester, 1973), p. 89. Nine of SF's candidates were in prison and others, including MacEntee, on the wanted list, which made for problems campaigning.
29 Dáil cabinet minutes, 6 Apr. 1921, Secretary to President de Valera to minister of Home Affairs, 29 Mar. 1921 (NAI, DT, 2/266, p. 94).
30 For details of election results see Elliott, *Northern Ireland parliamentary election results*, and Brian Walker (ed.), *Parliamentary election results in Ireland, 1918–22* (Dublin, 1992).
31 Ibid.   32 *Newsletter*, 20 May 1921.

CHAPTER EIGHT *The IRA campaign in County Antrim, 1919–21*

1 Feidhlim MacGuill (BMH WS 609, p. 8).
2 Brigade activity report, no. 2 Brigade Antrim, 3rd Northern Division, 7 Jan. 1937 (IMA, MSPC/A/49).
3 MacGuill (BMH WS 609, p. 4). The figure of 15 for Glenariffe is corroborated in the brigade activity report, 11 July 1921 (IMA, MSPC/RO/410).
4 Tom Fitzpatrick (BMH WS 395, p. 7).
5 Aiken et al., *The men will talk to me*, p. 190. See chapter 5 for a brief biography of McLogan.
6 Aiken et al., *The men will talk to me*, p. 190.
7 Brigade activity report, 7 Jan 1937 (IMA, MSPC/A/49).
8 Brigade activity report, 11 July 1921 (IMA, MSPC/RO/408).
9 Brigade activity report, 11 July 1921 (IMA, MSPC/RO/410).
10 Pension application, 30 Dec. 1936 (IMA, MSPC CMB/62).
11 Pension application, 30 Dec. 1936 (IMA, MSP34REF24159).
12 IMA, MSPC34REF17427.
13 Ibid. Cunning's whole family were heavily involved with the republican movement. Her brother, Hugh McCamphill, also received a pension. Her brother-in-law was Felix McCorley, a prominent IRA man in Belfast.
14 Ibid.
15 Brigade report, 2nd Brigade, 3rd Northern Division, 7 Jan. 1937 (IMA, MSPC/A/49).
16 Ibid.   17 Ibid.
18 Townshend, *Republic*, p. 115.   19 Ibid., p. 175.
20 Liam McMullan (BMH WS 762, p. 7).
21 Ibid., pp 8–10. The brigade activity report rather over-eggs the significance of the raid, describing Ballycastle RIC barracks as 'an important enemy station', 7 Jan. 1937 (IMA, MSPC/A/49).
22 Liam McMullan (BMH WS 762, pp 8–10).
23 The brigade activity report claimed the station was under observation from a destroyer in Torr Bay (IMA, MSPC/A/49).
24 Liam McMullan (BMH WS 762, pp 13–14).
25 Ibid. At the end of September the haul from Torr Head was supplemented by a successful gunrunning operation from Dublin which brought in six rifles and a dozen automatic pistols and ammunition – brigade activity report (IMA, MSPC/A/49).
26 Ibid.; McMullan (BMH WS 762, pp 13–14).
27 Charles Townshend, 'The Irish Republican Army and the development of guerrilla warfare 1916–21', *English Historical Review*, 94:371 (1971), 330.
28 Aiken et al., *The men will talk to me*, p. 190.   29 Ibid.
30 Kieran Glennon, *From pogrom to civil war: Tom Glennon and the Belfast IRA* (Cork, 2013), p. 46.
31 Brigade activity report, 7 Jan. 1937 (IMA MSPC/A/49). 32 Ibid.
33 CI Antrim, Jan. 1921 (TNA, CO 904/114).
34 Originally from Roscommon, Daly was the father of Cahal Daly who became cardinal archbishop of Armagh and primate of all Ireland.
35 Brigade activity report, 7 Jan. 1937 (IMA, MSPC/A/49).
36 CI Antrim, Feb. 1921 (TNA, CO 904/114).
37 Liam McMullan (BMH WS 762, p. 18).
38 Ibid., p. 19.   39 Ibid.
40 *Irish News*, 26 Mar. 1921.   41 Liam McMullan (BMH WS 762, p. 18).
42 O'Duffy's orders had produced similar developments in Derry and Tyrone, see Grant, *Derry*, p. 115.

43 Liam McMullan (BMH WS 762, p. 18).

44 *Belfast Newsletter*, 12 Apr. 1921. Glarryford station had been damaged by fire in the IRA attack on 24 March.

45 *Newsletter*, 21 Apr. 1921; CI Antrim, Apr. 1921 (TNA, CO 904/115).

46 Aiken et al., *The men will talk to me*, p. 183, nn 10 & 12.

47 Thomas Fitzpatrick, alias Robert McDonnell (BMH WS 395, pp 1–2). The following details all come from Fitzpatrick's witness statement.

48 Ibid., p. 5.   49 Ibid., p. 7.   50 Ibid., p. 6.

CHAPTER NINE *Election, truce and partition in Belfast and Antrim, 1921–2*

1 Kenna, *Pogrom*, p. 58.   2 Ibid.

3 The following account relies heavily on witness statements from Roger McCorley (BMH WS 389, pp 45ff.), Thomas Flynn (BMH WS 429, pp 10–12) and Tom Fox, who was one of the prisoners in Crumlin Road (BMH WS 365, pp 11–12).

4 Thomas Flynn (BMH WS 429, pp 10–12). The other men in the covering party were Hugh Elliott, Matt Quinn, William McGarry, James McDermott, Seán Keenan and Roger McCorley, see brigade activity report, 7 Jan. 1937 (IMA, MSPC-RO–401/A/48).

5 The brigade activity report corroborates McCorley's account (IMA, MSPC-RO–401/A/48).

6 The men sentenced to death were saved by the truce the following month and were finally released in January 1922, see Tom Fox (BMH WS 365, p. 12).

7 *Belfast Telegraph*, 11 June 1921; McDermott, *Northern divisions*, p. 87. Remarkably, the RIC men obviously could not recognize any of the IRA ASU standing at the street corner.

8 Ibid.; Abbott, *Police casualties*, p. 324.

9 Kenna, *Pogrom*, p. 59; *Belfast Telegraph*, 13 June 1921; Joe Baker, *The McMahon family murders and the Belfast troubles, 1920–22* (Belfast, 1993).

10 Roger McCorley (BMH WS 389, pp 14, 19–22); Joseph Murray (BMH WS 412, pp 4–6).

11 The account here is based on the following sources: *Belfast Telegraph*, 13 June 1921; *Irish News*, 13 June 1921; *Antrim's patriot dead*, pp 44–5, Baker, *The McMahon murders*; Kenna, *Belfast pogrom*; *Hansard (Commons)*, 14 June 1921, vol. 143, cols 211–13. The chief secretary, Hamar Greenwood, brushed aside Devlin's questions.

12 Dan O'Neill's Loney, or Loanin, a track leading to the Black Mountain, was where Britton's Parade stands today off the Whiterock Road in west Belfast. In 1921 it was on the outskirts of the city.

13 *Hansard (Commons)*, 14 June 1921, vol. 143, cols 211–13.

14 Ibid. On the reprisal policy see Fanning, *Fatal path*, pp 239, 251, 257; Farrell, *Arming*, appendix 2.

15 Street massacre, 1924 (NAI, DT, S1801); confidential report on DI Nixon file, 1924 (UCDA, Blythe papers, P24/175). The file, compiled in 1924, gives the usual names for the members of the Nixon gang: Sergeant Clarke, Constables Giff, Gordon, Cahar, Hare, Norris, Sterritt and Reid. The report contains many inaccuracies, including details of injuries sustained by the victims. It also claims only one murder gang was involved which is not possible logistically.

16 Abbott, *Police casualties*, p. 325.

17 Both the *Belfast Telegraph* and *Irish News* of 14 and 15 June give detailed accounts of the deaths and the shooting, though obviously with differing emphasis. These accounts have been relied on here.

18 *Irish News*, 15 June 1921.

19 *Hansard (Commons)*, 14 June 1921, vol. 143, cols 334–79. 20 Ibid.

21 Kenna, *Pogrom*, p. 60.   22 *Irish News*, 24 June 1921.

23 Fanning, *Fatal path*, pp 26off.
24 *Irish News*, 7 July 1921; Abbott, *Police casualties*, p. 335.
25 *Irish News*, 8–9 July 1921. 26 Tom Fitzpatrick (BMH WS 395, p. 7).
27 Aiken et al., *The men will talk to me*, p. 99.
28 Thomas Flynn (BMH WS 429, pp 6–8). The details that follow, of what came to be called 'the Raglan Street ambush', rely partly on Flynn's account. However, Flynn's account exaggerated the RIC casualties in the Raglan Street incident as well as embellishing the significance of other IRA operations.
29 Account by Seán Montgomery [n.d.] (NLI, Seán O'Mahony papers, MS 44,01/6).
30 Ibid.
31 *Irish News*, 11 July 1921; Abbott, *Police casualties*, p. 337. According to Montgomery, Conlon 'was good at giving tips of police raids'. He was an unlikely candidate to be in a murder gang. Montgomery (NLI, Séan O'Mahony papers).
32 Thomas Flynn (BMH WS 429, p. 7). 33 *Irish News*, 11 July 1921.
34 Aiken et al., *The men will talk to me*, p. 100.
35 Kenna, *Pogrom*, p. 61. Kenna says many more injured people were treated in their own homes; Parkinson, *Belfast's unholy war* (Dublin, 2004), p. 154.
36 *Irish News*, 11 July 1921.
37 McCorley (BMH WS 329, p. 25); *Irish News*, 12 July 1921.
38 McCorley (ibid., p. 26). Belfast was not known as 'Linenopolis' for nothing.
39 Kenna, *Pogrom*, p. 62; Parkinson, *Belfast's unholy war*, pp 124–5.
40 Kenna, *Pogrom*, p. 62. 41 Parkinson, *Belfast's unholy war*, p. 153.
42 Phoenix, *Northern nationalism*, p. 141.
43 Woods to chief of staff, 27 July 1922 (UCDA, Mulcahy papers, P7/A/23).
44 Reports of director of organisation, June/July, Aug. 1921 (ibid.).
45 Divisional strengths, Dec. 1921 (ibid., P7/A/32).
46 Farrell, *Arming the Protestants*, p. 65.
47 Liam McMullan (BMH WS 762, p. 19); Feidhlim MacGuill (BMH WS 609, p. 8).
48 MacGuill (ibid).
49 MacGuill (BMH WS 609, p. 7); Brigade activity report, 7 Jan. 1937 (IMA, MSPC/RO/410).
50 Brigade activity report, 30 Dec. 1936 (IMA, MSPC/RO/401–406A).
51 Thomas Flynn (BMH WS 429, pp 13–14). 52 Ibid.
53 Ibid., p. 14. 54 Ibid., p. 15.
55 McDermott, *Northern divisions*, p. 109.
56 Fanning, *Fatal path*, pp 264–72.
57 *Daily News*, 30 Aug. 1921; *Manchester Guardian*, 6 Sept. 1921.
58 Fanning, *Fatal path*, pp 266–9.
59 Marginal comments written on Belfast RIC City Commissioner Gelston's report about events at the beginning of September, including O'Duffy's reports about breaches by RIC, indicate a lack of confidence in the police line. RIC city commissioner bi-monthly report, Sept.–Nov. 1921 (TNA, CO 904/151).
60 Farrell, *Arming*, pp 66–7; Patrick Buckland, *The factory of grievances: devolved government in Northern Ireland, 1921–39* (Dublin, 1979), pp 186–9.
61 For the difficulties Craig placed in the way of talks with Sinn Féin see Fanning, *Fatal path*, p. 266.
62 Kenna, *Pogrom*, p. 66. 63 Farrell, *Arming*, pp 68–9.
64 Kenna, *Pogrom*, p. 67; *Irish News*, 24 Sept. 1921.
65 Ibid., 26 Sept. 1921. Kenna, *Pogrom*, p. 68. The main Protestant cemetery in Belfast was the city cemetery at the western end of the Falls Road. As an example of the bitterness and hatred between the two communities in Belfast, when the funerals of the two men killed by

the IRA bomb reached the cemetery, locals attacked the cortège. The IRA opened fire and killed a member of the funeral party, John Orr.

66 Intelligence Officer 3rd Northern Division to IRA GHQ, 26 Oct. 1921, Seán MacEntee to de Valera, 5 Nov. 1921 (UCDA, Mulcahy papers, P7/A/26, 29).

67 Farrell, *Arming*, p. 72.   68 *Belfast Telegraph*, 19 Oct. 1921.

69 *Hansard (Commons)*, 24 Oct. 1921, vol. 147, col. 464.

70 *Belfast Telegraph*, 19 Nov. 1921; *Northern Whig*, 14 Nov. 1921.

71 For a detailed account of the manoeuvring around this phase of the negotiations with SF see Fanning, *Fatal path*, pp 286–300.

72 Ibid., p. 288. Lloyd George deceitfully brushed aside objections from Joe Devlin and Lieutenant Commander Kenworthy MP on 10 November that the orders in council breached clause 72 of the Government of Ireland Act that no transfer of power could be made until the two parliaments of northern and southern Ireland were functioning. *Hansard (Commons)*, 10 Nov. 1921, vol. 148, cols 582–4.

73 Lynch, *The northern IRA*, p. 89; McDermott, *Northern divisions*, p. 141.

74 Farrell, *Arming*, pp 75–7; Kenna, *Pogrom*, p. 83.   75 Farrell, *Arming*, pp 79, 81.

76 Kenna, *Pogrom*, p. 71.

77 Ibid.; *Belfast Telegraph*, 25 Nov. 1921. The tram in Royal Ave. was bombed by an IRA man who had been ordered 'to do two trams', probably in York St. He moved to Royal Ave. because of the presence of Crown forces and threw the device from the front of the Grand Central Hotel. McDermott, *Northern divisions*, p. 130.

78 Ibid.   79 Kenna, *Pogrom*, p. 71.

80 Lynch, *Northern IRA*, p. 89. The Belfast IRA continued to operate the system with no reciprocation until 18 March 1922, McDermott, *Northern divisions*, p. 141.

81 *Irish News*, 10 Dec. 1921; Kenna, *Pogrom*, p. 72.   82 Ibid., 19 Dec. 1921.

83 Ibid., 28 Dec. 1921.

CHAPTER TEN *Endgame: Belfast and Antrim in 1922*

1 Niall Cunningham, 'The doctrine of vicarious punishment: space, religion and the Belfast Troubles of 1920–22', *Journal of Historical Geography*, 40 (2013), 52–66.

2 Aiken et al., *The men will talk to me*, p. 103.

3 Quoted in Phoenix, *Northern nationalism*, p. 170. Several historians have tried to account for Collins's motives in the actions he took about the north, E. Phoenix, 'Michael Collins: the Northern questions, 1916–22' in Gabriel Doherty and Dermot Keogh (eds), *Michael Collins and the making of the Irish state* (Cork 1998); John Regan, *The Irish counter-revolution, 1921–1936* (Dublin, 1999).

4 Aiken et al., *The men will talk to me*, p. 199.   5 Ibid.

6 Grant, *Derry*, pp 132ff.; McCluskey, *Tyrone*, p. 114ff.

7 *Irish News*, 2–6 Jan. 1922; Kenna, *Pogrom*, pp 98–9.

8 McDermott, *Northern divisions*, p. 153.   9 *Irish News*, 11 Jan. 1922.

10 Arthur Hezlet, *The 'B' Specials: a history of the Ulster special constabulary* (London, 1973), p. 58. Those released included the men sentenced to death for their part in the Lappinduff fiasco.

11 *Irish News*, 13 Jan. 1922.   12 Fanning, *Fatal path*, p. 313.

13 Paul Canning, *British policy towards Ireland, 1921–1941* (Oxford, 1985), pp 31–2.

14 John Anthony Gaughan (ed.), *Memoirs of Senator Joseph Connolly* (Dublin, 1996), p. 185. For details of the pact see Michael Hopkinson, 'The Craig–Collins pacts of 1922: two attempted reforms of the Northern Ireland government', *IHS*, 27:106 (1990), 149.

15 The boycott was officially ended on 24 January. Collins said its removal was to give unionists 'a chance of showing goodwill', Phoenix, *Northern nationalism*, p. 176.

16 McCluskey, *Tyrone*, pp 117–19; Grant, *Derry*, pp 130–3.

17 Coogan, *Michael Collins*, p. 346.   18 Ibid., p. 344.

19 Lynch, *Northern IRA*, pp 103–5.   20 Ibid., pp 107–13.

21 Exchange of letters Craig, Churchill, Cope, Collins, 11–15 Feb. 1922 (TNA, CO 906/20).

22 *Belfast Telegraph*, 14 Feb. 1922.   23 *Irish News*, 15 Feb. 1922.

24 Kevin Matthews, *Fatal influence: the impact of Ireland on British politics, 1920–1925* (Dublin, 2004), p. 78.

25 Fanning, *Fatal path*, p. 322.

26 *Hansard (Commons)*, 16 Feb. 1922, vol. 150, cols 1360–4, 1366–72.

27 *Belfast Telegraph*, 14 Feb. 1922.   28 *Irish News*, 13 Feb. 1922.

29 *Belfast Telegraph*, 14 Feb. 1922.   30 *Irish News*, 16 Feb. 1922.

31 For a detailed account of the City Guard, including Ernest Blythe's explanation in his memo on the north 1922–6, see McDermott, *Northern divisions*, pp 172–3.

32 Ibid.   33 Phoenix, *Northern nationalism*, p. 188.

34 Ibid.   35 Roger McCorley (BMH WS 389, pp 34–6).

36 Lynch, *Northern IRA*, p. 117.

37 Florence O'Donoghue, *No other law* (Dublin, 1954), p. 249.

38 RIC bi-monthly report, 31 Mar. 1922 (PRONI, ministry of home affairs files, HA/5/152).

39 *Irish News*, 16 Mar. 1922.   40 St Mary's Hall file (PRONI, HA/32/1/130).

41 Abbott, *Police casualties*, p. 361.   42 *Irish News*, 27 Mar. 1922.

43 For a detailed account of the murders and their aftermath see Baker, *McMahon family murders*; Glenravel Local history Project, www.glenravel.com; Phoenix, *Northern nationalism*, pp 195–7; Parkinson, *Belfast's unholy war*, pp 229–36.

44 *Hansard (Commons)*, 28 Mar. 1922, vol. 152, cols 1281–96.   45 Ibid.

46 Ibid.   47 Ibid.

48 For details see Phoenix, *Northern nationalism*, pp 197–200; Hopkinson, 'Craig–Collins pacts', 149.

49 *Northern Whig*, 3 Apr. 1922.

50 Northern Ireland House of Commons, vol. 2, cols 321–3, 327–8, 343–4.

51 He had spent seventeen years in the Royal Irish Rifles, serving through the Great War. Two of his brothers had been killed in the war and Hall had carried one of his wounded brothers a mile-and-a-half to safety during a battle, Abbott, *Police casualties*, p. 363.

52 *Belfast Telegraph*, 1 Apr. 1922.   53 Abbott, *Police casualties*, p. 363.

54 Kenna, *Pogrom*, pp 121–2; confidential file on DI Nixon, 20 Feb. 1924 (UCDA, Blythe papers, P24/176, pp 4–5).

55 Kenna, *Pogrom*, pp 122–4. G.B. Kenna was the nom de plume of Fr Hassan who witnessed the aftermath.

56 Séamus Woods to Mulcahy, 27 July 1922 (UCDA, Mulcahy papers, P7/B/77).

57 Ibid.   58 Roger McCorley (BMH WS 389, pp 34–5).

59 Ibid., p. 35.   60 Lynch, *Northern IRA*, p. 131.

61 Memo on the North, 1922–6 (UCDA, Blythe papers, P24/554, pp 12–13). The payments were substantial for men who had been unemployed and on the run: £5 a week for divisional officers, £4 10s. for brigade officers, £4 for battalion officers, see McDermott, *Northern divisions*, p. 199.

62 Lynch, *Northern IRA*, p. 134.

63 O'Donoghue, *No other law*, p. 249.

64 Lynch, *Northern IRA*, pp 128–40; Michael Hopkinson, *Green against green: the Irish Civil War* (Dublin, 2004 [1988]); Phoenix, *Northern nationalism*, pp 217–20.

65 Lynch, *Northern IRA*, pp 137–9.   66 *Irish News*, 18 Apr. 1922.

67 Kenna, *Pogrom*, p. 134.   68 Joe Murray (BMH WS 412, p. 25).

69 Roger McCorley (BMH WS 389, p. 29). Tom McNally, quartermaster 3rd Northern, said the figure was 200 rifles per brigade, Aiken et al., *The men will talk to me*, pp 106–7.

70 Although McCorley gave 19 May as the original date for launching the offensive, contemporary documents show it was 2 May, Woods to Mulcahy, 27 July 1922 (UCDA, Mulcahy papers, P7/B/77); Regan, *Irish counter-revolution*, p. 62. Antrim would eventually receive 100 rifles just before the offensive began on 18 May, Tom Fitzpatrick (BMH WS 395, pp 8–9).

71 For details of the confusion see Lynch, *Northern IRA*, pp 140–1.

72 Farrell, *Arming*, p. 128, Lynch, *Northern IRA*, pp 141–3; Aiken et al., *The men will talk to me*, p. 110.

73 McCluskey, *Tyrone*, pp 122–3.

74 Woods to Mulcahy, 19 May 1922 (UCDA, Mulcahy papers, P7a/173).

75 Ibid. McCorley claimed a policeman fired a shot which alerted the sleeping barracks. He does not mention that he shot a policeman, McCorley (BMH WS 389, pp 31–2); Joe Murray (BMH WS 412, pp 25–6); Abbott, *Police casualties*, pp 370–1.

76 McCorley (BMH WS 389, p. 32).

77 *Irish News*, 20 May 1922; *Belfast Telegraph*, 19 May 1922.

78 Damage was estimated at £1,500,000. Lynch, *Northern IRA*, p. 144.

79 *Irish News*, 22 May 1922; *Newsletter*, 22 May 1922.

80 *Irish News*, 20 May 1922. Despite its grand title, the 2nd Brigade amounted at best to fewer than 100 active men. For a detailed account of this short, intense campaign in Antrim see Tom Fitzpatrick (BMH WS 395, pp 9–11) and Felim MacGuill (BMH WS 609, pp 10–13).

81 *Belfast Telegraph*, 20 May 1922; *Irish News*, 22 May 1922.

82 Tom Fitzpatrick (BMH WS 395, p. 10).   83 Ibid., pp 11–12.

84 Mary Fitzpatrick (IMA, MSPC, 3430075); Lena Cunning (IMA, MSPC, 34REF17427).

85 Felim MacGuill (BMH WS 609, p. 13).   86 Ibid., p. 10.

87 Fanning, *Fatal path*, p. 327; Martin Gilbert, *Winston S. Churchill, IV, 1916–1922* (London, 1975), p. 716.

88 Farrell, *Arming*, p. 143.   89 Roger McCorley (BMH WS 389, p. 29).

90 Abbott, *Police casualties*, pp 370–1.   91 Ibid., p. 373.

92 Kenna, *Pogrom*, p. 142.   93 Abbott, *Police casualties*, pp 372–3.

94 *Irish News*, 30 May 1922.

95 Abbott, *Police casualties*, p. 374; McDermott, *Northern divisions*, p. 241.

96 *Irish News*, 1 June 1922.

97 Kenna, *Pogrom*, pp 143–4; *Irish News*, 1 June 1922.

98 Roger McCorley (BMH WS 389, pp 32–3). McCorley was operated on by Dr MacConaill, later professor of anatomy at UCC. Thomas Fitzpatrick (BMH WS 395, pp 13–14).

99 Kenna, *Pogrom*, pp 144–5; *Irish News*, 1, 2 June 1922.

100 Report on No. 2 (Belfast Brigade), 20 July 1922 (UCDA, Mulcahy papers, P7/B/77). Woods claimed there were 'upwards of 50 wounded' on 31 May.

101 Quoted in Farrell, *Arming*, p. 145.

102 *Irish News*, 6 June 1922.

103 Michael Collins has been implicated in ordering Wilson's assassination, but the motivation and instigation remain unresolved despite the extensive literature allocating blame, see Keith Jeffrey, *Field Marshal Sir Henry Wilson: a political soldier* (London, 2006); Coogan, *Michael Collins* (London, 1990); T. Ryle Dwyer, *The squad* (Dublin, 2005).

104 Kenna, *Pogrom*, p. 172; *Irish News*, 24 June 1922.

105 Anna Garson, '"Please give justice": the Cushendall incident, sectarian violence, and Anglo-Irish relations, 1920–22' (BA thesis, University of Pennsylvania, 2017). On 27 July Joe

Devlin successfully asked for an inquiry into the incident because British soldiers were officially in command of the Specials, *Hansard (Commons)*, 27 July 1922, vol. 157, cols 663–4. Nothing came of the inquiry.

106 Jonathan Bardon, *Belfast: an illustrated history* (Belfast, 1982), p. 202. The most detailed recent account of the events is in Parkinson, *Belfast's unholy war*. Anthony C. Hepburn, *Catholic Belfast and nationalist Ireland* (Oxford, 2008) examines the events from a historical geography viewpoint. T. Wilson, *Frontiers of violence: conflict and identity in Ulster and Upper Silesia, 1918–22* (Oxford, 2010) places the casualties in the context of politico-ethnic conflict.

107 Robert Lynch, 'Belfast' in Crowley et al., *Atlas of the Irish Revolution*, p. 630; Townshend, *Republic*, p. 176.

108 It is believed that fewer than a dozen of the original print run survived. The book was reprinted in 1997 and is readily available. It is also available in original format online. Fr Hassan was a member of the Belfast Boycott Committee and later the Northern Advisory Committee in 1922 to advise Michael Collins on northern policy.

109 Townshend, *Republic*, p. 176.

110 Werner Bergmann, 'Pogroms' in Wilhelm Heitmeyer & John Hagan (eds), *International handbook of violence research* (Dordrecht, 2003), pp 351–67.

111 *OED*.   112 Ibid.

113 *Daily News*, 1 Sept. 1920.

114 *Hansard (Commons)*, 25 Oct. 1920, vol. 133, col. 1329.

115 Bergmann, 'Pogroms', p. 351.

116 Cunningham, 'Doctrine of vicarious punishment', 52–66.

117 Lynch, 'Belfast', p. 630.

118 For details of IRA fatalities taken from the MSPC see Kieran Glennon, 'The boys of the old brigade – the IRA 3rd Northern Division', theirishstory.com. 5 June 2018.

119 Lynch, 'Belfast'.

120 See Devlin's detailed account of the role of USC in Belfast and Lisburn riots, *Hansard (Commons)*, 25 Oct. 1920, vol. 133, cols 1505–6.

121 Donald L. Horowitz, *The deadly ethnic riot* (Berkeley & Los Angeles, 2001).

122 Brendan O'Leary, *A treatise on Northern Ireland*, vol. 2, *Control* (Oxford, 2019), p. 28.

Select bibliography

PRIMARY SOURCES

A. MANUSCRIPTS

Armagh
Cardinal Ó Fiaich Memorial Library & Archive
Cardinal Michael Logue papers.
Cardinal Joseph MacRory papers.

Belfast
Public Records Office of Northern Ireland
Abercorn papers.
Antrim papers.
J.B. Armour papers.
Belfast UVF papers.
Cabinet secretariat.
Craigavon political papers.
Crawford papers.
Ministry of Home Affairs.
Ministry of Home Affairs, secret series.
Ulster Unionist Council papers.

Dublin
Military Archives
3rd Northern Division reports, 1921–2.
Belfast, Antrim & East Down Brigade reports, 1919–21.
Bureau of Military History witness statements.
IRA nominal rolls.
Military Service Pensions Collection.

National Library of Ireland
Seán O'Mahony papers.

University College Dublin Archives
Ernest Blythe papers.
Richard Mulcahy papers.
Ernie O'Malley papers & notebooks.
Eoin O'Neill papers.
Sinn Féin minutes, 1919–22.

London
The National Archives
Cabinet papers.
Colonial Office papers.
Home Office papers.

B. OFFICIAL RECORDS

Census of Ireland, 1901–11.
Dáil Éireann debates, 1919–22.
Hansard House of Commons parliamentary debates.
Report of the 1911 census, Province of Ulster, County Antrim (London, 1911).
Royal Irish Constabulary and Dublin Metropolitan Police. Appendix to the Report of the Committee of Inquiry, 1914 (Cd. 7637).

C. NEWSPAPERS AND PERIODICALS

Andersonstown News
An Phoblacht
Belfast Newsletter
Daily Mail
Daily News
Freeman's Journal
Irish Bulletin
Irish Freedom

Irish Independent
Irish News
Irish Times
London Daily News
London Morning Post
Manchester Guardian
Northern Whig
Times

D. PRINTED PRIMARY MATERIAL

Gaughan, J. Anthony (ed.), *The memoirs of Constable Jeremiah Mee RIC* (Cork, 2012 [1975]).
—— (ed.), *Memoirs of Senator Joseph Connolly* (Dublin, 1996).
Kenna, G.B., *Facts and figures of the Belfast pogrom, 1920–22* (Dublin, 1922).

SECONDARY SOURCES

E. PUBLISHED WORKS

Abbott, Richard, *Police casualties in Ireland, 1919–1922* (Cork, 2000).
Adgey, R.J., *Arming the Ulster Volunteers, 1914* (Belfast, 1952).
Aiken, Síobhra, Fearghal Mac Bhloscaidh, Liam Ó Duibhir & Diarmuid Ó Tuama (eds), *The men will talk to me: Ernie O'Malley's interviews with the Northern Divisions* (Kildare, 2018).
Bardon, Jonathan, *A history of Ulster* (2nd ed., Belfast, 2005).
——, *Belfast: a century* (Belfast, 1999).
Bartlett, Thomas, 'Defence, counter-insurgency and rebellion: Ireland, 1793–1803' in Thomas Bartlett & Keith Jeffrey (eds), *A military history of Ireland* (Cambridge, 1996), pp 247–93.
Bergmann, Werner, 'Pogroms' in Wilhelm Heitmeyer & John Hagan (eds), *International handbook of violence research* (Dordrecht, 2003), pp 351–67.

Bew, Paul, *Conflict and conciliation in Ireland, 1890–1910: Parnellites and radical agrarians* (Oxford, 1987).

Borgonovo, John, *Florence and Josephine O'Donoghue's War of Independence* (Dublin & Portland, 2006).

Bowman, Timothy, 'The UVF and the formation of the 36th (Ulster) Division', *IHS*, 32:128 (2001), 498–518.

——, 'The Ulster Volunteers 1913–14: force or farce', *History Ireland*, 1:10 (2002), 43–7.

——, *Carson's army, the Ulster Volunteer Force, 1910–22* (Manchester, 2007).

Brett, Charles, *Buildings of Belfast, 1700–1914* (Belfast, 1985).

Brewer, John D., *The Royal Irish Constabulary: an oral history* (Belfast, 1990).

Brock, Michael and Eleanor Brock (eds), *H.H. Asquith, letters to Venetia Stanley* (Oxford, 1982).

Brooke, Peter, *Ulster Presbyterianism: the historical perspective* (Dublin, 1987).

Buckland, Patrick, *Irish unionism: the Anglo-Irish and the new Ireland, 1885–1923: a documentary history* (Dublin, 1972).

——, *Irish unionism, 1885–1923: a documentary history* (London, 1973).

——, *The factory of grievances: devolved government in Northern Ireland, 1921–39* (Dublin, 1979).

——, *James Craig: Lord Craigavon* (Dublin, 1980).

Callanan, Frank, *T.M. Healy* (Cork, 1996).

Canning, Paul, *British policy towards Ireland, 1921–1941* (Oxford, 1985).

Cawood, Ian, *The Liberal Unionist Party: a history* (London, 2012).

Coleman, Marie, *The Irish revolution, 1916–23* (Abingdon, 2013).

Colvin, Ian, *The life of Lord Carson* (3 vols, London, 1934).

Coogan, Tim Pat, *Michael Collins* (London, 1990).

Crowley, John, Donal Ó Drisceoil, Mike Murphy & John Borgonovo (eds), *Atlas of the Irish Revolution* (Cork, 2017).

Cunningham, Niall, 'The doctrine of vicarious punishment: space, religion and the Belfast Troubles of 1920–22', *Journal of Historical Geography*, 40 (2013), 52–66.

——, 'The social geography of violence during the Belfast Troubles, 1920–22', CRESC Working Paper No. 122, Manchester, Mar. 2013.

Dangerfield, George, *The damnable question: a study in Anglo-Irish relations* (London, 1977).

Elliott, Marianne, *The Catholics of Ulster: a history* (London, 2000).

Elliott, Sydney, *Northern Ireland parliamentary election results, 1921–72* (Chichester, 1973).

Ervine, St John, *Craigavon: Ulsterman* (London, 1949).

Fanning, Ronan, *Fatal path: British government and the Irish revolution, 1910–1922* (London, 2013).

Farrell, Michael, *Arming the Protestants: the formation of the Ulster Special Constabulary and the Royal Ulster Constabulary, 1920–27* (London, 1983).

Feeney, Brian, *Sinn Féin: a hundred turbulent years* (Dublin, 2002).

——, *Seán Mac Diarmada* (Dublin, 2014).

Finley Bowman, Rachel E., 'An ideal Unionist: the political career of Theresa, marchioness of Londonderry, 1911–19', *Journal of International Women's Studies*, 4:3 (2003), 15–29.

Fitzpatrick, David, *The two Irelands: 1912–1939* (Oxford, 1998).

Follis, Bryan A., *A state under siege: the establishment of Northern Ireland, 1920–1925* (Oxford, 1995).

Foy, Michael, 'Ulster unionism and the development of the Ulster Volunteer Force' in Jürgen Elvert (ed.), *Nordirland in Geschichte und Gegenwart* (Stuttgart, 1994), pp 99–127.

——, 'Ulster unionist propaganda against home rule, 1912–14', *History Ireland*, 4:1 (1996), 49–53.

Garvin, Tom, *Nationalist revolutionaries in Ireland, 1891–1922* (Oxford, 1987).

——, *The evolution of Irish nationalist politics* (Dublin, 2005 [1981]).

Gibbons, Ivan, *The British Labour Party and the establishment of the Irish Free State, 1918–24* (London, 2015).

Gilbert, Martin, *Winston S. Churchill, vol. iv: world in torment, 1916–22* (London, 1975).

Grant, Adrian, *Derry: the Irish Revolution, 1912–23* (Dublin, 2019).

Grayson, Richard, *Belfast Boys: how unionists and nationalists fought and died together in the First World War* (London, 2009).

Haines, Keith, *Fred Crawford: Carson's gunrunner* (Donaghadee, 2009).

Hepburn, A.C., *A past apart: studies in the history of Catholic Belfast, 1850–1950* (Belfast, 1996).

——, *Catholic Belfast and nationalist Ireland in the era of Joe Devlin, 1871–1934* (Oxford, 2008).

Hezlet, Arthur, *The 'B' Specials: a history of the Ulster Special Constabulary* (London, 1972).

Hittle, J.B.E., *Michael Collins and the Anglo-Irish War: Britain's counterinsurgency failure* (Washington, DC, 2011).

Hobson, Bulmer, *Yesterday, today and tomorrow* (Tralee, 1968).

Holmes, Janice & Diane Urquhart (eds), *Coming into the light: work, politics and religion of women in Ulster, 1840–1940* (Belfast, 1994).

Hopkinson, Michael, *Green against green: the Irish Civil War* (Dublin, 2004 [1988]).

——, 'The Craig–Collins pacts of 1922: two attempted reforms of the Northern Ireland government', *IHS*, 27:106 (1990), 145–58.

Horowitz, Donald L., *The deadly ethnic riot* (Berkeley & Los Angeles, 2001).

Hughes, Brian, *Defying the IRA? Intimidation, coercion and communities during the Irish Revolution* (Liverpool, 2016).

Hyde, H. Montgomery, *Carson, the life of Sir Edward Carson* (London, 1953).

Jackson, Alvin, 'Craig, James' in James McGuire and James Quinn (eds), *Dictionary of Irish biography* (Cambridge, 2009).

——, *Ireland, 1798–1998: politics and war* (Oxford, 1999).

——, *Home rule: an Irish history, 1800–2000* (London, 2003).

Jeffrey, Keith, *Field Marshal Sir Henry Wilson: a political soldier* (Oxford, 2006).

Kostick, Conor, *Revolution in Ireland: popular militancy, 1917–1923* (London, 1996).

Laffan, Michael, 'The unification of Sinn Féin in 1917', *IHS*, 17 (1971), 353–79.

——, *The resurrection of Ireland: the Sinn Féin party, 1916–23* (Cambridge, 2005).

Lawlor, Pearse, *The burnings 1920* (Cork, 2009).

Lynch, John, *An unlikely success story: the Belfast shipbuilding industry, 1880–1935* (Belfast, 2001).

Lynch, Robert, *The northern IRA and the early years of partition, 1920–22* (Dublin, 2006).

——, 'The People's protectors? The Irish Republican Army and the "Belfast Pogrom" 1920–22', *Journal of British Studies*, 47:2 (2008), 375–91.

——, 'Belfast' in Crowley et al. (eds), *Atlas of the Irish Revolution*, pp 630–5.

Lyons, F.S.L., *John Dillon: a biography* (London, 1965).

McCarthy, Pat, *Waterford: the Irish Revolution, 1912–23* (Dublin, 2018).

McCluskey, Fergal, *Tyrone: the Irish Revolution, 1912–23* (Dublin, 2014).

McColgan, John, *British policy and the Irish administration, 1920–22* (London, 1983).

McCullagh, David, *De Valera: rise, 1882–1932* (Dublin, 2017).

McDermott, Jim, *Northern divisions: the old IRA and the Belfast pogroms, 1920–22* (Belfast, 2001).

McGarry, Fearghal, *Eoin O'Duffy: a self-made hero* (Oxford, 2005).

McKenna, John, *A beleaguered station: the memoir of Head Constable John McKenna* (Belfast, 2009).

McKeever, Gerry (ed.), *Up The Falls* (Belfast, 1988).

McMinn, J.R.B. (ed.), *Against the tide: a calendar of the papers of Rev. J.B. Armour: Irish Presbyterian and home ruler, 1869–1914* (Belfast, 1985).

McNally, Jack, *Morally good: politically bad* (Belfast, 1987).

Macaulay, Ambrose, *Patrick McAlister, bishop of Down and Connor, 1886–95* (Dublin, 2006).

Mansergh, Nicholas, *The unresolved question: the Anglo-Irish settlement and its undoing, 1912–72* (New Haven, CT, 1991).

Maume, Patrick, 'T.H. Sloan 1870–1941' in James Quinn & Patrick Maume (eds), *Ulster political lives* (Dublin, 2009), pp 285–91.

Mercer, Eric, 'For king, country and a shilling a day: Belfast recruiting patterns in the Great War', *History Ireland*, 11:4 (2003), 29–33.

Morgan, Austen, *Labour and partition: the Belfast working class, 1905–23* (London, 1990).

Morrissey, Conor, '"Rotten Protestants"': Protestant home rulers and the Ulster Liberal Association, 1906–1918', *Historical Journal* (published online 2017), 1–23.

Munck, Ronaldo, 'Class and religion in Belfast – a historical perspective', *Journal of Contemporary History*, 20:2 (1985), 241–59.

Murphy, R., 'Walter Long and the making of the Government of Ireland Act, 1919–20' *IHS*, 97 (1986), 211–35.

National Graves Association, *Antrim's patriot dead, 1797–1953* (Belfast, 1966).

O'Donoghue, Florence, *No other law* (Dublin, 1954).

O'Leary, Brendan, *A treatise on Northern Ireland* (3 vols, Oxford, 2019).

Parkinson, Alan F., *Belfast's unholy war: the troubles of the 1920s* (Dublin, 2004).

——, *Friends in high places: Ulster's resistance to Irish home rule, 1912–14* (Belfast, 2012).

Patterson, Henry, 'Independent Orangeism and class conflict in Edwardian Belfast', *Proceedings of the Royal Irish Academy*, 80, Sect. C, 1 (1980), 1–27.

Phoenix, Eamon, *Northern nationalism: nationalist politics, partition and the Catholic minority in Northern Ireland* (Belfast, 1994).

——, *Feis na nGleann* (Belfast, 2005).

Radford, Mark, '"Closely akin to actual warfare": the Belfast riots of 1886 and the RIC', *History Ireland*, 7:4 (1999), 27–31.

Regan, John M., *The Irish counter-revolution, 1921–1936* (Dublin, 2001).

Sheehan, William, 'The British army in Ireland' in Crowley et al. (eds), *Atlas of the Irish Revolution*, pp 363–70.

Stewart, A.T.Q., *The Ulster crisis: resistance to home rule, 1912–14* (London, 1967).

Townshend, Charles, *The British campaign in Ireland: 1919–21* (Oxford, 1975).

——, 'The Irish Republican Army and the development of guerrilla warfare, 1916–1921', *English Historical Review*, 94:371 (1979), 318–45.

——, *The Republic: the fight for Irish independence, 1918–1923* (London, 2013).

Walker, Brian M. (ed.), *Parliamentary election results in Ireland, 1801–1922* (Dublin, 1978).

Ward, Margaret, *Unmanageable revolutionaries: women and Irish nationalism* (London, 1983).

——, *The women of Belfast and Cumann na mBan: Easter Week and after* (Belfast, 2016).

Yeates, Padraig, 'Dublin' in Crowley et al. (eds), *Atlas of the Irish Revolution*, pp 588–95.

——, '"Have you in Ireland all gone mad?", the 1918 General Strike against conscription', *Saothar*, 43 (2018), 47–53.

F. THESES AND UNPUBLISHED WORK

Garson, Anna, '"Please Give Justice": The Cushendall incident, sectarian violence and Anglo-Irish relations, 1920–22' (BA thesis, University of Pennsylvania, 2017).

G. INTERNET SOURCES

www.36thulster.com/north-antrim-uvf.html
www.quincey.info.
Ulster Covenant online, PRONI: http: // www.proni.go.uk/

Index

Abercorn, *see* Hamilton
Adair, Major-General Sir William, 23
Aherne, Dr Leo 'Stetto', 69
Aiken, Frank, O/C 4th Northern
   Division, 113, 126
Ancient Order of Hibernians (AOH), 19,
   20, 29, 32, 45, 46, 48, 51, 97,111, 112
Antrim, 1, 7, 10, 11, 23, 25, 27, 30;
   Antrim Brigade; *see* IRA; economy, 2;
   GAA, 8; geography, 1; Glens of, 1, 2,
   14, 27, 28, 92, 97, 141; population 3;
   religion, 2; Westminster constituencies,
   14
Ardoyne, 4, 48, 72, 74, 95, 108, 116, 127
Armour, Revd John A., 28
Arnold-Foster, Hugh Oakley, MP, 12
Arnon Street, 136–7
Asquith, H.H., 15, 22, 36, 43
Auxiliaries, 90, 91

Ballycastle, 1, 28, 57, 96, 104, 106, 118,
   141; IRA company, 97–102; Irish
   Volunteers, 36; conscription crisis, 53–4;
   RIC barracks, 100
Balfour, Arthur, 17, 39, 46, 76
Ballymena, 2, 3, 103, 104, 106, 140, 141,
   142, 144; newspapers, 9; RIC barracks,
   100
Ballymacarrett, 60, 65, 78
Ballymoney, 2, 9, 25, 28, 103, 104, 141
Balmoral, Royal Ulster Agricultural
   Showgrounds, 18–19, 25, 34
Banbridge, 58, 76, 86, 147
Bann, River, 1, 10, 30, 47, 123
Barnes, Councillor Denis, 82, 95
Bates, Richard Dawson, hon. sec. UUC,
   18, 52, 64, 119, 120, 121
Belfast, 10,18, 23, 25, Belfast Boycott, 85–
   7; Belfast Celtic, 7; Celtic Park, 7;
   cinemas, 7; economy, industry, 3;
   engineering strike, 52–3; GAA, 8;
   geography, 4; housing, 6–7; Linfield
   FC, 7; literacy, 7; population, 2–3;

railways, 3; schools, 7; shipyards, 3;
   Westminster constituencies 11–12
Beechfield Street, 65, 66
Belfast City Guard, *see* IRA
Belfast Newsletter, 8, 9, 57, 105
Belfast Protestant Association, 12
Belfast Telegraph, 9, 57, 85, 110, 122, 129
Bigger, Francis Joseph, 27
Birrell Augustine, 19, 22
Black and Tans, 62, 76, 88, 90, 91, 92, 102
Black Mountain, 41, 69
Blythe, Ernest, 32, 85, 86, 132
Boland, Harry, 86
Bombay Street, 65, 67
Bonar Law, Andrew, 17, 18, 19, 21, 39,
   46, 76
Bone (The) or Marrowbone (The), Belfast,
   4, 48; houses burnt, 139
Boyle, Lizzie, 98, 99
Brown Square RIC barracks, 78
Brugha, Cathal, 69
Bryson Street, 65, 78
Byrne, Paddy, 82

Campbell, Joseph, 27
Carney, Winifred, 50, 55
Carnlough, 1, 98, 99, 100
Carolan, Michael, 95
Castlereagh, Lord, 23
Carson, Edward, 17, 18, 21, 24, 28, 34, 35,
   36, 39, 40, 46, 52, 57, 58, 62, 75, 76,
   100, 148
Carrick Hill, Belfast, 4, 75, 93, 114, 143,
   147; USC assault, 116
Carrickmore, 42, 88
Castledawson, 19, 20, 35
Celtic Park, 7, 30
Chamberlain, Colonel Sir Neville,
   inspector-general RIC, 22
Churchill, Winston, 30, 62, 127, 128, 129,
   131, 135, 141
Clark, Sir Ernest, 77, 84, 93
Clark, George MP, 11, 18

Clark, Tom, 40
Clarke, Sergeant Charles, RIC, 83
Clarke, Constable Joe, RIC, 78
Clifton Street, 131, 132
Clonard, 41, 1, 60, 64, 65, 66, 67, 74, 110,
    112, 116, 127
Cloughmills, 97, 98, 105
Coalisland, 41, 42, 96
Cody, Jack, 69
Collins, Michael, 68, 69, 82, 86, 94, 124,
    125, 126, 127, 128, 129, 132, 133, 134,
    136, 137, 138, 141, 143
Connolly, James, 12, 41, 42, 50
Connolly, Ina, 42
Connolly, Nora, 42
Conway Street, 81
Cope, Andy, 119, 120, 121, 129
Corkey, 98, 105
Cotton, Alf, 33
Covenant, Ulster, 22, 23, 25
Cowzer, Richard, 18
Craig, Charles, MP, 14, 21
Craig, Sir James, MP, 14, 16, 17, 18, 22,
    24, 34, 58, 62, 63, 113, 117, 119, 121,
    122, 123, 129, 142, 144; Craig-Collins
    pacts, 128, 135–6; mobilizes USC 1921;
    plan for special constabulary, 76; prime
    minister Northern Ireland, 107; Special
    Powers Act, 134
Crawford, Frederick, 16, 24, 72, 122;
    gunrunning 17–18
Crumlin, 2
Crumlin Road, 75, 90, 109
Crummey, Frank, 85, 115, 143
Culhane, Seán, 58, 69, 70, 71
Cullen, Seamus, 33
Cullybackey, 100
Cumann na mBan, 16, 50, 98, 99, 104,
    106, 141; *see also* Boyle, Lizzie; Carney,
    Winifred; Cunning, Lena; Fitzpatrick,
    Maggie; Fitzpatrick, Mary; McCullagh,
    Agnes; Neeson, Nellie; Ward, Annie
Cunning, Brian, 98
Cunning, Lena (née McCamphill), 98, 99,
    141
Cunningham, James, 18
Cupar Street, 64, 109, 112
Cusack, Seán, 33, 35, 36, 37

Cushendall, 28, 73, 145; IRA company,
    54, 97–9.
Cushendun, 27, 99, 140, 141

Delaney, Elizabeth, 51
Dempsey, Patrick, 31, 45
Dempsey, Seán, 33
Derrytresk, 42
Devlin, Bernard, 65
Devlin Joe, MP, 8, 11, 32, 37, 38, 46, 63,
    71, 78, 111, 112, 113, 131, 134, 135;
    election 1918, 51–2; election 1921, 94–6;
    Irish Volunteers, 35–7; MacMahon
    murders, 134–5; partition conference
    1916, 44–5; RIC reprisals, 111–3;
    shipyard expulsions, 20–1
de Valera, Eamon, 51, 52, 88, 94, 113,
    119, 120, 132, 136
Dillon, John, MP, 30, 43, 51
Divis Street, 31, 41, 51, 52, 131, 142
Dobbyn, Seamus, 33, 102
Donaghy, E. & Sons, 71
Downpatrick, 68
Duffin, Dan, John, Patrick, 91, 92
Dungannon, 2
Dungannon Clubs, 31, 32, 96
Dunloy, 97, 98, 103, 104, 105, 140
Dunmurry RIC barracks, 105

Fair Head, 104
Falls Road, Belfast, 4, 6, 7, 8, 29, 31, 33,
    37, 52, 79, 81, 109, 112, 116, 139, 142,
    144
Fanning, Ronan, 40, 77
Feis na nGleann, 27, 28
Feis Uladh, 31
Ferris, DI RIC, 92
Feystown, 98
Finaghy, 57, 58
Finn, Seamus, 92
Finnegan, Francis, 65
Fitzpatrick, Maggie, 90
Fitzpatrick (née O'Loan), Mary, 98, 99,
    141
Fitzpatrick, Thomas, alias Bob
    McDonnell, 48, 105–6, 115, 137, 138,
    140, 143
Flynn, Thomas, 79, 108, 115, 118

Fox, Aloysius, 55
Fox, Ignatius, 82
Fox, Tom, 69, 70, 92

GAA (Gaelic Athletic Association), 8, 31, 48
Gaelic League, 8, 31, 34
Gaynor, Liam 33, 82, 86
Gaynor, Seán, 82, 83, 109
Gelston, J.F., RIC commissioner, 112, 120, 127
Giff, head constable, RIC, 83
Gilmartin, sergeant, RIC, 89
Glarryford, 104
Glenann, 98
Glenariffe, 1, 27, 73 145; Gaeltacht, 27; IRA company, 97–9
Glenarm, 97, 98, 143
Glendun, 27
Glennon, Tom, 102, 104, 105, 106
Glenravel, 54, 92, 97, 98, 99, 100, 101, 106
Glenravel Street, 63
Gleichen, Brigadier-General Lord, 17
Glover, Sergeant, RIC, 83, 109, 110
Government of Ireland Act 1920, 78, 93, 94, 107, 117, 123, 149
Grant, William, MP, 117
Greenwood, Sir Hamar, chief secretary, 119
Griffith, Arthur, 32, 50, 86

Halfpenny, Malachy, 111, 112
Hall, Captain Frank, 18
Hamill Street, 81
Hamilton, James, 3rd duke of Abercorn, 11
Hannahstown, 41, 69
Harland, Edward, MP, 11
Harland & Wolff, 3, 12, 19, 21, 59, 114
Harrison, DI, RIC, 82, 90
Haskins, Rory, 33
Hassan, Fr John, alias G.B. Kenna, 85, 145, 146
Healy, Tim, 30, 39
Heffron, Constable, RIC, 89
Heron, Archie, 33
Heron, Sam, 33
Hicks, Sergeant, RIC, 83

Hobson, Bulmer, 8, 31, 32, 53, 96
Holmes, County Inspector, RIC, 22
Holywood, 4, 5, 6, 71
home rule, 15, 18, 36, 45
Horne, Robert MP, 76

Imperial Guards, 122, 123, 142
Independent Orange Order, 12
IRA, Irish Republican Army, 67–8, 81, 83, 86, 88, 97, 103, 104, 108, 114, 131, 138, 144, 145, 147; Antrim Brigade, 36, 54, 56, 97, 104, 105, 106, 125, 128, 139, 140; May 1922 operation, 141,142; organization, 54, 97–8; training camp, 118; Belfast Brigade, 56, 60, 66, 67, 81–2, 89, 108, 117–18, 123, 125, 128, 145; attack on Musgrave Street RIC, 140; Belfast City Guard,132; burning tax offices, 55, 78–9; defending Ballymacarrett; defending west Belfast, 79–80, 93; Lappinduff, 92; leadership split, 137–8, 139; St Mary's Hall raid, 133–4; truce, 116; 3rd Northern Division, 54, 78, 99, 108, 118, 125, 132, 133, 139, 142, 144; formation, 88; leadership split, 137–8; organization, 48–9, 54, 104; 139, 142, 144; Raglan Street ambush, 115–16; weapons, 101–2, 106
IRB (Irish Republican Brotherhood), 7, 28, 30, 31, 32, 33, 37, 40, 41, 67, 82, 132
Irish Parliamentary Party (IPP), 8, 15, 19, 29, 30, 32, 36, 45, 47, 48, 57, 81, 94, 95, 108
Irish News, 8, 9, 43, 44, 45, 51, 54, 59, 72, 121, 123, 143, 146
Irish Volunteers, 34, 35, 36; Belfast, 41, 42, 43, 47; Tyrone, 41, 42
ITUC/ILP, 49, 50

Johnson, Thomas, 49, 50
Jones, Jack, MP, 113

Kashmir Road, 64, 110, 112
Keenan, Seán, 91
Kerr, William, 111, 112
King George V, 107, 113

Lagan, River, 1, 4, 6, 59
Lambeg, 72
Lansbury, George, MP, 19
Lansdowne, Lord, 46
Lappinduff, 92
Larne, 2, 9, 18, 27, 35, 56, 71, 103
Leonard, Seán, 70
Leonard, Constable Thomas, RIC, 81, 82
Lester, Seán, 33
Liberal government 15, 19
Liberal Unionist, 14, 28
Ligoniel, 72, 111
Lisburn, 2, 8, 24, 54, 58, 60, 68–9, 78, 86,
    97, 105, 142, 147; arson of town, 70–3;
    population, 72
Listowel, 58
Lloyd George, David, 43, 44, 45, 46, 68,
    76, 88, 93, 107, 113, 119, 122, 129, 130
Logue, Michael Cardinal, 44
Londonderry, *see* Stewart Vane-Tempest-
    Stewart
Londonderry, Theresa, marchioness, 16–
    17
Long, Walter, MP, 17, 39, 46, 113
Loughguile, 54, 56, 97, 98, 99, 101, 103,
    104, 105, 106
Lough Neagh, 1, 2, 30, 41, 97, 140
Lynch, Robert, 89, 145
Lynn, Willie John, 98, 99, 101

MacCracken, Henry Joy, 27
Macready, General Sir Cecil Frederick
    Nevil, GOC Ireland, 62
Mac Curtain, Tomás, 54, 68, 69, 92
Mac Diarmada, Seán, 31, 32, 33, 34, 40,
    41
MacDonald, Ramsay, MP, 21
Mac Guill, Feidhlim, 54, 97, 117, 140, 141
MacRory, Bishop Joseph, 44, 45, 85, 92,
    125, 130, 131, 135, 136, 148
MacEntee, Seán, 48, 85, 89, 94, 95
Mackies (engineering factory), 6, 37, 59,
    64, 65, 86
MacNeill, Eoin, 27, 34, 40, 42, 143
Maghera, 19
Mansergh, Nicholas, 16
Martinstown, 92, 98, 99, 140, 141
McAllister, James, 144, 145

McBride, Alexander, 110, 112
McCalmont, Colonel James, MP, 14
McCalmont, Robert, MP, 14
McCammon, Colonel, 24
McCartan, Dr Pat., 42
McCarthy, Sergeant Maurice (Matt), RIC,
    68, 69
McCartney, Seán, 92
McConnell, J.J., DI RIC, 79, 117
McCorley, Roger, 55, 56, 67, 68, 69, 70,
    78, 80, 83, 89, 90, 91, 92, 108, 109, 115,
    116, 125, 137, 138, 139, 140, 143
McCotter, Revd, 45
McCullen, Agnes, 50
McCullough, Denis, 27, 31, 34, 35, 36, 37,
    82, 96, 132, 144; Belfast Boycott, 85;
    Belfast IRB, 32–3; Easter Rising,
    Coalisland, 41–3; election 1921, 94–5;
    president, Supreme Council IRB, 40
McDermott, Jim, 75
McDevitt, Daniel, 55, 90
McFadden, Seán, 82, 83, 109
McHugh, Bishop Charles, 44
McKay, Charles, 52, 59
McKelvey, Joe, 55, 67, 68, 69, 78, 83, 88,
    89, 103, 104, 106, 126, 132, 137, 138
McKenna, Seamus, 48, 55, 79, 89, 90, 92,
    109
McLogan, Paddy, 54, 97–8, 99, 102
McMahon, Owen, 112, 134, 135
McMullan, Liam, 36, 53, 54, 100, 101,
    103
McNulty, Constable, RIC, 79
McSweeney, Con, 69
McVeagh, Jeremiah, MP, 44
Markets (The), Belfast, 4, 48, 54, 56, 60,
    64, 65, 121, 142
Markievicz, Countess, 48, 86
Millfield, 136, 143
Moneyglass, 102
Montgomery, Seán, 91, 115
Morgan, Brother, 65
Mountpottinger Road, 74
Mountpottinger RIC barracks, 79
Mulcahy, Richard, 69, 92, 126, 134, 137,
    138
Murphy, Dick, 69, 70, 71
Murray, Joseph, 79, 80, 83, 89, 140

Na Fianna Éireann, 31, 33
Neeson (née O'Boyle), Nellie, 50
Newtownards Road, 66, 74
Nixon, John William, DI RIC, 90, 111, 115, 127, 134
Noade, Margaret, 65
Nolan, Revd John, 45
Norfolk Regiment, 64, 65, 71, 73, 132
North Street, 75
Northern Whig, 9, 57

O'Boyle, Manus, 78, 79
O'Boyle, Neal John, 30, 31
O'Brien, Bill, 55
O'Brien, William, 30
O'Connell, W.H., deputy inspector-general RIC, 22
O'Connor, T.P., MP, 81, 111, 112, 113
O'Donoghue, Florence, 138
O'Duffy, Eoin, 92, 104, 129, 133, 137, 138; establishes 3rd Northern Division, 88; and Northern Command, 126; truce liaison officer, 117–20
O'Hare, Andy, lieutenant, IRA, 81
O'Leary, Brendan, 149
O'Malley, Ernie, 97, 126
O'Neill, Arthur Edward Bruce, MP, 14, 23
O'Neill, Joe, 42
O'Neill, Seán, 108, 138
O'Neill, Terence, 14
O'Shannon, Cathal, 33, 34
O'Sullivan, Seán, 33
Old Lodge Road, 75, 92, 114, 132, 143, 147
Oldpark Road, 75
Orange Order, 12, 16, 21, 29, 116, 117
Osborne, Harry, 33
Osborne, Patrick, 33

Pain, Colonel George William Hackett, chief of staff UVF, 18, 24, 63, 64, 71, 76
Pakenham, Head Constable, RIC, 83, 90
Parliament Act 1911, 15, 16
Pim, Herbert Moore, 33
Portadown, 2, 4
Portglenone, 97

Portrush, 2
Presbyterian, 1, 2, 9, 10, 11, 14, 27, 28

Quinn, Constable, RIC, 89

Raglan Street, 115, 116
Railway Hotel, *see* Roddy's
Rasharkin, 103
Rathlin Island, 1, 27, 118
Redmond, John, MP, 15, 23, 30, 32, 38, 39, 43, 45, 46; Woodenbridge, 36, 37
RIC, 16, 22, 25, 37, 41, 43, 48, 50, 55, 57, 58, 63, 64, 67, 70, 73, 81, 90, 91, 110; County Antrim districts, 5; numbers, 5; Belfast districts, 5; reprisals, 82–3, 110–12, 134–5
Richardson, Lieutenant-General Sir George, 18, 24
Rodgers, Hugh, 41
Roddy's Hotel or Railway Hotel, 89

Sailortown (Docks), Belfast, 4, 6, 110, 112, 113, 120, 123, 140, 147
Scotland, 1, 28
Seaforde Street, 65, 66, 108
Shaw, Councillor William, 71
Short Strand, 4, 48, 54, 60, 67, 81, 93, 95, 108, 120, 121, 123, 139, 147; loyalist assaults, 64–6, 74, 78–9
Sinn Féin, 10, 11, 32, 33, 36, 43 46, 47, 54, 67, 70, 71, 93, 108, 111, 113, 114, 122, 148; growth in support, 48; anti-conscription, 50; 1918 election, 51–3; local government elections 1920, 57; 1921 elections, 94–6
Somerset Light Infantry, 71
Springfield Road, 74, 86, 111, 112; RIC barracks, 92
Smyth, Colonel G.B.F., RIC, 58, 68
Staines, Michael, TD, 86
Stewart, Charles, Vane-tempest-Stewart, 6th marquess of Londonderry, 11, 16, 22
Sturdy, Thomas, USC, 112
Sandy Row, 7, 144
Savage, Councillor Archie, 95
Shankill Road district, 6, 60, 64, 65, 67, 74, 75, 90, 92, 111, 123, 147

Shiels, Henry, 33
Sisley, DI, RIC, 66
Skeffington, Algernon William John
  Clotworthy, Viscount Massereene, 24
Sloan, Thomas, MP, 12
Smithfield, 6
Spender, Captain Wilfrid, 18, 58, 77
St Mary's Hall, Belfast, 35, 37, 44, 46, 48,
  51, 72, 117; USC raid, 133, 134, 137,
  139
St Matthew's church, 65, 66, 74, 126
Stranraer, 2
Swanzy, Oswald, DI RIC, 68, 69, 70, 72,
  73, 74, 80, 148

Tennant Street, 75
Titanic, 19
Tomney, James, 41
Toome/Toomebridge, 30, 97, 102, 106,
  140
Torr Head, 101, 104
Townsend Street, Belfast, 4
Townshend, Charles, 49, 102, 145
Trodden, Edward 'Ned', 82, 83, 109
Tudor, General Sir Henry Hugh, RIC, 62,
  119, 121
Turley, Dan, 33
Twaddell, William, MP, 142

Ulster Brigade, 64
Ulster Clubs, 16, 19, 20, 21, 22
Ulster Liberal Association, 28
Ulster, Plantation of, 1
Ulster-Scots, 1
Ulster Special Constabulary (USC), 4, 60,
  80, 81, 93, 103, 104, 105, 106, 107, 108,
  112, 116, 120, 122, 123, 125, 140, 142,
  147, 148; Arnon Street massacre, 136–7;
  assault on Millfield and Carrick Hill
  143; attacks on Ardoyne, 127; 'Clones
  affray', 129; Cushendall murders, 144–5;
  establishment of, 77; occupy west

Belfast, 144; offences in Lisburn and
  Belfast, 78; murder gangs, 79; St Mary's
  Hall raid, 133–4; sweep of the Glens,
  141
Ulster Unionists, 11, 15, 18, 22, 25, 28,
  34, 35, 43, 44, 62, 107, 108, 109, 113,
  114, 122
Ulster Unionist Council (UUC), 12–13,
  15, 17, 18, 22, 24, 34, 64, 100, 122
Ulster Volunteers (UVF), 10, 13, 16, 17,
  32, 35, 58, 62, 63, 71, 76, 77, 100;
  Antrim regiments, 23–5; Belfast
  regiments, 24–5; gunrunning, 35;
  organization, 18
Ulster Women's Unionist Council
  (IWUC), 16
United Irish League (UIL), 36, 48
United Irishmen, 27

Victoria barracks, Belfast, 5, 90, 108, 119,
  120

Walker, William, 12
Walsh, Louis, 53, 57, 94, 95
Ward, Annie, 51
Waring, William, 131, 132
Waters, Vincent, 89, 90
Waterford, 2
Weaver Street, 131
Whitehouse, 19, 20
Wickham, Charles, divisional
  commissioner RIC, 123
Wolff, Gustav Wilhelm, MP, 11
Woods, Seamus, 55, 67, 80, 89, 91, 108,
  117, 137, 139, 143
Workman Clark shipyard, 3, 18, 20, 21,
  59, 75, 123, 114,

York Road, Belfast, 4
York Street, 75, 95, 110, 112, 113, 126,
  147
Young Ulster Society, 16